The University of Nevada, 1874–2024

The University of Nevada, 1874–2024

150 Years of Inspiring Excellence

JOHN TRENT

With a Foreword by President Brian Sandoval

UNIVERSITY OF NEVADA PRESS | *Reno & Las Vegas*

University of Nevada Press | Reno, Nevada 89557 USA
www.unpress.nevada.edu
Copyright © 2024 by University of Nevada Press
All rights reserved

Manufactured in Canada

FIRST PRINTING
Cover designer: Diane McIntosh
Cover photographs courtesy of University Archives (front cover and inside back flap) and UNR Marketing / Communications (back cover)

LIBRARY OF CONGRESS CATALOGING-IN-PUBLICATION DATA
Names: Trent, John, 1963– author. | Sandoval, Brian, 1963– writer of foreword.
Title: The University of Nevada, 1874-2024: 150 years of inspiring excellence / John Trent; with a foreword by Brian Sandoval.
Description: Reno, Nevada: University of Nevada Press, [2024] | Includes bibliographical references and index. | Summary: "The University of Nevada, Reno, has seen everything from an initial enrollment of seven students on October 12, 1874, in Elko, to its status today as a nationally classified Carnegie R1 'Very High Research' university located in Reno with one of the most productive faculties in the country and a student body that has reached record levels of achievement and diversity. This 150th anniversary book highlights some of the University's history in explaining why the University of Nevada, Reno, truly has been a catalyst for success in the state's higher education story."—Provided by publisher.
Identifiers: LCCN 2024003544 | ISBN 9781647791698 (cloth) | ISBN 9781647791704 (ebook)
Subjects: LCSH: University of Nevada, Reno—History. | State universities and colleges—Nevada—Reno—History.
Classification: LCC LD3763 .T74 2024 | DDC 378.793/55—dc23/eng/20240619

LC record available at https://lccn.loc.gov/2024003544

ISBN 978-1-64779-169-8 (cloth)
ISBN 978-1-64779-170-4 (ebook)
LCCN: 2024003544

The paper used in this book meets the requirements of American National Standard for Information Sciences—Permanence of Paper for Printed Library Materials, ANSI/NISO Z39.48–1992 (R2002).

Half Title: Students walk near the Mathewson-IGT Knowledge Center and through the center of the modern campus. Courtesy of UNR Marketing / Communications.

Frontispiece: On the pillars of the University's Honor Court are carved the names of the students, faculty members, and benefactors who have made an indelible impact on campus. Courtesy of University Advancement / Theresa Danna.

Contents

Foreword by President Brian Sandoval
The University–A Community Unlike Any Other vii

Preface
James Hulse, in Memoriam xi

Acknowledgments xv

Chronology xix

INTRODUCTION 1

THE BEGINNING, 1864–1908 5

THE UNIVERSITY TAKES HOLD, 1909–1938 29

THE UNIVERSITY REFLECTS THE CHALLENGES OF NEVADA AND THE NATION, 1939–1978 55

THE UNIVERSITY FINDS ITS PURPOSE AND PLACE, 1979–PRESENT 89

EPILOGUE 163

Honor Court 167

References 171

Contributors 173

Notes 175

Index 181

Foreword

The University—A Community Unlike Any Other

We all have stories about our first days at the University of Nevada, Reno, and this is mine. And I don't know if it's a story so much as it was a feeling. I was scared to death when I walked onto campus as a first-year student for my first day of classes on Monday, August 31, 1981. The University had already reached out to first-year students such as myself in a variety of ways. A student orientation was on August 25, student sponsor meetings on August 27, advisement sessions with representatives from the University's nine colleges, a convocation address by President Joe Crowley, and during that first week of classes, the traditional all-school picnic in Manzanita Bowl on September 2. Yet, as one of 7,680 students who were registered for classes for that semester—registration was actually up 3.7 percent that fall, even with an increase in tuition and fees—I wasn't sure if I was going to last that first week, let alone that first semester.

Why? I was an extremely shy kid from Sparks. I'd enjoyed my time and made several good friends at Bishop Manogue Catholic High School in Reno. How time has changed. Bishop Manogue was then in a quiet neighborhood on Bartlett Street off Valley Road. I'd developed a sense of comfort and familiarity during my time at Manogue, but the University, only a few hundred yards away over a set of railroad tracks and up on a hill, was something different entirely. What were the professors like? Did I have the academic chops to survive in a college classroom? Were the students who were already attending the University very nice people? What would they think of me, a quiet kid who had grown up doing 4-H projects, often tending sheep in the morning, and hadn't had other members of my family who had ever gone to college?

Maybe there was still time to back out. Maybe attending the University of Nevada, Reno, had been a foolish mistake.

As it turned out, attending the University of Nevada, Reno, wasn't a mistake at all. It was a fateful and important decision. It was perhaps the best decision I would ever make in my life. First, I needed to get beyond the feeling that I was too scared to ask for help. This is an extremely difficult thing to do when you are eighteen years old. You don't want to look like you don't know what you are doing—when in fact you have no idea about anything at all. Eventually this feeling of not wanting to ask for help dissipated. In the coming days, I decided to open up and let the University in. I found not isolation, nor loneliness, nor the dejection of knowing you've made a wrong decision. I began to find my way. Throughout my time as a student at the University, I found friends who would remain friends throughout the decades that followed.

President Brian Sandoval addresses the emeriti faculty at an annual celebration in the University's Honor Court. Courtesy of UNR Marketing / Communications.

Esteemed English professor Anne Howard, geography professor Chris Exline, and many others simply went beyond classroom lectures and had a profound influence on my life. Howard, one of the driving forces in establishing the Women's Studies Program on campus, was a leader in championing women's rights throughout Nevada. And who can forget "Professor Ex" and his incredible Mackay Science classroom slideshows of Northern Nevada and Northern Nevada topography? They saw something in me before I could see my own true potential. They encouraged me to stretch myself academically and socially. I learned from them I could become self-sufficient and independent and navigate my way through college. And when it came time to find my next chapter in life, professors such as Howard wrote me letters of recommendation for law school.

I went from feeling scared to feeling that the University of Nevada, Reno, has a way of getting in your bones because of the people you meet and the experiences that you have here. It is a university that helps you find your purpose. And it's a university that never leaves you. The University has awarded more than 125,000 degrees since the conferral of our first degree back in 1891. During that time, we have transformed countless lives. We have been an indispensable lever in helping Nevada find its economic and social path to the future. And we have made dreams become reality. Since we first opened our doors to a student body of seven students in Elko on October 12, 1874, our University has become a silver gate of opportunity for a state that is constantly evolving.

With the University's sesquicentennial upon us in 2024, this idea of service to Nevada—whether it is through our tripartite mission of teaching, research,

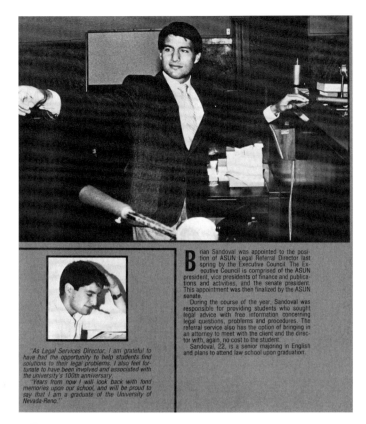

The University's seventeenth president, Brian Sandoval, pictured as an undergraduate student and ASUN member, featured in the 1986 edition of the *Artemisia* yearbook. Courtesy of University Archives.

and engagement or through the successes of our students, faculty, staff, alumni, and friends in the community—is something that I believe will continue to be at the heart of the University's story for years and years to come. During our spring commencement ceremonies in 2021, held in Mackay Stadium for the first time in our history, the long shadow of the COVID-19 pandemic was still with us. Mackay Stadium provided us with an outdoor venue where we could hold eight ceremonies over four days, all in a safe open-air environment. What was apparent over those days of celebration, which included the class of 2020, whose spring commencement was celebrated virtually, was how our

President Brian Sandoval (class of 1986) and his wife, Lauralyn (class of 1992), are proud Wolf Pack alumni. Courtesy of UNR Marketing / Communications.

University had met the challenge of the previous year-plus and had done so in a highly human and impactful way. I called this "The Wolf Pack Way," the idea that what our University has always done in times of challenge is to help build communities in the sense of where we live throughout Nevada or in the sense of where we can find acceptance and belonging. This is what we must always do if we are to realize the long-ago words of professor N. E. Wilson, who wrote movingly in celebration of our thirty-year anniversary. In a 1904 essay, "What the University Stands For," Wilson said, "This University is yours; it should be your pride. Take it; nurture it; support it; sustain it. It depends entirely upon the state—upon the people of the State—what the future of this institution shall be." During my time as president of the University, I have found that the Wolf Pack Way is collaborative and that an individual's success can only be attained when we enjoy collective success. That we are at our best as a University when we think not about ourselves, but about the lives, dreams, and opportunities of our friends and neighbors. That in the common hopes and dreams of all people, we can find the intersections of hope and possibility that have characterized our 150-year history as an institution, and that will help guide us into our next 150 years.

We all find our purpose at the University of Nevada, Reno. This is true of all of us: our students, our faculty, our staff, our alumni, or our friends in the community. Together, we strive each day to make the University the best institution of higher learning it can possibly be. More than forty years after my first day of classes on our campus, I can say without hesitation or equivocation that the University of Nevada, Reno, is the place where we find our path and, perhaps more importantly, where we beckon others to come along with us. Of all the communities we shall know, our University serves community, generates community, and *is* community in a way unlike any other.

On our 150th anniversary, we celebrate this fact, and pledge to carry it with us into our future. Go Pack!

—Brian Sandoval, May 2024

Preface

James Hulse, in Memoriam

When James Hulse took on the task of writing the University of Nevada's history in 1970, he was already an extremely busy professor. The clock to completing what became 1974's *The University of Nevada: A Centennial History* was already ticking. Hulse, then forty years old, had been a professor of history at the University since 1962. His life to that point spoke to a Nevada of a different time. One of seven children, he was born in the small mining town of Pioche, in Lincoln County, about 180 miles northeast of Las Vegas. He enrolled at the University of Nevada thanks to a Harolds Club scholarship. From the beginning of his time at the University, whether as a student and certainly later as a professor, Hulse was a writer. He studied journalism, graduated from the University in 1952, and was drafted into the US Army during the Korean War. Once his military commitment ended, Hulse was a reporter for the *Nevada State Journal* newspaper. Always fascinated with history, Hulse took graduate courses at the University as he worked in newspapers, eventually earning his master's degree from the University, followed by his PhD in Russian history from Stanford University. Hulse's primary academic interest was in European history, and during his thirty-five-year career at the University he would write several books on subjects such as the Communist International and Greek history. But the pull of Nevada was always strong. Throughout his life, Hulse and his wife, Betty, and their two children, Jane and Jimmy, traveled to all points in Nevada, hiking, fishing, and camping.

In typical Hulse fashion, what became *The University of Nevada: A Centennial History,* published by the University of Nevada Press, was a product of the deep collaborative respect he always felt toward the University's faculty. He only agreed to write the history on his own after he had the blessing of Department of History professor Russell Elliott, a venerated Nevada historian who was his mentor and friend. Charles Armstrong, the University's president 1958–1967, and N. Edd Miller, the University's president 1967–1974, both felt strongly that a history of the institution needed to be written. Miller, in particular, was able to free Hulse of several of his campus duties, including serving on the

Opposite: Even the trees that line the historic Quad started small. Courtesy of University Archives.

Above: James W. Hulse graduated from the University of Nevada with a BA in 1952 and an MA in 1962, and he became a professor of history in 1962. He wrote one of the two major collections of the institution's history, *The University of Nevada: A Centennial History,* in 1974. Courtesy of University Archives.

James W. Hulse's Nevada roots were deep and strong. He grew up in the tiny mining town of Pioche. Members of the Hulse family stand in front of their house in Pioche, including (*back row, left to right*) Berene C. Hulse, Delora Hulse, and James G. Hulse; (*front row*) Delora Rose and James W. Hulse. Courtesy of University Archives.

Faculty Senate, so that he could turn his attention to researching and writing the one-hundred-year history.

Hulse wasn't motivated by making extra money when he embarked on the project. He said in a University oral history: "I didn't want any reduction in teaching load, and I didn't want any compensation in addition to my salary. But I did want to be liberated from that kind of thing [administrative duties associated with being a fully tenured professor of history], because I'd become convinced that I was not effective on the University Senate, I was not effective on the Undergraduate Council, or the Public Occasions Board, etc."[1] Hulse's only monetary request was a budget of about $7,900 for travel, research, and to retain the services of graduate student Lenore Kosso, who helped comb through the University's archives and conduct interviews. The project took Hulse about three and a half years to complete. Later, Hulse estimated that he only used about $5,000 of the allotted budget. Hulse made sure the remaining money went to the book's production and marketing costs.[2]

In the preface of *The University of Nevada: A Centennial History*, Hulse made clear his intent: although "there is no such thing as 'objective' history, where all of the author's prejudices are put into a deep-freeze during the research and writing," he wanted to make sure all the book's readers understood that it was a "historian's history, not a public relations piece that would ignore the institution's shortcomings and handicaps."[3] The entire process, which included submitting what turned out to be a 258-page manuscript to the University of Nevada Press, had been gratifying to Hulse. "At no time have I been asked to modify any of my findings or interpretations," he wrote.[4]

A theme emerged in Hulse's book:

> The making of a university in an environment like Nevada was a difficult procedure. . . . The University was created as a result of the Morrill Land Grant Act to meet some specific technical needs of the frontier. To transform that collegiate idea into a university where important research goes on, where sophisticated investigation can go on, whether or not it serves the needs of Nevada's economy, to make that transition from what I call the small college idea to the university idea was a major challenge. And that's part of the theme that I try to develop in the book.[5]

Hulse asserted the University's story of success picked up steam during the 1950s and 1960s. That was when faculty members Robert Gorrell and Charlton Laird wrote one of the most successful English grammar textbooks in the country and Department of Psychology researchers Allen and Beatrix "Trixie" Gardner earned national and international headlines for teaching American Sign Language to a chimpanzee named Washoe. Hulse wrote:

> The university idea grew and developed very rapidly in the '60s. There was more money available. A number of scholars did some rather remarkable things. (We've had some people trying to do the university job over the years, but by and large, they were few in number.) Up until the late '50s or early '60s, the state really didn't fund much university work. It didn't really encourage much of what I'm calling the university approach to scholarship until late '50s, into the '60s, when we began to get more national endowment money, when the state legislature provided sufficient money for the library, for graduate student aid, for sabbatical leaves, the kind of resources and time instructors need to do real research and to reach out to the larger academic world.[6]

Ultimately, *The University of Nevada: A Centennial History* succeeded on all levels. It was a book about the University's origins and how it struggled to survive in its early years. It was how (although Hulse never wrote this, but this was true then and remains true today) the University succeeded because it had talented, hardworking, and honest people such as Jim Hulse pouring their heart and soul into the University's everyday existence. With the book's publication in 1974, Hulse said the University, even with some misfires and some moments when its future was in doubt, was "a splendid undertaking." It was splendid because Hulse, and so many others before him and after him, had felt that "this is a special kind of thing to be doing."[7]

Hulse lived the ideals and purposes of the University of Nevada (and later the University of Nevada, Reno) from the day he first arrived on campus as an eighteen-year-old freshman in 1948 until the day he died in Reno on May 9, 2023, only about a week before the University's 133rd commencement. As he was retiring from the faculty in 1997, Hulse would be inducted into the Nevada Writers Hall of Fame. In addition to his centennial history of the University, Hulse would also write a history of higher education in the state, *Reinventing the System: Higher Education in Nevada, 1968–2000,* in 2002 and two textbooks of Nevada history. And for years afterward, Hulse could be seen regularly walking on campus, or eating breakfast of cereal and toast in the Overlook above Manzanita Lake, or coming out of the Mack Social Science Building after visiting with old and new faculty in the Department of History.

One day, a passerby asked Hulse why he kept coming back to campus, long after his teaching days had ended. The man, with his horn-rimmed glasses, gentle disposition, and white hair that sometimes looked combed and sometimes did not, smiled. He looked about him. The campus was still a special place to him.

"This," James Hulse said, pointing to the Quad, "has always been my home."

Since their formal dedication in 1908, the Mackay School of Mines Building and a statue of its namesake, John Mackay, have been iconic features of campus. Courtesy of University Advancement / Jordan S. Buxton.

Acknowledgments

During the 2016–2017 academic year, I had the good fortune of serving as a member of the University of Nevada, Reno, Faculty Senate. Our chair that year was College of Engineering professor David Sanders. David was not only an excellent leader, he was also a great storyteller. He would often launch into stories about past and present College of Engineering faculty, invoking lines from these colleagues that were often witty and were also spot-on in their application of a greater universal truth that somehow always circled back to Faculty Senate business. David shared his thoughts during one meeting by first starting with yet another story. Then he caught himself midsentence. "Oh no," he said, half-repentant and half-reflective and with a wide smile. Although he had made an important discovery, the grin indicated, it wasn't about to slow him down from his storytelling momentum. He asked for our forgiveness and said, "I guess I'm so old now where everything I say is a story." And then David proceeded to tell us . . . yet another story.

This is how I feel about the acknowledgments regarding this book. There are stories behind the relationships I've had with the people who are in these acknowledgments, stories that speak to how good they are as people and why they are so good at what they do. I'll try to spare you the stories. But I do wish to acknowledge how central all of them have been in the creation and the completion of this book.

Let me start with Brian Sandoval, president of the University of Nevada, Reno. I have known Sandoval since our time here as students together in the 1980s. He loves the University and has always given it credit for helping him find a personal purpose that led him eventually to two terms as Nevada's governor and his appointment as the institution's seventeenth president. It was Sandoval's idea to do this book as part of a conversation about ways the University could bring more attention to its 150th anniversary. To Sandoval's credit, other than the foreword he has graciously provided, he has given me full editorial freedom in attempting to tell the University's story. I wish to thank him for this trust. Patricia Richard, the longtime chief of staff to not only Sandoval but also former presidents Marc Johnson and Milton Glick, was also one of the earliest people to encourage me to write this book.

I've known Catherine Cardwell, the University's dean of libraries, for a lot less time than Sandoval. Catherine began her appointment at the University in the summer of 2021, after serving as regional associate vice chancellor of academic affairs and campus dean of the Nelson Poynter Memorial Library at the University of South Florida. I share these titles for a reason. This is an extremely accomplished person who very quickly on our campus has become one of our best leaders. The idea for this book only took form because of Catherine's willingness to share the tremendous treasure of resources that are part of our libraries, most notably University Archives and Special Collections. I've come to learn that this is what Catherine does with our entire campus. She invites us in. She shares the experience, expertise, and talents of her tremendous staff in any way that she can. Throughout this process, I've been incredibly impressed and inspired by the "can-do" enthusiasm of people such as Laura Rocke, community and university archivist, and Maggie Ressel, libraries director of access services, who embody why our libraries aren't just cold repositories, but living and thriving places where we can reimagine and rethink our history and what it means to us.

Without the ongoing support of my boss and good friend, Kerri Garcia Hendricks, the executive director of marketing and communications at the University, this project might not ever have reached completion. Throughout her time as the leading voice and champion of the work that is done in marketing and communications, Kerri has demonstrated to me time and again what great leadership is all about. She trusts the talents of her people and always finds the means to support our work. So this is a thank-you not only to Kerri, but to all my colleagues in marketing and communications for the collegial and positive workplace we enjoy, and our team-wide belief in the meaning of our work and its value to our campus community.

I need to also thank JoAnne Banducci and Curtis Vickers and the great team at the University of Nevada Press for making this book a reality. Throughout every step of this project, JoAnne, the Press's director, and Curtis, acquisitions editor, have been the encouraging presences a writer needs in fending off the neurotic self-doubt that is often an ongoing affliction in the writing profession. JoAnne and I are both runners, and I've marveled at her ability over the years to always find new, exciting goals for running and fresh, innovative ways to keep the more than sixty-year-old University of Nevada Press at the forefront in an ever-changing publishing world. Curtis, without a doubt, is a gifted writer and editor who is able to make suggestions and improvements that always "feel" right—and needed. I don't know if I've ever worked with a more humanistic and empathetic editor. He is the best kind of collaborator, a trusted voice who understands the structure and the soul of a book.

I also want to thank the contributors of the essays that are in this book. Some of these writers are good friends of mine, some are people I've admired from afar, and all of them, I think, have unique and insightful experiences with our University that help give this book an added dimension. I am indebted to all of them for the essays they've provided.

On a personal note, I must thank my wife, Jill, and our daughters, Annie and Katie, for always being there for me. They understand how much the University has meant to me throughout my life. Their lives have always inspired me to be a better person, and to be willing to stretch myself personally and professionally.

Along these same lines, just like any graduate of our University, professors here, both past and present, have changed my life. I wish to thank them all, as well as all the incredible faculty, staff, students, administrators, and alumni whom I've had the good fortune of writing about during my career as a writer and editor on campus. They've all shared their stories with me with grace and goodness—and with an uncommon generosity of spirit that speaks to why our University is such a special place. The late, great English professor Robert Gorrell once told me that he came to our campus during the 1940s not expecting to work and teach here for more than a couple of years. "But the stories were too good, and the people were just too damned interesting," Bob said. "So I never left."

And there I go again. Just like my esteemed Faculty Senate colleague David Sanders, I'm getting so old everything I say eventually turns into a story. It is my hope that you forgive me for these rambling personal stories . . . and that you enjoy the most remarkable story of them all—the story of the University of Nevada, Reno.

—John Trent, Reno, October 2024

The October 2023 kickoff of the University's yearlong sesquicentennial celebration was selfie worthy. Courtesy of UNR Marketing / Communications, Damian Gordon.

Chronology

1864

Nevada entered statehood with a constitution providing for a state university.

1873

Governor L. R. Bradley signed a legislative bill locating the University in Elko.

1874

University Preparatory School opened in Elko with seven students.

1885

Governor Jewett Adams signed a legislative bill moving the University to Reno. Morrill Hall constructed.

1886

The University formally reopened as a preparatory school in the new Morrill Hall on the Reno campus. Classes began with seventy-five students enrolled.

1887

The administration of President LeRoy D. Brown, the first president, began.

Fifty students enrolled in the 1887–1888 academic year for the first year of college-level instruction.

President Brown and Hannah K. Clapp began as faculty. Two additional faculty members were hired within the first year.

1888

The School of Mines launched, with Robert D. Jackson, PhD, as director.

Following the provisions of the Morrill Act, and with the support of Congress, the University established the Agricultural Experiment Station.

1890

Stephen A. Jones, the second president, began his term on January 6.

1891

Frederick Bristol, Henry Colman Cutting, and Frank Norcross received the first three degrees in the School of Liberal Arts.

McKissick Opera House in Reno hosted the first graduation exercises.

1892

The Schools of Mines and Agriculture graduated their first classes.

Electric lights were installed on campus.

Blanche Davis became the first woman to graduate from the University. Along with four other people, she received a bachelor of arts degree.

1893

The first issue of the student newspaper, *The Student Record,* appeared on October 19.

1894

Joseph Edward Stubbs, the third president, began his tenure on July 1.

Students formed the Independent Association of the University of Nevada.

Graduates organized the Alumni Association of the University of Nevada.

1895

The Mining Analytical Laboratory launched an assay service for citizens of the state.

The University established a preparatory department and University High School.

1896

The first freestanding dormitory, Lincoln Hall, opened as a men's dormitory.

Manzanita Hall opened as the first women's dormitory.

1898

An intercollegiate men's football team began competing.

1899

The *Artemisia* yearbook appeared for the first time.

The University adopted silver and blue as the school colors.

Washoe County presented the University with a sixty-acre farm valued at $12,000 to be used in connection with the Agricultural Experiment Station.

1900

The University opened a school of commerce, making it the fourth university in the nation to offer a four-year business degree.

With a final price tag of more than $8,000, construction of the President's House was completed.

1902

Because of a possible smallpox epidemic, University leaders and local health officials required students living in the dormitory to stay on campus.

1903

Joseph Williams earned the first advanced degree from the University, a master of arts in social sciences.

1904

The University celebrated the thirtieth anniversary of its founding. James E. Church, professor of classics, edited a memorial volume for the event.

1906

The University's name officially changed from Nevada State University to the University of Nevada.

A devastating earthquake destroyed large parts of San Francisco, including the printer responsible for that year's *Artemisia* yearbook.

1907

The University received a bronze statue of Comstock pioneer John W. Mackay created by Gutzon Borglum and commissioned by Mackay's family.

The Department of Physics began offering classes.

1908

The Mackay family donated $1.5 million to support a new mining building and its equipment, landscaping for the Quad, and an athletic field and training house.

The Mackay School of Mines Building was dedicated.

The Mackay Mineral Museum opened to showcase minerals, rocks, and fossils from Nevada and around the world.

1909

The Mackay Athletic Field and Training Quarters opened.

1910

The student newspaper, *The Student Record,* changed its name to *The U. of N. Sagebrush.*

Audrey W. Ohmert and Dorothy F. Riechers received the first R. Herz Gold Medals, given to the graduates who achieved the highest grade-point average.

1911

A ceremony commemorated the completion of the Orr irrigation ditch dam and Manzanita Lake.

1912

The Mackay family established a $150,000 endowment for the Mackay School of Mines.

Students enrolled in the first summer session.

1913

Campus held the first Mackay Day celebration.

Students placed and whitewashed thousands of rocks to form a 140-by-150-foot "N" overlooking the campus on Peavine Peak.

1914

President Stubbs died May 27.

Archer W. Hendrick assumed the presidency on September 14. He was the University's fourth president.

The Smith-Lever Act invigorated the Cooperative Extension program, leading to the creation of the Agricultural Extension Division.

1915

The first graduates in electrical engineering earned their degrees.

1917

The University purchased 213 acres to establish the University Farm.

1918

Walter Ernest Clark was inaugurated as the University's fifth president on September 1.

The University ordered a quarantine to contain the spread of the flu pandemic. No one was allowed to go from or to the campus without permission.

1920

Classes began in the newly formed School of Education.

The University established a federal radio station on campus.

The University of Nevada received accreditation from the National Association of American Colleges and Universities.

The University held its first homecoming activities.

The football team became the first from the mainland to play a game in Hawaii.

President Clark initiated the "Book of the Oath," to be signed by each successive class as a pledge to service and high ideals.

1921

The University established an Engineering Experiment Station.

James "Rabbit" Bradshaw, a standout football player, became Nevada's first All-American.

Enrollment surpassed five hundred students for the first time.

1922

Faculty member Laura Ambler matriculated the first journalism department students.

1923

The "Wolf Pack" officially became the team name.

1924

Samuel B. Doten published his *History of the University of Nevada*.

1927

Thanks to funds donated by William A. Clark Jr., construction of Memorial Library was completed.

Wá·šiw tribe member Lloyd Barrington became the first Native American to graduate from the University with a bachelor of arts in economics.

1929

The Mackay School of Mines established the Nevada Bureau of Mines.

1930

Clarence H. Mackay dedicated Mackay Science Hall on October 24 and presented it to the University.

Theodore H. Miller, the first African American graduate of the University, completed a bachelor of science in electrical engineering.

1936

Clarence H. Mackay purchased and donated almost twenty-seven acres of adjacent land, increasing the campus footprint by almost 50 percent.

Enrollment surpassed one thousand students for the first time.

1938

The Northwest Association of Secondary and Higher Schools accredited the University.

Max C. Fleischmann initiated the then largest giving program in University history, including scholarships for Native American students.

President Clark resigned on September 30.

1939

President Leon W. Hartman was inaugurated on December 15 after serving as interim president for more than a year. He was the sixth president.

Campus held the first winter carnival.

1941

The Nevada Legislature authorized a bond issue to construct a new gymnasium. The University's original gymnasium was converted at this time into an ROTC rifle range and space for a military department.

Commencement ceremonies included celebrations for the fiftieth anniversary of the graduation of the first four-year class.

1942

After no major capital improvements for thirty years, the University constructed an engineering facility, later named the Stanley Palmer Engineering Building.

The University's war effort included the development of additional special summer session offerings.

1943

The US Army and US Army Air Force training contingents arrived at the University.

President Hartman died on August 27.

1944

John O. Moseley was inaugurated as the seventh president on October 12.

1946

The University canceled a football game at Mississippi State University when its athletics director requested that Nevada play without African American players.

1948

Twentieth Century Fox filmed *Apartment for Peggy* on campus, one of several movies shot on campus during the 1940s.

1949

Gilbert E. Parker became acting president on July 1 after the resignation of John Moseley.

1951

On June 10 and 11, the University marked the inauguration of Malcolm A. Love as its eighth president.

One full-time and two part-time instructors began offering classes in Las Vegas. A total of thirty-eight students enrolled.

1952

Stella Mason Parson became the first African American woman graduate, with a bachelor of arts in English.

1953

Minard W. Stout was inaugurated as the ninth president on June 8.

1954

The University established a Nevada Southern branch in Las Vegas with 269 students.

1956

The legislature funded a new building to support business education. The building was named for Silas E. Ross, a former regent who served for twenty-five years.

1957

The first Las Vegas campus building opened.

Students began taking classes in the Orvis School of Nursing, which received funding from Arthur E. and Mae Zenke Orvis.

1958

Construction concluded on Jot Travis Student Union, which alumni helped to fund.

1959

The University established the Desert Research Institute.

Charles J. Armstrong was inaugurated as the tenth president on April 19.

1960

The Winter Olympic Games selected the University as host university for the 1960 Games in Squaw Valley (now known as Olympic Valley).

1961

The University of Nevada Press began operation with Robert Laxalt as director.

1962

Getchell Library, named after Nevada mining tycoon Noble H. Getchell, opened.

1963

The only planetarium in the shape of a hyperbolic paraboloid, the Fleischmann Planetarium and Science Center opened.

The University's FM radio station, KUNR, began broadcasting on October 7.

1964

University Archives opened as a department within Getchell Library.

The Oral History Program commenced.

Roger Barron Morrison received the first doctoral degree from the University, a PhD in geology.

1965

The Las Vegas branch became known as Nevada Southern University.

Kenneth J. Carpenter founded Black Rock Press.

Students organized a chapter of the Student Nonviolent Coordinating Committee (SNCC) on campus.

Enrollment exceeded 5,000.

1966

On February 11, N. Edd Miller began his tenure first as chancellor, then as the eleventh president of the University.

The University finished construction on the new Mackay Stadium in the northern end of campus.

1967

The Center for Basque Studies, originally part of the Desert Research Institute, hired William Douglass as the founding director.

The NAACP created the first campus chapter.

The Upward Bound program started offering support and services to low-income students, one of the first in the nation.

The student newspaper, *The U. of N. Sagebrush,* changed its name to *Sagebrush.*

1968

Black students founded the Black Student Union, an organization dedicated to serving Black students in the University community, local high school students, and minorities in the area.

The American Indian Organization launched a campus chapter.

The Board of Regents restructured the rapidly growing network of campuses into the University of Nevada System (UNS).

The Human Relations Action Council formed, faculty members and students calling for "immediate and drastic action" by the University to address "the social problems created by racism and apathy."

1969

The Regents officially named the Reno campus the University of Nevada, Reno, while changing the name of the southern campus to the University of Nevada, Las Vegas.

The Desert Research Institute and Community College Division also became separate units of the University of Nevada System.

The first African American faculty member, Ben Hazard, began teaching in the art department.

Nevada and UNLV played their first football game on November 22. Nevada won, 30–28.

Reno campus enrollment surpassed seven thousand, and Las Vegas exceeded five thousand.

1970

Students and faculty staged the Governor's Day anti-war protest on campus, ultimately resulting in the dismissal of English professor Paul Adamian.

UNLV won the second annual rivalry game, taking home the replica Fremont Cannon in its first year. At one point, the cannon was the largest and most expensive trophy in college football.

1971

Howard Hughes made the first payment on a $4 million, twenty-year gift in support of the new two-year School of Medical Sciences in Reno.

1972

Comprising faculty, staff, and students, the Committee on the Status of Women organized and began its ongoing advocacy work.

The Faculty Women's Caucus formed.

1974

James Hulse published *The University of Nevada: A Centennial History*.

The University celebrated its one hundredth birthday in Reno with a convocation combined with the inauguration of Max C. Milam as the twelfth president.

1978

The thirteenth to hold the office, Joseph N. Crowley became president on February 24, beginning the longest presidential tenure at the University.

1979

Morrill Hall reopened in a rededication ceremony after years of major renovations.

1981

The University established the University of Nevada, Reno Foundation to generate private support for the University.

1982

Laxalt Mineral Engineering Center building opened.

A new business building opened, later named in honor of Nazir Ansari, a faculty member in the College of Business.

To encourage international students, the University started the Intensive English Language Center.

1983

The Office of the Provost established the Foundation Professor program to recognize professors for outstanding achievements in research and teaching.

Construction on Lawlor Events Center was completed.

1984

The University established the Donald W. Reynolds School of Journalism and Center for Advanced Media Studies.

The Campus Transportation Service, intended for the safety of students, began.

1985

The Nevada Legislature named the campus grounds a state arboretum.

1986

The University celebrated one hundred years in Reno.

1989

The College of Human and Community Sciences opened.

Enrollment surpassed 10,000.

1991

The ElderCollege began offering continuing education opportunities for retirees.

1992

The University of Nevada System (UNS) rebranded as the University and Community College System of Nevada (UCCSN).

1993

The Reynolds School of Journalism building was completed and named after Donald W. Reynolds, a businessman and journalist whose support catalyzed the transition from department to school.

1994

History professor Michael Coray was named the first special assistant to the president for diversity to improve recruitment and retention of diverse students and faculty.

1997

The University created the Honor Court to highlight the students, faculty, and donors who had a great impact on the University, both historically, and into the future.

1999

Legacy Hall opened, housing the athletic department under one roof and capping $20 million in athletic facility improvements during the decade.

Wolf Pack Radio, a student-operated AM radio station, began broadcasting.

2000

Nevada established the Millennium Scholarship for high-achieving high school students.

The Fitzgerald Student Services Building opened.

2001

John Lilley was inaugurated as the fourteenth president on October 8.

2003

Enrollment surpassed 15,000.

2004

A massive campus reorganization divided the College of Arts and Sciences into the College of Liberal Arts and College of Science.

The Mackay School of Mines merged into the College of Science as the Mackay School of Earth Sciences and Engineering.

The Latino Research Center opened with startup funds from the US Department of Education, supported by Harry Reid, US senator, and Sheila Leslie, Nevada assemblywoman.

The student newspaper, *Sagebrush,* changed its name to *The Nevada Sagebrush.*

2005

The University and Community College System of Nevada (UCCSN) was renamed the Nevada System of Higher Education (NSHE).

The Kennedy Index rated the University as the best in the nation overall for providing opportunities for women in sports.

The Redfield campus, a joint educational venture between Truckee Meadows Community College and the University, opened.

The Tahoe Science Consortium formed. It was composed of the Desert Research Institute; the University of California, Davis; the University of Nevada, Reno; the US Geological Survey, and the USFS Pacific Southwest Research Station.

2006

Milton D. Glick was inaugurated as the fifteenth president on September 29.

2007

Construction of the Joe Crowley Student Union finished, primarily paid for by the student body.

The ElderCollege became the Osher Lifelong Learning Institute (OLLI).

Hixson Softball Park opened on the site of the former Bishop Manogue High School to provide improved and dedicated playing and practice fields for women's sports.

2008

The Mathewson-IGT Knowledge Center opened. It is one of the most technologically advanced libraries and campus technology services facilities in the country.

Marguerite Wattis Petersen Foundation Athletics Academic Center opened.

The Davidson Academy, a free public school for profoundly gifted young people, and the Black Rock Press opened in the Jot Travis Building, formerly the Student Union.

The Nevada Agricultural Experiment Station Greenhouse Complex opened on Valley Road.

The UNR Student Concrete Canoe team won both the regional and national competitions with their entry, *Argentum.*

After several years of appearing as a magazine, *Artemisia* changed its name to *Insight Magazine.*

2010

The Davidson Mathematics and Science Center opened.

The Center for Molecular Medicine, housing the Whittemore Peterson Institute, opened.

The multi-institution Redfield campus launched the National Geothermal Institute.

2011

President Milton D. Glick died on April 16, and Provost Marc Johnson stepped in as interim president.

2012

Marc A. Johnson was inaugurated as the sixteenth president on September 28.

Wolfie Jr. won the tenth annual Capital One Mascot Challenge.

2013

Demolition of the Getchell Library building made way for the William N. Pennington Student Achievement Center.

The Earthquake Engineering Laboratory, housing one of the world's largest shake table experiential floors, opened.

2014

NevadaFit completed the first campus-wide freshman boot camp, after expanding from the successful BioFit the previous year.

2015

The Innevation Center, a collaborative space designed to stimulate innovation and entrepreneurship, opened in downtown Reno.

The University established the Museum District, featuring twelve diverse museums, galleries, and attractions, in and around campus.

Enrollment surpassed 20,000.

2016

The William N. Pennington Student Achievement Center opened.

2017

The E. L. Wiegand Fitness Center opened.

2018

The University attained the prestigious R1 status as measured by the Carnegie Foundation for the Advancement of Higher Education.

2019

The University offered the first-ever Paiute language course.

The University Foundation Arts Building opened.

2020

The University closed on-campus operations in March to slow the spread of COVID-19. Faculty pivoted to online instruction.

Brian Sandoval was inaugurated as the seventeenth president on October 5.

2021

The University launched the Digital Wolf Pack Initiative to reduce digital inequity by providing iPads to all incoming first-year students.

Commencement was held in Mackay Stadium for the first time to recognize 8,350 graduates from 2020 and 2021 after exercises were canceled because of the pandemic.

A partnership agreement between the School of Medicine and Renown Health established the first fully integrated health system in Nevada and expanded clinical training and clinical research programs as well as access to clinical care for all Nevadans.

The University signed concurrent enrollment agreements with the Clark County and Washoe County School Districts, allowing high school students to take university-level courses.

Faculty and staff returned for in-person classes and experiences in August while the University managed the impact of COVID-19 on campus.

2022

The University began operations at the University of Nevada, Reno, at Lake Tahoe on July 1 after entering into an agreement to acquire Sierra Nevada University.

The University established the Office of Indigenous Relations with Daphne Emm-Hooper as the inaugural director.

2023

President Sandoval held a ribbon-cutting for the Mathewson University Gateway District.

The Mackay Muckers Women's Team won the International Collegiate Mining Competition in Australia.

The Associated Students of the University of Nevada (ASUN) revived the *Artemisia* yearbook.

The University formally kicked off its 150th anniversary on October 12.

Source: University of Nevada, Reno, Archives

The University of Nevada, 1874–2024

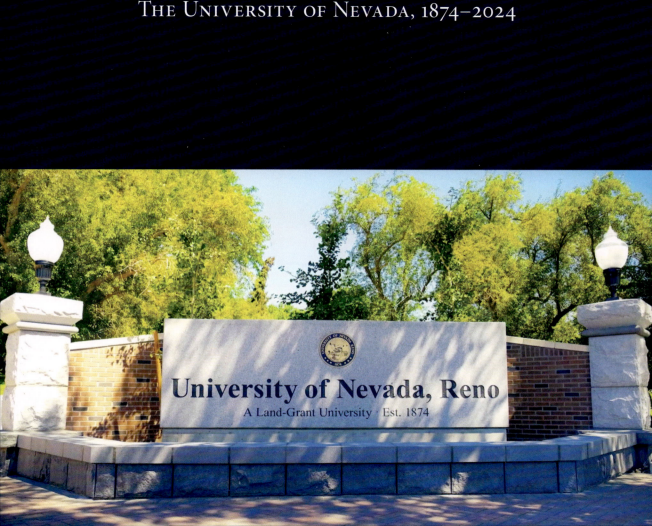

In the campus's early days, there was no place to park a car, but visitors could hitch a horse near Morrill Hall. Courtesy of University Archives.

Introduction

The Sierras shut us in on the Pacific side, and a weary stretch of almost uninhabited plain separated us from the Atlantic Coast. These were pioneers, indeed, and their spirit was worthy the opportunity.

—HANNAH K. CLAPP, the University's first faculty member[1]

Every university, even before it fully develops the intricacies of its institutional mission, must find its sense of human constancy first. Without a person such as Hannah K. Clapp, the mission of the University of Nevada, Reno, would not have become its true purpose. Clapp brought a deep-rooted belief in the power of education and the potential of the institution itself to the University when her presence was needed most and when its future was clearly in doubt. For a little more than a decade since its creation by the Nevada Legislature in 1873, the State University of Nevada had struggled to find a foothold. Originally in Elko, more than three hundred miles away from the state capital of Carson City, the University and its "Academic or Preparatory" Department could not seem to capture the public's imagination or even the support of the public education system that existed in Nevada. An editorial in the *Reno Evening Gazette* in 1879 wrote that "to dub that Elko public school, supported by the state, a 'University' is about as appropriate as to call a canoe a man-of-war. . . . It should be done away with and a school of mines established in its stead."[2]

Above: Hannah Clapp was the first faculty member, along with President LeRoy Brown, when the University moved from Elko to Reno. Courtesy of University Archives.

By 1885, the legislature voted to move the institution to Reno. But even after the purchase of twenty acres and construction of the new campus's first building—Morrill Hall—in spring 1886, the University's prospects were still not promising. The Nevada Board of Regents noted in its report that the state's support to that point was "hardly sufficient" and that if the same "indifference" were to continue "in respect to the career of the University at Reno . . . the people may only look for a repetition of the results attained in Elko."[3]

It was about this time that the University hired Clapp. She was the first faculty member at the new Reno location, and her duties included serving as President LeRoy D. Brown's assistant and the institution's librarian. Given her background and her personality, it shouldn't be too surprising that her duties at the University would increase over the next fourteen years.

Hannah Keziah Clapp was born in Albany, New York, in 1824. A teacher in the Michigan public school system throughout her twenties, she became a principal at the Lansing (Michigan) Female Seminary by the time she was thirty. As gold and silver discoveries still fevered the nation, she came by wagon train to California in 1859 and settled in Carson City by the next year. Clapp's belief in the transformative value of education and her dedication in advocating for women's rights defined her and made her a formidable presence. When she learned that there were no schools in Nevada, she founded the first one, the Sierra Seminary, in 1861. By the time she joined the faculty of the University, Clapp was in her sixties. She was a known quantity in Northern Nevada. Mark Twain, among many others, had reported about her school in the *Territorial Enterprise*.[4]

Her investment in the future of the new University, on a hopeful bluff overlooking the farm and ranchland that would one day connect it with Reno, was total. Clapp's professional productivity and personal determination accelerated at an age when most others would consider slowing down. Her wish to remain in place and to keep pushing forward so that the University could eventually realize a true sense of place—a place that students would find enticing and be drawn to learn—set her apart. Clapp always viewed the University as an exciting destination. In her mind, it was a place to live and learn, and to work and grow:

> Providence has a special care for the young, whether human beings or their creations. Surely it was true of this university. When I think of this fine scholarly work that was done in those early days of this institution and of the enthusiasm, consecration, and special fitness of each member of the faculty, it seems it could have been nothing short of a special direction that led to the choice of them.
>
> The Sierras shut us in on the Pacific side, and a weary stretch of almost uninhabited plain separated us from the Atlantic Coast. These were pioneers, indeed, and their spirit was worthy the opportunity.[5]

During her fourteen-year tenure on faculty at the University, Clapp helped the University acquire more than eleven thousand books and pamphlets while serving as the University's librarian; helped found the Nevada Historical Society; taught history and English; and became one of the University's most notable faculty members.

When Clapp died in Palo Alto, California, on October 8, 1908, at the age of eighty-four, the *Reno Evening Gazette* wrote that "her friends in this state are numberless." The Reno Kindergarten Association wrote that "a list of those whom she has aided to an education would startle some who pose as philanthropists. . . . It is doubtful that any single individual has had a wider influence in the forming days of Nevada than Miss Clapp."[6]

For 150 years, the students, faculty, staff, alumni, and friends in the community of the University of Nevada, Reno, have embraced the purpose-driven ideal that Hannah Clapp lived, that one's spirit should be worthy of the opportunity that has come to represent the University.

Seven students initially enrolled on October 12, 1874, in an entirely different part of the state, Elko, whose moment in history must stretch on its tip-toes to even be considered modest. Today, the University of Nevada, Reno, is a nationally classified Carnegie R1 "Very High Research" institution with one of the most productive faculties in the country and a student body that has reached record levels of achievement and diversity. If the aspirations of the Morrill Act that created it never quite spelled it out in bold letters, the University today is achieving it: the state's oldest institution of higher learning reflects Nevada's increasingly diverse population. In 150 years, the University has seen

Walter McNab Miller (*standing, light-colored jacket*), a University faculty member in anatomy, physiology, and geology at the University of Nevada 1887–1906, poses in front of Morrill Hall, 1888. Courtesy of University Archives.

The graduating class of the University of Nevada, June 12, 1890. Included in the photo are (*first in line*) Christine Harriet Andrews and (*seventh*) Jenny Lockman. Courtesy of University Archives.

its fortunes mirror that of the state it has served. Out of the Morrill Act the University has grown to become more than an "Academic or Preparatory" state university. Over time, the little university that was widely derided in newspaper editorials such as the *Reno Evening Gazette*'s has come to represent one of Nevada's best ideas in providing opportunity and making the dreams of Nevadans a reality. No matter the era, no matter the challenges faced throughout the University's history, the constant has always been the unique character of the people of the University. Hannah Clapp was the first of many.

For 150 years, there has been more to the University of Nevada, Reno, than what meets the eye. It is something more than today's "smart" classrooms and cutting-edge laboratories. More than books by the esteemed scholars and the lectures presented by a masterful faculty. More than transformative research and innovation. More than impactful community engagement and outreach. The University of Nevada, Reno, has always been about the possibilities of the human condition, about finding a path and beckoning others to share that path. In fall 1985, as the University prepared to celebrate its one hundredth anniversary of its relocation from Elko to Reno, President Joe Crowley mulled what the University's ultimate value needed to be. He started with the idea that a University must always be changing and evolving, not just to meet the needs and answer the challenges of a particular era, but because "not evolving means stagnation." But then Crowley took it a step further. "Did we make a difference?" was the most important standard for the University, he said.[7]

In 2024, the standard, and the people who work every day at the University in meeting it, remains the same. Hannah Clapp's initial immersion and embrace of what the University could be, should be, wasn't wrong. There isn't another place like the University of Nevada, Reno. This 150th anniversary book attempts to highlight some of the University's history in explaining why this is so.

An 1874 photograph of a building at the University's original location in Elko. Courtesy of University Archives.

The Beginning, 1864–1908

This year has been the happiest and most useful of my life.

—LeRoy D. Brown, the first president of the University of Nevada

Before the University found its constancy and purpose in people such as Hannah Clapp who saw it not for what it was but for what it could eventually be, its beginnings were mired in political haggling and public disinterest. The Morrill Land Grant Act of 1862 created an endowment fund specifically for colleges throughout the country and laid the groundwork for the modern public university. It led to the enabling language written during the Nevada State Constitutional Convention by an education committee in July 1864 that created a state university. Nevada historian and longtime University faculty member James Hulse, in his book *The University of Nevada: A Centennial History*, wrote:

> If any members of the convention had aspirations to create a great seat of learning where the traditional studies of the older universities would flourish—where philosophy, theology, history, the sciences, fine arts, and literature would find a home—they did not record such hopes.... They wanted a school to train teachers, miners, mechanics, and farmers, and they wanted it open to all students. They did not rule out the more traditional fields of study, but they provided for them only in a most general way.[1]

He noted Article XI, Section 4, of the Nevada Constitution: "The Legislature shall provide for the establishment of a State University, which shall embrace departments for Agriculture, Mechanic Arts, and Mining to be controlled by a Board of Regents, whose duties shall be prescribed by law." In addition, Section 5 called for the establishment of "normal schools and such different grades of schools, from the primary department to the University." The governor, secretary of state, and superintendent of public instruction were chosen to constitute "a Board of Regents to control and manage the affairs of the University and the funds of the same."[2]

At the time of the convention, Nevada was still sparsely populated and had only a handful of high schools. When the Nevada Legislature met in 1873 to finally make the University a reality, competitors for the institution's home included Carson City, Washoe City, and Reno. Elko, benefiting from the political rivalry between Reno and Carson City's elected representative and with the support of the state's new governor, Lewis R. Bradley, who was from Elko County, was chosen as the site of the new state university. The former Carson City newspaperman D. R. Sessions, only four years removed from graduating from Princeton, was appointed the founding principal of the Preparatory Department of the University of Nevada.

Sessions went to work quickly. He penned a front-page solicitation that appeared in newspapers throughout the state:

The Academic or Preparatory department of the State University, at Elko, Nevada, will be opened for admission of pupils on Monday, October 12, 1874. Requirements for admission: In written arithmetic, Eaton's high school arithmetic . . . in English grammar, will be required a familiarity with the rudiments and the ability to apply the general rules of syntax to the correction of false English; in geography, intermediate No. 2, Eclectic Series; orthography and reading—it will go towards recommending applicants for admission, and will be rigidly required they spell correctly and read with becoming expression; History of the United States—Swinton's Condensed History or its equivalent.

Sessions also noted that the preparatory course would "embrace" a two-year period and that "those branches will be taught which are required for admission into the Freshman Class in colleges. French and German will be taught as optional. For further information, apply to the Principal, D. R. Sessions, at Elko. Tuition free."[3] Hulse noted, "It had been obvious to the legislature that Nevada had no hope of launching a regular college. The opening of a Preparatory Department seemed the most expedient course of action."[4]

Sessions welcomed the institution's first seven students on October 12, 1874. The Preparatory Department was on a parcel of land donated by Central Pacific Railroad. It was located just outside of Elko. The single brick building was described by one visitor as being "two stories high and fronts the railroad. It is erected on a plateau to the rear and east of the town, commanding an excellent view of the surrounding country. . . . It is a handsome piece of work, a credit to the state, and the people of Elko."[5] The first year showed promise. Reports of Sessions and his work with the students, which numbered thirteen as the academic year ended, were greeted positively: "Professor Sessions, a young man of culture and ability, is the instructor in charge and is giving universal satisfaction."[6] The next few years, however, would prove increasingly more difficult. Regional rivalries to relocate the school began to flare up again. Enrollment, even after a dormitory was added, never exceeded thirty-five students. The school lost one of its prime assets when Sessions left in 1878 to become superintendent of public instruction for Nevada. An attempt to retool its purposes occurred in 1882 when a professor of assaying of mining, J. E. Gignoux, was hired. But interest in that new emphasis was tepid.

The 1885 Nevada Legislature reluctantly moved to consider moving the institution. Although the University had struggled, several Nevada locations coveted it. The Nevada Senate and Assembly finally agreed to a bill designating Reno as the University's new home. The Board of Regents in June 1885 acquired ten acres of "land on a hill north of Reno and took an option on another ten acres," Hulse wrote.[7] A sense of hope came with the land's acquisition. The expectation of a new, more optimistic chapter in the short history of the state's University grew when ground was broken in August for the first Reno campus building, the structure that would become Morrill Hall.

The *Reno Evening Gazette* editorialized on August 3, 1885:

> Our various exchanges note the departure of many young gentlemen and ladies, who are about to enter

some of the many excellent institutions of learning in California. The citizens of Nevada who have been and are patronizing these schools should bear in mind that the ground is broken for the State University at Reno and it is the purpose of those in charge to have the University open for the reception of pupils at the beginning of the ensuing school year.

It will be the aim of the Regents to make it what its name implies, and if the citizens of Nevada will take pride in elevating it, as they should, our children can receive a thorough education at home. . . . Local jealousies and seeming grievances should be laid aside, and all should aid in making the University one of the State's ornaments; make it demand the patronage and the good will of all lovers of learning; make it the peer of any other institution of the kind on the coast.[8]

Such lofty and idealized praise masked an unfortunate reality for the Indigenous people. They had been a part of the land well before the white colonization that occurred during the gold and silver rushes of the Comstock Lode. The University's founding in Elko and its relocation to Reno as part of the Morrill land-grant university movement throughout the country displaced Native tribes that included the Paiute, the Western Shoshone, and the Washoe. Severe sociological stress occurred as the Native tribes were forcibly relocated. The economic exchange through the creation of land-grant institutions such as the University bolstered the white society while severely undercutting the upward mobility of the tribes, who had honored and made the land the center of their existence for thousands of years. The signing of the Morrill Act by President Abraham Lincoln in 1862 distributed "public land" to raise funds for the creation of public universities. It was hailed in the twentieth and twenty-first centuries as one of the watershed moves that helped democratize college educations by making them more accessible for average Americans. However, in a March 2020 investigation in partnership with the Pulitzer Center, the *High Country News* noted that it caused massive disruption for Native people. For all its lofty aspirations, the Morrill Act created a huge transfer of wealth that only benefited white society. "The Morrill Act worked by turning land expropriated from tribal nations into seed money for higher education. In all, the act redistributed nearly 11 million acres," the *High Country News* wrote. The challenge for higher education today, it went on to say, is "to re-evaluate the foundations of their success by identifying nearly every acre obtained and sold, every land seizure or treaty made with the land's Indigenous caretakers, and every dollar endowed with profits from dispossession."[9] The land grab still haunts higher education today as students from Northern Nevada's tribes seek fair access and enrollment at the University. Brian Melendez, a member of the Reno-Sparks Indian Colony of Northern Paiute, Southern Paiute, and Western Shoshone, has worked in recent years with the Nevada Legislature to find equitable paths for Native students to colleges and universities. "It seems really ironic and strange that we have to petition the institutions for access, when these institutions are built on the blood and bones of our people," Melendez said in a 2021 interview with *The Nevada Independent*. "It's a fair ask."[10]

Reno, the county seat of Washoe County, in August 1885 was described by the *Nevada State Journal* as "situated on the line of the Central Pacific Railroad, fourteen miles east of the California state line on both sides of the beautiful Truckee River" featuring a population of 3,500. "At the northwest corner of the beautiful and fertile valley known as the 'Truckee Meadows,'" Reno and the surrounding area "presents to the observer a living landscape of green fields, beautiful gardens and groves of towering trees, a veritable paradise, surrounded on all sides by rugged and strange mountain scenery."[11] While Nevada's first chapter as a mineral-rich and quickly created new state in 1862 was coming to a close, Reno, founded in 1868, felt like it was only beginning. The *Nevada State Journal* echoed this sense of Reno's future and prized place in Nevada's history: "Mining towns may be approaching desolation, like other mining camps in the Rocky and Sierra Nevada mountains, but Reno, depending on an agricultural basis for its wealth and life, must continue to grow and flourish for all time." The town had five churches. In addition, there was "one large theater, numerous public halls and several large and well-kept hotels," the edifice of the "imposing" high school building, a "Young Ladies Seminary" ("which will ever add dignity and culture to the town") founded by Bishop Whitaker of the Episcopal Church, and several more new buildings coming online. One was being constructed in the new location of the state's relocated University. "Work is now in active operation on the State University building, the last Legislature having removed the institution from Elko to this place. It is the intention of the Regents to have the building so far completed that the school may be opened by the first of November next."[12] The first term at the University's new location, in Morrill Hall, which had a price tag of $13,500, began on March 31, 1886. J. W. McCammon was the principal and director of literary courses, and A. H. Willis was head of mining and science courses.[13]

An examination was conducted on March 31 "when all persons in Reno who expect to enter the University may submit themselves to the test" to be admitted. A few days later the number tested for admission had grown to thirty-nine students. Professors Willis and McCammon announced that all students were requested "to be present at the University to be assigned to their classes" at 9:00 a.m. on Thursday, April 15.[14] The *Reno Evening Gazette* reported that day that "the practical educational work" of the University had begun earlier that day with attendance "much greater than anticipated" with "twenty-three young ladies and thirteen young gentlemen" enrolled. The University's doors were "open to all the youth of Nevada who are qualified to enter its portals. The tuition is free. . . . Should the institution receive the patronage and encouragement it should from our citizens it will not be long till the efficient corps of professors are increased; it will not be long till we have men and women educated, not only as educators, but as local metallurgists and scientific men and women, hence there will soon be a new era in the development of all our great resources."[15]

The University's formal opening exercises were on the afternoon of April 22 in front of Morrill Hall. The Rev. Henry Ashton offered a benediction, trees were planted, and the speakers included McCammon, Willis, and Regent Henry G. Shaw.[16] Shaw was editor of the influential *Territorial Enterprise* newspaper and had developed the plan for Morrill Hall. Shaw urged the students to be diligent, and that if they showed "zeal and enthusiasm" they would find that "success would crown the labor so auspiciously begun."[17] An obvious centerpiece of the opening exercises was Morrill Hall, named after US Senator Justin Morrill of Vermont, who sponsored the legislation that had created land-grant universities. The *Nevada State Journal* reported that the new brick three-story building had a stone foundation with a basement and mansard roof floors and was "well lighted." The basement consisted of four rooms "for the janitor, stores, assay furnaces, quartz crushers and workshops." On the first floor were the principal's office, reception room, regents' room, library, museum, an assayer's office, assaying room, weighing room, lavatory, and gymnasium. The second and third floors, which were still to be finished, would feature a lecture hall and two classrooms. A "general assembly" room would be on the third floor.[18] "A simple classroom was dignified by the name of the physiological laboratory," Hannah Clapp remembered. "The basement represented the laboratory of physical sciences, as was befitting this foundation of knowledge, and with equal fitness our crowning glory was the department of normal training in the attic—it was an airy attic."[19]

The luster of the University's fresh start, however, soon began to fade. The new location and a new building were not enough to mask several problems the institution faced. More state support was needed, with only $5,833 having been appropriated annually by the state since the University was founded in 1874. There was also the question of purpose. Should the University be preparing teachers through a normal school model? Should its emphasis be on mining and agriculture? And what about the literary or liberal arts? How could any of this be accomplished in a still-unfinished Morrill Hall? By early 1887, political passions also stirred when the Nevada Legislature removed the incumbent members of the Board of Regents and the institution's two professors, McCammon and Willis, were fired. LeRoy D. Brown, who had served as an Ohio commissioner of education, was chosen to become the University's first president that summer. Brown, who had served in the Civil War, was a somewhat stern and formal person. He was an extremely hard worker, though. He believed deeply in the promise of the new University, according to his son Thomas, who went on to become a University graduate: "Of that first year my father said to me: 'I worked from sixteen to eight hours a day; I spent the nights planning for the days that not a minute be lost in getting under way.' To my father these difficulties were a test of strength, in which he rejoiced. . . . And so, at the close of the year, he wrote to a friend, 'This year has been the happiest and most useful of my life.'"[20] Brown made some clear delineations in academic offerings, which included the School of Mines and Mining Engineering; the School of Agriculture; the Normal School; the Business Department; and the Academic Department (English, Latin, Mathematics, and Natural Science).[21] And perhaps just as importantly, Brown was able to build the faculty with individuals who filled their work with a shared sense of purpose.

The faculty, Clapp recalled later, was small but enthusiastic. In many ways, she thought, they echoed the community of which they were a part:

We were not long in want of anything. They were an ambitious and energetic community, who keenly appreciated having a university in their midst, and who inspired the regents to nurse with all care the infant institution. The first addition they made to our faculty was Professor (Walter) Miller, who came as a special instructor in physiology and as a general all round assistant. Soon followed Professor (Robert) Jackson from the University of California, who opened the mining department. A little later Miss (Kate) Tupper came to grace a new departure, our department of normal training. There were five of us, representing twice as many departments packed into one building.[22]

Very early on, it became apparent to Clapp that the faculty was industrious and devoted to the University's success. Each faculty member possessed special intellectual and personal traits that were beginning to stamp the experience at the University as something special. The Nevada faculty was multitalented and multidimensional, Clapp believed: "Providence has a special care for the young, whether human beings or their creations. Surely it was true at this university. When I think of the fine scholarly work that was done in those early days of this institution, and of the enthusiasm, consecration and special fitness of each member of the faculty, it seems it could have been nothing short of a special direction that led to the choice of them." Lieutenant Arthur Ducat, a West Point graduate, taught military science. "He was not only a thorough military man, but a whole host in himself," Clapp recalled. "He found occasion to show himself a good carpenter and splendid clerk. I recall watching him one morning when the drill was in progress. As his sharp, quick orders brought instant obedience, I thought, 'How stern he is.' The next morning, I happened into his house and found him with sleeves turned back and a towel across his lap, tenderly bathing his week-old baby and I thought, 'How tender he is.'" Professor Fred Hillman, who came from Michigan Agricultural College, led the botany and entomology departments. Hillman published a book about the flora of the Truckee Meadows, and he was also known as a fine musician, "constantly in demand in society, where he shone," Clapp said. "I am glad to tell this of him; it is true of so few scientists [to be a musician as well as a scientist]. I take it that it showed added power in the man." Richard Brown, who taught mechanics, was a teach-by-doing sort, who "got hammers and saws and planes and various other implements and he set his pupils actually to work," Clapp said. "He got an old second-hand engine, took it apart with them, put it together again, and that so well that it was a sound engine when it finished and the boys understood its mechanism thoroughly. He was then, as he is today, the right man in the right place."[23] Kate Tupper, wrote Samuel Doten in his *An Illustrated History of the University of Nevada*, was known for her "marvelous" memory that held her students "enthralled while she quoted page after page from the noble works of English literature. In personality Miss Tupper was unusually sweet and charming; the lonesome girls from other towns, homesick in their new surroundings, came to her constantly for advice, and sympathy, of which they were always sure."[24]

Clapp was equally impressed by the hard-working nature of her students: "The students were not one whit behind the teachers, but worked with enthusiasm that was an inspiration. They were thankful for what they got and helped us bear the inconveniences with so kindly a spirit that we actually rejoiced in the circumstances."[25] Clapp was herself known as a person who was beyond reproach and whose teaching was known as kind and caring. "Miss Clapp was energetic and fearless to an extraordinary degree," Doten wrote of her. "Miss Clapp brought to Reno a matured mind and judgment and a kindly force of character that made her a power for good throughout all the early history of the University."[26] Added an observer in 1893, "Miss Hannah K. Clapp . . . knows right where to turn to find any event since, and even before, the landing of Columbus."[27] It was, Clapp recalled later, a team effort to build the University back from the ashes of its Elko beginnings: "But as has been often proved in economic and social life, the success of an institution, or enterprise, does not depend on any one woman or man; in spite of these frequent changes, the University kept its equilibrium and moved on in the even tenor of its way."[28]

By 1889, the faculty numbered ten, and the student body had grown to 127. In that same year, the Normal School graduated its first class.

The University celebrated the conferral of its first college degrees in 1891. The three college graduates from the College of Arts and Sciences were Frederick Amos Bristol, Henry Colman Cutting, and Frank Herbert Norcross. On the evening of June 11, 1891, as the University marked the closing exercises of commencement and before an overflow crowd at McKissick Opera House, the three graduates presented their "orations" as the capstone of their college work. Bristol's "Overtaught" was "a protest against the teaching of those branches in college which were totally impractical in

The class of 1890 commencement of the State Normal School was held on June 12, 1890. Twelve graduating women, members of the second graduating class from the State Normal School, were: Lizzie Savage, Persia Lemon, Lattie Shaber, Jennie McFarland, Mary Clow, Annie Oleevich, Frances Frey, Helena Joy, Blanch Atherton, Hattie Rhodes, Mary Snow, and Addie Morton. The State Normal School was established in 1887 to train teachers who would work in rural elementary and secondary schools. Courtesy of University Archives.

after life." Cutting's "Toadyism in America" criticized the aristocracy in Europe. "Genesis of Socialism," delivered by Norcross, was perhaps the best of the three: "Mr. Norcross held the close attention of all his listeners."[29] His oration was a portent. Norcross would go on to marry University graduate Adeline Morton (1890 Normal) in 1895 and graduated from Georgetown University Law School. He later became principal at Verdi Elementary School, county surveyor for Washoe County, clerk of the US Census Office, Washoe County district attorney, a state assemblyman, an esteemed attorney in Reno, a trustee of the Reno Public Library, chief justice of the Supreme Court of Nevada, and after

Class of 1891 commencement, the first University of Nevada graduating class. The first three students to graduate from the University of Nevada were (*left to right*) Frank H. Norcross, Fred C. Bristol, and Henry Cutting. Courtesy of University Archives.

being nominated by President Calvin Coolidge, served as a federal judge for almost twenty-five years.

President Joseph E. Stubbs brought leadership stability and sparked growing recognition of the University's value to Nevada upon his appointment in 1894. Before Stubbs, leadership at the University had been a revolving door of good intentions and relatively swift exits. From hard-working presidents LeRoy Brown to Stephen Jones, as well as the six principals in Elko, no University chief executive had lasted more than five years. Stubbs would serve as president for almost twenty. Stubbs was a graduate of Ohio Wesleyan University and was president of Baldwin University in Berea, Ohio, when he was appointed as the University's third president in April 1894. Stubbs's inauguration address on September 10, 1894, before a crowd at McKissick Opera House that was tightly packed "from gallery to orchestra," showed an immediate grasp of the moment's importance. He spoke to an understanding of the history of the University: "Out of the mine, from the fragrant fields of your beautiful valleys, and the contribution of your local commerce came the means to erect this University, which speaks of the magnificence of your ideals"—as well as what the future would hold for it. "The ideal University," Stubbs said, "is a place of special training; it focalizes the best in art, in science, in philosophy and is an embodiment of the best spirit of the age. . . . The great fault I have to find with the instructors of this University is their modesty, and I will not be content until the valuable work they are doing is known throughout this and adjoining States. We hope during these coming months to extend the knowledge of this University throughout the State, so that the faces of the professors will be familiar and inspiring guides in every hamlet of Nevada." He concluded: "And from your University that sits upon the hill, guarded by the enduring mountains, and under the serene splendor of the eternal skies, will go out unseen and unmeasured a wave of influence and power that will raise us all in world of living."[30] Stubbs would go on to earn a reputation for speeches that sounded almost as if they were sermons, with messages that were colored by his training in story-driven Greek and Latin studies.

Over the course of his tenure, Stubbs would provide stability, vision, and a missionary-like zeal in relating the importance of the University to the community. In 1894, the University had five buildings; by 1900, there were eleven, including two student dormitories and a gymnasium. He encouraged the establishment of more high schools in the state to ensure the University's students were well-prepared for the rigors of higher education. He stressed the value of the University's land-grant mission and was the first president to take the University's resources into rural Nevada. He was also the first University president to actively take a stand on the moral issues of the day, stressing "ethical values" in his speeches. For the time, Stubbs was progressive in his attitudes and his words regarding racial discrimination: "The land today is the American Negro's land, this country is his country and the Stars and Stripes his flag. He has proved himself possessed of the highest virtues of patriotism."[31] By Stubbs's final year in office in 1914, the University had forty-one members of its instructional faculty, had implemented summer school for the state's teachers, opened a new library building with 27,000 volumes, and was considered the best location in Nevada to process scientific and technical information.

It was also during this time that the University made its first significant foray into philanthropy. In 1907, Comstock Lode pioneer John Mackay's family funded the Mackay School of Mines, the Mackay Athletic Field, and the Mackay Training Quarters. The donation also helped create the University Quadrangle and a statue of John Mackay that would be commissioned to Mount Rushmore sculptor Gutzon Borglum. The "Magnificent Gift" announced in May 1907 created

Joseph E. Stubbs, the third University president (1894–1914), stands with officers of the Cadet Corps on the Mackay Athletic Field, 1911. Courtesy of University Archives.

a $250,000 endowment, which Clarence Mackay, the son of John Mackay, said "was the only way he could repay this great state for the riches it had bestowed upon his father, John W. Mackay, and to his heirs."[32] On June 10, 1908, the fruits of the Mackay endowment were the centerpiece of a commencement ceremony that the *Reno Evening Gazette* breathlessly declared to be "the greatest day in the history of the University of Nevada. It will be a public holiday throughout the entire state in recognition of the proclamation issued by Governor (Denver) Dickerson, who has proclaimed that the day shall be observed as a holiday in honor of Mr. and Mrs. Clarence Mackay and party, and that Mr. and Mrs. Clarence Mackay shall be guests of the State of Nevada."[33]

In addition to the graduation of the class of 1908 in the gymnasium, Clarence Mackay commemorated the unveiling of the John Mackay statue with a long address. Accepting the gift for their constituencies were Governor Dickerson, on behalf of the state; O. J. Smith, president of the Board of Regents, on behalf of the University; and notable graduate Norcross, now on the Nevada Supreme Court, on behalf of the alumni. The big day would conclude that evening with a "brilliant" ball in the gymnasium. The campus was stirring with excitement even before the statue was unveiled. The night before, the Mackays, who were staying downtown in the Riverside Hotel, were made aware of a group of University students who had marched onto the hotel's porch and began calling Clarence Mackay's name: "We want Mr. Mackay. We want Mr. Mackay!" Clarence Mackay, who was dining with President Stubbs and several other guests in the Riverside's dining room, was impressed by the students' spirit. Mackay stood up from the table and made his way to the porch and proceeded to talk to the students. He expressed how pleased he was to meet them and how much their enthusiasm for his visit had meant to him."[34]

The ceremony itself, "under a radiant sun and skies of softest blue," on what is today's Quad, included the unveiling of the statue and the dedication of the new mining building, also named after the Mackays. Clarence Mackay and a long collection of dignitaries spoke in lofty, reflective tones. They appraised the contributions of Comstock Lode figures such as John Mackay as affirmation of the courage and determination that was needed for Nevada to become a state and to realize its bright future. Smith said he accepted the gifts of the day on behalf of the University "to build up the University of Nevada and to make it one of the leading colleges of the United States."[35] As he had almost twenty years earlier upon his graduation, Norcross nearly stole the show. The University had grown tremendously since his senior oration at McKissick Opera House in 1891. What Norcross saw on that sunny day—a shimmering new mining building behind an equally dazzling bronze statue on grounds that would come to have trees and grass and other new buildings—was "an artistic improvement of the landscape," he said. Norcross asked the estimated ten thousand people who attended to take a step back with him. He wished that they would all simply reflect on what the moment really meant. It was a new mining building and a beautiful statue of a miner, yes, he seemed to be saying. But there was something more afoot. The University, in Norcross's estimation as one of its most successful graduates, had finally arrived. "In a broader and higher sense," he said, "through the lives and the characters of those who will here receive an education, the name of this school will live and be familiar to a vastly larger field than that occupied by those who have the privilege of knowing it in its material form. The young men and women who in the past have found this university their only opportunity for a higher education, which has been the case with many of us, know how to appreciate the value of an institution of this kind."[36]

Of the Mackay statue, Clarence Mackay noted that he had "the honor of presenting to the state and the University of Nevada this representation in bronze of John William Mackay, the miner and pioneer, his hand upon the pick and his eyes turned towards Virginia City, the scene of his struggles, his early manhood life, his hopes, his fears, his first great successes."[37] Over the years the John Mackay statue would come to represent many things to the students of the University. The statue became one of the focal points of Mackay

Week, a celebration of the school's mining roots. Students, sometimes wishing for divine intervention for their final examinations, would sometimes pay "tribute" to the Mackay statue with gifts or messages placed below it.

The statue also could not fully escape some of the personal history of its sculptor. Gutzon Borglum was forty-one years old in 1908. Born in the Idaho Territory to a family of Mormon polygamists, Borglum eventually converted to Catholicism and was living in the East and was a sculptor of modest acclaim. He gained renown in 1907 with his bust of Abraham Lincoln, which is displayed in the US Capitol. Following completion of the Mackay statue, he was commissioned by the elderly president of the United Daughters of the Confederacy in 1914 to create a "shrine to the south" near Atlanta that would include Confederate generals Robert E. Lee and Stonewall Jackson. Borglum had no real ties to the Confederacy, according to *Smithsonian Magazine*'s October 2016 article, "The Sordid History of Mount Rushmore," but "he had white supremacist leanings. In letters he fretted about a 'mongrel horde' overrunning the 'Nordic' purity of the West, and once said, 'I would not trust an Indian, off-hand, 9 out of 10, where I would not trust a white man 1 out of 10.'" Above all, however, he was an opportunist. According to *Smithsonian*, "He aligned himself with the Ku Klux Klan, an organization reborn—it had faded after the Civil War—in a torch-light ceremony atop Stone Mountain in 1915."[38] Of all the personal baggage Borglum carried with him, there is no reason to believe, nor is there anything from the historical record concerning John Mackay or his family's past, to indicate that Mackay had white supremacist leanings.

Clarence Mackay is held on the shoulders of a group of supporters during the Mackay Athletic Field dedication ceremony in 1909. (*Left to right*) Claude Teel, Dudley Homer, Ernest Folsom, Kenneth Tillotson, Neil McVicar, Cecil Creel, Walter C. Harris Jr., Frank Hobbins, and Leon Long. Clarence Mackay is holding Walter Harris's 1910 class hat. Courtesy of University Archives.

The Mackay statue cost $12,000 to create and anchors the north end of the Quadrangle where spring commencement exercises are traditionally held each May. The statue was one of many gifts given by the Mackay family to the University. From 1907 to 1936, Clarence Mackay donated about $2 million. For the first time in its history, philanthropy was helping pave the way forward for the University—for what Norcross called "a very full realization of this University to the state at large."

When the University celebrated its thirtieth anniversary from May 28 through June 2, 1904, it needed someone to compile its history. The University turned to a likely and trusted faculty member: James Edward Church. He collected the texts of momentous speeches;

James Edward Church, the Father of Snow Surveying and a professor of classics, was perhaps the most known of all early University faculty. Church developed the Mount Rose Snow Sampler to accurately measure the water content of snow. In 1935, Congress created the Federal-States Co-Operative Snow Survey, based on Church's method, which continues to be used today. Courtesy of University Archives.

found lists of special guests who attended celebrations; gathered the rolls of honor for graduating classes; commemorated the high, lows, and unexpected achievements following times of deep challenge; and produced facts and figures that were part of the celebration. As with everything else Church did in his long and remarkable life, his editing skill adroitly created what became the *Nevada State University Tri-decennial Celebration, May 28 to June 2, 1904.* James Hulse wrote of Church's many talents: "No Nevada faculty member traveled more than Church or contributed more to the University's intellectual and scientific life in the early years. He not only offered most of the courses in Latin for a half century, but he often lectured on classical art and history, and he gained an international reputation as a snow scientist."[39]

Church arrived in Reno in 1892 and had already been on the faculty for twelve years by 1904. He would remain a vital part of campus life until he died in 1959. Church was a professor of Latin and the classics. The Michigan native was an expert in Greco-Roman art and earned his PhD in Germany. As much as he was an admired academic, Church was known also for possessing an adventurer's spirit and for not being afraid of taxing himself physically. He would often hike up and down nearby Mount Rose. He was sometimes accompanied by his wife, Florence, a leading suffragist who earned two degrees from the University of Nevada and was the first woman to ever ride horseback from Yosemite to Mount Shasta. Beginning in 1905, Church began to pioneer "systematic meteorological tests and snow surveys on the slopes of Mount Rose in an effort to predict frosts and water supplies for the valleys below."[40] Church's work led to the first international acclaim any University researcher would ever receive. His work provided the foundation for today's study of snow science, which is particularly critical in measuring the water content of snow and in understanding and predicting the levels of snow-fed runoff in western states such as Nevada and California. Church's energy was legendary and seemingly never waned throughout his life. He helped set up snow survey programs in the United States, Europe, Canada, and South America. At age seventy-eight in 1946–1947, Church organized a snow survey in India in the Himalayas. Once he had successfully completed that survey, he did the same thing for Argentina in the Andes Mountains. Although he often globetrotted, Church was a fixture in the Reno community. He lived in a small home on Washington Street (where his beloved wife died after a stroke in 1922), raised two sons, and was one of the founders of what is today the Nevada Museum of Art. The Church Fine Arts Building, opened in 1960, is named in James Church's honor.

The snow survey equipment used by James Church was considered revolutionary. He was known the world over as a leading expert on how to measure snow and evaluate how water content affected agriculture, development, and growth in the arid western United States. Courtesy of University Archives.

The Extraordinary Life of James E. Church, from Classics Professor to Father of Snow Surveying

by Jacquelyn K. Sundstrand

There was little in James Edward Church Jr.'s background that hinted of what he would accomplish during his lifetime in Reno. Born in Michigan in 1869, he joined the University of Nevada in 1892 as a classics professor, teaching Latin and Greek languages and literature, which he continued throughout his tenure, later adding German and art history and appreciation after receiving his PhD from the University of Munich in 1901. He was captivated by the Sierra Nevada Mountains rising in the east. While struck by the beauty of the mountains, he wanted to understand the role the seasons played in supporting life in his new desert home.

The relationship of the winter's snow accumulation to the amount of water in streams fed by the snowmelt later in the season was known, but there was little hard data on which to rely. Finding the depth of the snow was not enough. One needed to know the amount of water contained in the snow per foot of depth. The drive to understand this relationship between snow and runoff became Church's consuming interest for the rest of his life.

His first experience with the Sierra Nevada was in 1895 when he made a midwinter ascent to the summit of the 10,800-foot Mount Rose on a dare. He spent as much free time in the mountains as he could for "the sheer joy of it." He became interested in mountain meteorology and wanted to establish a high-elevation weather station on Mount Rose. Along with Samuel B. Doten, professor of entomology and later longtime director of the Agricultural Extension Service, he decided to place weather instruments at the mountain's summit in 1905. However, taking measurements at such a high elevation could not always be executed in a single day. A shelter was needed to safeguard those who made the trek. Along with members of his Latin classes, they built the four-bunk Mount Rose Observatory in Reno, hauled it to the summit, and reassembled it.

The weather station had to be fitted with a meteorograph to capture and record on graph paper, in both summer and winter, the daily data for temperature, humidity, and barometric pressure. The station also needed a robust anemometer to capture and record wind velocity and direction at the station. The weather instruments supplied by the US Weather Bureau, however, were not made for the demands of the Mount Rose elevation. Church began work with S. P. Fergusson, a Massachusetts-based designer, who devised early meteorological instrument designs and further improvements. Fergusson came to the University in 1911 and became a professor at the Experiment Station and continued his collaborative work with Church.

Church continued to work on the problem of finding the density of water held in snow. No equipment was available. He came up with an answer in what became known as the world-famous Mount Rose Snow Sampler. It consisted of a steel tube long enough to reach through the snow cover and a scale to weigh the tube and its core of snow. A cutter on the end of the tube helped to drive it into densely packed snow and hold it in place when the tube was weighed by the snow surveyors.

Snow measurements were needed each winter at the same geographical locations to gain the data needed for the later seasonal runoff forecasts. To accomplish this, several fixed snow course locations were mapped where snow surveyors used the sampler. These measurements, collected by Church and other snow surveyors, were given to Horace P. Boardman, who came to the College of Engineering in 1907. Boardman did not get out into the field much with Church but spent time back in his office computing Church's surveys. As a result, he worked out an accurate system of forecasting water runoff based on statistical data painstakingly gathered over many years, previously just a matter of guesswork. He also worked out a mathematical equation which helped make forecasts more scientific.

Church became a working member of the Agricultural Experiment Station staff during the snow survey development's pioneer period (1906–1917) while continuing to teach. His personal connection to understanding snow science continued when he joined a scientific expedition in 1926 and again in 1927–1928 to discover the effect of climate and geography of Greenland on North Atlantic navigation. His own snow-surveying methods became known nationally and then spread internationally, and he shared his knowledge at scientific conferences and with foreign governments. He traveled to Canada and most European countries, including Russia, during the 1930s and 1940s and assisted in streamflow forecasting. He was invited by the government of India in 1947 to assist with forecasts for runoffs from the Himalayas, occasionally traveling to elevations of more than 14,000 feet. The following year he went to Argentina and traveled the entire length of the Andes to locate snow course sites.

His love and appreciation of nature and art were reflected in his attempts for many years during the 1930s to establish a campus art museum. Thwarted in these campus efforts, Church was the principal figure in establishing a museum off campus, called the Nevada Art Gallery. The need for a campus fine arts building as a center for music, art, speech, and drama became a reality with the groundbreaking and dedication of the James Edward Church Fine Arts Building in February 1959. James Church died in August 1959 at the age of ninety.

In 1939 at the mandatory retirement age of seventy, he said that "the science of snow and ice has never been any more than a sideline with me. My students and the classics were my basic interest, and both kept me young." Nevertheless, James Edward Church will always be known as the Father of Snow Surveying, a man for all seasons.

The Beginnings of a Campus on the Hill: Buildings from the Past

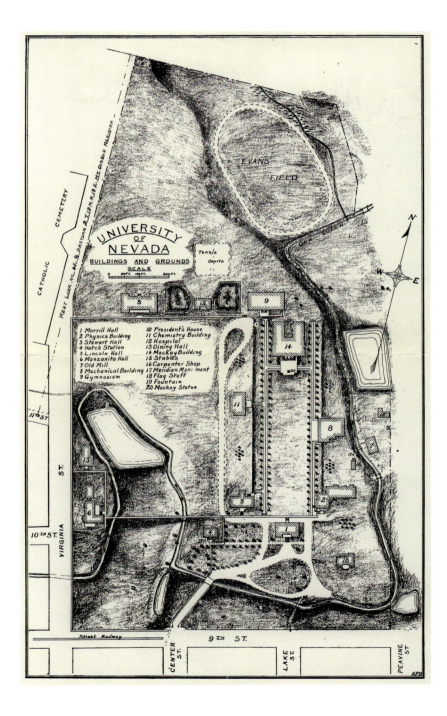

Map showing how the campus looked in 1908.
Courtesy of University Archives.

As the University found its footing from its beginnings in Elko to its relocation to Reno, its physical setting began to take root. Morrill Hall, the first building built on the Reno campus, would prove to be the campus's enduring anchor. But soon other needs were being met—Lincoln Hall (the first men's dormitory, built in 1896), a new gymnasium, an athletic field, and the beautification of campus grounds including the Quad truly gave the University its historic and lasting flavor.

Above: The entrance to the University of Nevada in Reno, 1899; Morrill Hall, Stewart Hall, and the Hatch Hall are visible. Courtesy of University Archives.

Left: Lincoln Hall, the first men's dormitory built at the University in 1896, with a wooden boardwalk leading through grassy areas up to the entrance. Before its opening, up to four male students to a bed slept on the top floor of the Mechanical Arts Building until the fall of 1895 when a fire destroyed the living area. Lincoln Hall maintained its status as the oldest continuously operating residence hall in the western United States until 2015. Courtesy of University Archives.

The gymnasium, built in 1896 with students providing most of the labor, was located where the western side of the Ansari Business Building stands today. This gymnasium housed all kinds of events, including early commencements, until it was demolished in 1964. Courtesy of University Archives.

The Nevada Agricultural Experiment Station in 1900, later known as the Physics Building. The campus's second building, it opened in 1889 to house the growing group of agriculture students. The top part was destroyed in a fire the following year. The building was reconstructed after the fire and housed the mining school and then the physics school until 1929, when it was demolished to make space for construction of the Mackay Science Hall. Courtesy of University Archives.

The Tram across the University ditch (Orr Ditch) and Manzanita Bowl, 1902, with the Chemistry Building and Gymnasium (*right*) and the University Hospital (*back center*). The Tram was built as a wooden walkway across the original Orr Ditch and eventually separated the lake from the grassy knoll known as Manzanita Bowl. It was converted to concrete in 1937. Courtesy of University Archives.

The Mackay School of Mines Building dedication on June 10, 1908, featured the unveiling of the Mackay statue during the dedication ceremony for the Mackay School of Mines. Courtesy of University Archives.

This 1904 view of the campus from the northwest shows the gymnasium, the Hospital Building, the Mechanical Arts Building, Morrill Hall, Lincoln Hall, the Nevada Agricultural Experiment Station Building, and the Chemistry Building. Courtesy of University Archives.

The Tram is photographed with Manzanita Hall in the background and the future site of Manzanita Lake. The Tram was a wooden walkway that stretched over the Orr Ditch and was changed into a concrete structure in 1937. Manzanita Hall, originally known as "The Cottage," was built in 1896 in an L-shape half the size it is today. An addition and an eastern-facing porch were constructed in 1910. The porch was removed when the building was remodeled in 1950. This was the second all-women dormitory built on campus. Courtesy of University Archives.

Morrill Hall, viewed from the south near the campus's Lake Street entrance, circa 1890. Morrill Hall, originally known as the Main Building, was the first building constructed in 1885 and still stands at the southern part of the Old Quad. This building housed classrooms, dorm rooms, and administrative offices until expansion began. Named for Justin S. Morrill, a US senator from Vermont, who wrote the Morrill Land Grant Act of 1862 that helped create universities across the country, the building cost $13,000. The building was renovated in 1979. Courtesy of University Archives.

The Agriculture Building was built in 1918, named after beloved biology professor and 1895 graduate Peter "Bugs" Frandsen. The building housed classrooms and laboratories for the College of Agriculture and Home Economics, until they both moved into other buildings in the late 1950s. The building then housed the philosophy and foreign language departments until it underwent a two-year remodel and reopened in 2000 to house the Department of English. Courtesy of University Archives.

A look across Manzanita Lake and lawn in front of Lincoln Hall in 1930. Courtesy of University Archives.

Faculty members lead the academic procession into Palmer Engineering for the building's dedication on May 10, 1941. Courtesy of University Archives.

The President's House, pictured in 1950, was built east of Morrill Hall and south of today's Mackay Science. The building was the president's home until it was torn down in 1956. Courtesy of University Archives.

This 1911 view looks south over the Quad, with Morrill and Stewart Halls in the background (*left to right*) and the John Mackay statue (*right*). The Quad was created with trees lining its sides as part of the beautification of the campus funded by Clarence Mackay. Courtesy of University Archives.

The University Takes Hold, 1909–1938

One cannot be witness of the proceedings of this day without absorbing a renewed confidence for the future of Nevada, and having a feeling that in this university lies the fountain-head for the future greatness of the state.

—Judge Frank Norcross, one of the University of Nevada's first graduates

The community of Reno mourned the loss of President Joseph Stubbs, who died of heart failure on May 27, 1914. The University's third president had taken ill following a grueling six-week trip during which he and the president of the Nevada Board of Regents visited several universities in the East and federal government and business leaders. That week's commencement exercises were called off. Tasker L. Oddie, governor of Nevada, said in a statement that Stubbs "was our greatest citizen. If we had only known it before! His monument for all time to come will be the University of Nevada, destined to become, as he planned, more and more, as years go by, the center and source of Nevada's true development and awakening."[1]

By the time he died, Stubbs had helped elevate awareness of the University. James Hulse wrote that the "Stubbs administration had started a process of transforming the little college on the Hill into a university. He had found many of the faculty members who became many of the University's most respected teachers of the next generation. In the year of his death, there were forty-one members of the instructional faculty; ten of them reported some kind of publication or scholarly work."[2] Stubbs was the first University president to have a national reputation. He had served as president of the Association of American Agricultural Colleges and Experiment Stations. He had honed the University's land-grant focus with the development of state public service resources on campus. They included the Nevada Analytical Laboratory, Food and Drug Control, and Weights and Measures Department. He had toiled with a near-evangelical fervor for almost two decades in sharing the University's story with the citizens of Reno and throughout the state. When the Mackay statue was looking for a home, it was Stubbs who had taken the initial request from the Mackay family and had found a place for it on campus. Author Rufus Steele later wrote a letter of condolence to Stubbs's widow: "I wish that another monument might be placed at the other end of the Quadrangle—a statue of Dr. Stubbs. . . . the gold that Dr. Stubbs developed was in the lives of men and women, and he formed characters that are more lasting monuments than ever bronze might be."[3]

In fall 1918, the influenza pandemic, which would eventually claim about 675,000 lives of Americans and more than fifty million worldwide, hit Reno. On October 11, 1918, University President Walter Clark issued the following order: "Beginning (on October 11) a military guard will be set about campus and no one will be allowed to go from the campus or come on the campus except by express permission." The University said the order was needed to "check the spread."[4] The quarantine

Joseph E. Stubbs (University president, 1894–1914) stands to the left of US President Theodore Roosevelt during Roosevelt's visit to Reno in 1911. Courtesy of University Archives.

Two University students exhibit a bull at the Agricultural Experiment Station, California State Fair, 1911. Courtesy of University Archives.

was lifted about a month later, but great uncertainty prevailed. World War I had been four years of hellish and brutal warfare. Now there was a pandemic. And if that wasn't enough, at one point, in December, the chemistry building even caught on fire.

Against this backdrop, students demonstrated their willingness to make a difference. Some had gone off to fight in the war, and some had made numerous sacrifices at home. In March 1919, the Associated Students of the University of Nevada (ASUN) brought before the Board of Regents a petition essentially asking to tax themselves. The student organization had become keenly aware over the months of the influenza pandemic how important health care was. They requested that a compulsory $2.50 medical fee be levied on each student each semester. Some of the funds would pay for the recurring services of a physician who would serve the campus. A few months later, the class of 1919 held its commencement exercises. The twenty-two graduates who received bachelor's degrees and the two who received advanced degrees were indicative of a new generation of students at the University. They were part of a group of young people who took the challenges they and the country had weathered as a personal call to do more, to become more involved in their community, and to make a difference wherever they could.

The class of 1919 included Isabelle Slavin, who became a women's rights leader in Nevada. The class also included Frank Harriman, who had been student body president, enlisted for the war, then returned to campus to finish his degree. His family established a trust with the University to help students whose academic careers were interrupted by unforeseen events. It also included a young woman named Laura Louise Ambler, who quietly created ripples of achievement that would be felt years later by students at the University.

On August 1, 1922, the University announced that Ambler would teach its first journalism class, which had eleven students. After spending two years as a newspaper reporter in the Reno area, she had moved to New York City, where she was among a handful of women who earned a degree in journalism from Columbia University in 1922. Her appointment to teach journalism for fall semester 1922 was actually in the English Department. "Miss Ambler has accepted the appointment for one semester only, as she intends to return to New York in order to complete her course at the Columbia School of Journalism at the beginning of the new year," the *Nevada State Journal* reported.[5] Her approach to the class was very much in the spirit of "learning by doing," which would become a hallmark of teaching at the University. "Acting as special correspondent for the city and state newspapers, students enrolled in the first course in journalism offered that the University of Nevada will furnish the public each week with the latest news of college activities," the *Reno Evening Gazette* reported. "According to the plan now in operation, every member of the class is given a weekly assignment to cover. . . . It is designed to give the young journalist practical training in both newspaper writing and interviewing. . . . Though open to only third and fourth year students, some fifteen have already enrolled and intend to follow journalism as a profession. The majority of the students are women."[6] In early 1923, professor Alfred Higginbotham, who would become known as "Higgy" during his forty-three-year career at the University, began teaching the journalism course. Eventually, Higginbotham established journalism as a stand-alone department in 1943. Ambler would marry another journalist, Paul Fredericksen, in 1923, and would go on to become a travel writer and teach at several public and reservation schools. In 1967, she became one of the oldest volunteers for Vista—the domestic Peace Corps—and spent a year working for

An aerial photograph of the campus in 1924. Courtesy of University Archives.

Vista in Kansas City, Missouri. Her Vista experience in some ways mirrored her all-in approach to teaching the University's first journalism course some forty-five years earlier. "How well I remember arriving at the home of a welfare family with my suitcase and air mattress, courageously prepared to spend twenty-four hours a day with them for three long weeks," she said. "It turned out all right. We became good friends."[7]

Walter Clark, like Stubbs, would prove to be a long-serving president whose tenure saw the University continue its steady growth in practically every key area. A native Ohioan, Clark had trained at Ohio Wesleyan University and Columbia. He was known for research in economics and business, and he had a distinguished fifteen-year teaching career at City College of New York. Clark took office in 1918 and served as president until he resigned in September 1938 because of ill health. The growth of the University's physical facilities continued under Clark. They included the expansion of the football stadium, construction of $415,000 Mackay Science Hall, and the opening of a new $250,000 library. Clark supported academic freedom, and often defended the faculty in the cause. "The University grew substantially in the 1920s," Hulse wrote of the period, "approximately tripling its student body in the first six years of Clark's tenure and reaching an enrollment of a thousand for the first time in 1922–23."[8]

The University held a fifty-year celebration in May 1924. Ten graduates were honored through a vote of alumni as part of the University's Hall of Fame. They were: Delle Boyd (1899), a forty-one-year Washoe County auditor so widely respected she rarely faced opposition; Emmet D. Boyle (1899), a native of Gold Hill, who was the first Nevada governor born in the state; Florence Church (1902), a respected Reno suffragist and wife of professor James Church; Sam B. Doten (1898), University historian and longtime faculty member; Peter Frandsen (1895), a biology professor for more than forty-two years; Frank Hobbins (1911), a graduate of the Mackay School of Mines who was killed in action in France during World War I in 1918; Charles Lewers (1893), a prominent attorney and member of the Board of Regents; Margaret E. Mack (1910), a longtime biology faculty member and dean of women; Anne Martin (1894), a faculty member from 1897 to 1901, founder of the Department of History, and an Independent candidate for the US Senate in Nevada in 1918 and 1920; and Frank Norcross (1891), who by 1924 had served as chief justice of the Nevada Supreme Court and who would be appointed to the federal bench a few years later by President Calvin Coolidge.

In his remarks, Norcross noted that "the history of the state has been the history of this university, one of struggles against obstacles, one of triumph over

Department of History founder and professor Anne Henrietta Martin was awarded an honorary degree in 1945. Martin played a key role in the women's suffrage movement and was the first woman in Nevada to run for the US Senate. Courtesy of University Archives.

difficulties. To one who has watched the growth of this university, today is one of deep significance. One cannot be witness of the proceedings of this day without absorbing a renewed confidence for the future of Nevada, and having a feeling that in this university lies the fountain-head for the future greatness of the state."[9]

Cars are parked near the Mackay Science Hall during its construction in 1930. Samuel Doten took the photo, and a copy was given to Clarence H. Mackay, who funded the building's construction. Designed by renowned Reno architect Frederic DeLongchamps and built to house the physics and chemistry schools, the building was praised as one of the most modern places to teach science in the western United States. Courtesy of University Archives.

President Walter E. Clark, architect Frederic DeLongchamps, and donors Clarence Mackay and daughter Katherine Mackay O'Brien participate in the Mackay Science Hall cornerstone ceremony on October 24, 1930. Clarence Mackay holds a trowel with DeLongchamps standing behind him. President Clark (*left*) and an unidentified man help to push in the cornerstone. Courtesy of University Archives.

The Legacy of the Clark Family: From a University President to a Renowned Author, a Family History Still to Be Written

by Guy Clifton

Walter E. Clark was a native Ohioan who came to Nevada in 1917 by way of New York's Madison Avenue to leave an indelible mark—and continuing legacy five generations deep—at the University of Nevada.

Clark, the fifth president of the University, served twenty-one years, from January 1918 to his retirement in 1938—one of the longest tenures for a president in the University's history and a time of significant growth for the campus on the hill. When he took office, student enrollment was 285. By the time he retired, the student population was almost one thousand and the number of buildings on campus had more than doubled.

More importantly, he proved to be a calming force and trusted guide for a campus enduring a crisis of confidence in the mid-1910s. The sudden death of President Joseph Stubbs in 1914 and the tumultuous tenure of his successor Archer Hendrick had everyone from students to faculty to state legislators to the public questioning how things were being run both financially and as an institution of higher education.

In Clark, they found a leader who understood both. The son of an educator, he was born June 9, 1873, in Defiance, Ohio. He earned his undergraduate degree at Ohio Wesleyan University before moving to Columbia University in New York City, where he earned a PhD in economics in 1903. He authored several books on economics and was a popular lecturer in New York's business circles. Among the businessmen he impressed was Clarence Mackay, son of the Comstock Lode pioneer John Mackay and a major benefactor of the University of Nevada.

In September 1917, he was head of the economics department at the City College of New York when the opportunity to lead the Reno campus came about. He was offered a salary of $20,000 and a home to be built on campus for him, his wife, and their four children. He accepted and started on January 1, 1918. Upon news of his selection, the *Reno Evening Gazette* wrote in an editorial, "Now that the regents have chosen a president for the University of Nevada, it is the duty of the people of Nevada to get behind him."

Athletics had been a part of campus life since the 1890s. The University's first official intercollegiate sports victory came in women's basketball on April 11, 1899, when Nevada surprised Stanford University, 3–2. As Kimberly Roberts, University Special Collections archivist noted in her 2018 *Nevada Today* story, "It was startling enough that both the *Nevada State Journal* and the *Reno Evening Gazette* took notice, running prominent articles celebrating the win and anticipating the large crowd and loud ovation that would greet the team when they returned to Reno. The student newspaper proclaimed, 'This is the first time in which Nevada has defeated a college team and we feel duly proud of our victorious girls. Let us follow up this victory with others, and the time is not far off when Nevada will be recognized in athletics among the colleges of the West.'" Roberts further notes why the game was so important:

> The university formed the Athletic Association in 1898, marking the start of organized sports on campus. Before that, less formal co-ed and scrimmage teams had formed among students who quickly discovered that Reno's isolation from other

History showed Walter Clark was the right man at the right time for the University of Nevada, first ushering the campus through World War I and then turning it into a time of expansion. During the two decades Clark served as president, the University saw a great upsurge in growth and development. Among the physical assets added on campus were the Education Building, the Bureau of Mines building, the Agriculture building, Mackay Science Hall, and the Alice McManus Clark Memorial Library.

"He gave the university a stability that it had not enjoyed for several years in the teens," history professor William Rowley said.

Clark, who died in Reno in 1955 at the age of eighty-one, also left an incredible legacy. The Clark children—Walter, Euphemia, David, and Miriam—were graduates of the University of Nevada. Walter Van Tilburg Clark became a noted American novelist and educator. Two of his novels, *The Ox Bow Incident* and *The Track of the Cat*, were turned into films and a third novel, *The City of Trembling Leaves*, is a tribute to growing up in Reno. He and fellow author Robert Laxalt were the charter inductees in the Nevada Writers Hall of Fame.

Daughter Euphemia married James Santini after her graduation from the University; son David became a noted surgeon who spent much of his career in New Mexico; and daughter Miriam married John Chism of the pioneering Reno family. She served as First Lady of Reno when her husband was mayor.

The third generation—the eight grandchildren of Walter Clark—included four-term US Representative Jim Santini and his brother, Clark, who served in numerous state and county government roles and helped secure Rancho San Rafael in Reno as a public park. Both men were University of Nevada, Reno, graduates. As were the Chism grandkids. "It was a given, you weren't going to go away for school. You were going to the University of Nevada," David Chism said.

Calder Chism, a graphic artist who works at NV Energy in Reno and part of the fourth generation of the family to attend the university, agreed: "It's a source of pride, really," he said. "I went there. My kids are going there."

The legacy of the Clark family is still being written at the University of Nevada.

universities made finding opponents and scheduling games difficult. These teams included football, baseball, track, and basketball. The results entered the university record via the student newspaper and yearbooks, predating official collegiate record keeping. According to these records, the football team had in fact won games prior to the women's basketball victory in 1899, playing prep schools, athletic clubs, small private colleges, and second-elevens (the equivalent to second strings or junior varsity teams). Once the university began keeping score, these scrimmage games with non-university teams no longer counted. The win over Stanford did count. It stands to this day as the first official victory of the University of Nevada.[10]

The women of the 1899 Nevada team were indicative of a growing trend in the country, where female athletics and athletes were gaining prominence. Roberts writes:

> Women were interested in playing sports and basketball was their sport of choice. The *Student Record* noted in September of 1896 that "the co-eds of the class of '99 who have always taken an interest

in athletic sports have organized a team to play basketball. This is the first team of the kind organized in this State." Over the next few months, student reporters tracked the practices, often as early as 4:30 a.m., noting that no visitors were allowed in and that people were very intrigued by this group of young ladies, with anticipation palpably building on campus. A large crowd formed when a game was finally organized. Both teams were composed of university students: the Class of 1899 and a second group of students from the women's dormitory, Manzanita Hall, called the Girl's Cottage team. The Class of 1899 won 2–1 after 50 minutes of play with a ten-minute intermission. According to the *Student Record*, the Cottage team remained undaunted while the Class of 1899 intended to find other teams to play.[11]

The members of the 1899 women's basketball team included Elizabeth Stubbs (daughter of President Joseph Stubbs), Amelia North, Edith Brownsill (coach), Mary Eugenia Arnot, Mattie McIntyre, Julia Beckman, Louise Ward, Winnie Strosnider, Elizabeth Webster, Ida Holmes, Maude Patterson, Maude Nash, and Ruby North.

During the late 1890s, some of the first athletic facilities were built on campus. The gymnasium, envisioned as a multiuse facility to host commencements and physical education courses, was completed in 1896, capping a two-year effort that included fundraising drives by students, faculty, and the community. At what is now approximately the site of the Mack Social Science Building, the University's first football field was constructed following the Mackay family donations in 1908: "That new $23,000 athletic track and football

The 1899 University of Nevada women's basketball team. Standing (*top row, left to right*) are Zena Blakeslee, head coach Robert Frazier, M. Grayson, and Vive Hickey. Sitting in the middle row (*left to right*) are Delle Boyd, Elizabeth Stubbs, and Mattie McIntyre. Sitting in the front row (*left to right*) are Enid Williams, Louise Ward, and Mattie Parker. They were the first athletics team, male or female, to record an intercollegiate victory for the University. Courtesy of University Archives.

field donated to the University by [Clarence Mackay], is rapidly assuming shape and will be ready for the athletes of the Nevada college when the University opens next month," the *Reno Evening Gazette* reported in August 1908.[12]

The football program's first star was James "Rabbit" Bradshaw. Known as "Rabbit" because of his size—he was five-foot-eight and 135 pounds—and his shifty elusiveness while carrying the ball, Bradshaw was a native of Kansas. He followed his college assistant at the University of Illinois, Raymond "Corky" Courtright, to Nevada in 1919. Bradshaw led the country in rushing in 1920 with 1,586 yards as the Sagebrushers (Nevada was not yet the "Wolf Pack") finished the year with a 7–3–1 record. That season included a 14–0 victory at

Hawaii, the first game ever played on the Hawaiian Islands by an American mainland team. In 1921 Bradshaw again was the country's top rusher, with 1,534 yards. He was named a fourth-team All-American by Walter Camp. He was also selected for the inaugural East-West Shrine Game. After playing semiprofessionally, Bradshaw became a coach and joined Glenn "Pop" Warner's staff at Stanford. He coached under the Stanford legend for nine years before becoming head coach at Fresno State University in 1936. Bradshaw guided the Bulldogs to a 59-18-5 record in eight seasons. Maxwell Stiles, a longtime Los Angeles newspaperman, remembered the magic Bradshaw had whenever he carried the ball: "Bradshaw was the only man I have seen who could do a tap dance in one place on a football field and, without moving in any direction for a few seconds—defy you to tackle him, then go scooting away like a scared rabbit."[13]

Lloyd Harold Barrington's graduation from the University on May 14, 1928, was historic. Barrington was the first Native American to graduate from the University of Nevada. Barrington, who received a bachelor of arts degree, was one of 143 graduates that year.

Barrington was born on July 9, 1904, in Loyalton, California. His parents were Jessie and Richard Barrington. Richard, born in the town of Boca along the Truckee River, was a member of the Washoe tribe. Richard is generally considered the first student enrolled at the Stewart Indian School in 1890, was one of the first graduates of the school in 1901 and for a time, from July 1898 until June 1900, was also a student at the Carlisle Industrial Indian School in Pennsylvania, where he was known as "Dickie Jack."[14, 15] The Stewart Indian School, which operated in Carson City

Former Nevada football players (*left to right*) James "Rabbit" Bradshaw, Tommy Kalmanir, Stan Heath, and Marion Motley, 1960. All four players belonged to the inaugural Nevada Athletics Hall of Fame class in 1973 and were selected to the University of Nevada's Team of the Century. Courtesy of University Archives.

from 1890 to 1980, was one of several Native American boarding schools throughout the country modeled after the Carlisle Indian School. Native American children were forced to attend schools such as Stewart and Carlisle, where vocational training was emphasized. The Native American children were forbidden to speak their Native languages or practice Native customs. How Richard became a student at Stewart provided a glimpse into how Native American families often had little say about the educational futures of their children and how often "enrollment" for their children at a school such as Stewart was almost like kidnapping. According to the winter 2020 issue of the Sierra County Historical Society newsletter:

> [Richard's] parents heard that a new school for Indian children would be opening, so they walked to Carson City, Nevada to find out more. Richard

was ten years old at the time and was playing with other Washoe children near a pond when William Gibson, the new Superintendent of the Stewart Indian School, approached in a wagon. The children ran, but Richard hid in the willow bushes. He was found and taken to the school. Ninety students that year were brought to the school in a similar manner.[16]

To his credit, Richard excelled as a student and a singer. Known for his rich baritone, he toured the country as a member of Carlisle Indian School's band before returning to Stewart to become one of the school's first graduates in 1901. Richard later became Stewart's band director and took students on band tours throughout Nevada and California. He also directed Stewart's orchestra and taught students how to make shoes and harnesses. Richard's life was notable in how it was extremely focused on providing help and guidance for all Native people in Nevada and California. The University honored him as a "Distinguished Nevadan" during its May 1964 commencement exercises. He was one of the first persons of color to be so honored and without question one of the most notable and well-known Washoe Tribe members. His influence went far beyond music and business. "Richard Barrington worked for the welfare of Native Americans throughout his life," the Sierra County Historical Society noted. "He testified before Congress for the Washoe Tribe of Nevada and California's Indian Claims Commission. His testimony was helpful in establishing the Washoe Tribe as a distinct unit. He also provided scholarships for Native American students at the University."[17] Richard died at his home on the main street in Sierraville, California, at age eighty-five, in 1967.

Wá·šiw tribe member Lloyd Barrington became the first Native American to graduate from the University of Nevada with a bachelor of arts in economics in 1928. Courtesy of University Archives.

Son Lloyd was an honor roll student at Carson High School, playing on the school's football, tennis, and track teams, and graduated in 1923. Lloyd served in the US Army in World War II and for a time was stationed near Nevada's copper mines, which were helping Nevada play an important role in the country's war effort.[18] Following the war, Lloyd worked alongside his father in the lumber industry in northern California, serving as vice president of Richard's Sierraville Lumber Company. Lloyd died at his Sierraville home following a short illness on his birthday, July 9, 1959, at the age of fifty-five. The *Sierra Booster* newspaper wrote of his passing that Lloyd was "one of the Sierra Valley's finest gentlemen," and that he was a "main cog" in the operation and success of his father's lumber company.[19] More than one hundred delegates from the Indian Association of California attended Lloyd's funeral, providing further testimony of Lloyd's and his family's significance to the Native American people of Nevada and California.[20]

Theodore H. Miller's graduation from the university in 1930 did not receive the kind of fanfare that it deserved. Miller, who received a degree in electrical engineering in May 1930, was the first African American to graduate from the University. Since its inception in 1862, the Morrill Act had promised to make a college education more accessible to more people throughout the United States. The nation's reality was far different than the promises the Morrill Act seemed to make. "Access to higher education for black Americans did not improve dramatically after the Civil War," wrote Robert Bruce Slater in the comprehensive study of land-grant educational opportunity, "The First Black Graduates of the Nation's 50 Flagship State Universities" in The Journal of Blacks in Higher Education. "W. E. B. Du Bois' research concluded that from 1865–1900 only 390 blacks had graduated from predominantly white colleges and universities." The introduction of a second Morrill Act, in 1890, wrote Slater, "was a mixed blessing for the higher education for African Americans. Although it opened the door to the establishment of dozens of black public land-grant institutions, the act assured a half century of more of strict racial segregation of American public higher education."[21]

Many major obstacles faced young Black Americans such as Miller, who in the late 1920s chose to seek higher education at western universities. In Nevada in 1930, for example, the US Census Bureau reported that 526 African Americans were living in the state. About 143 African Americans were in Washoe County,

Senior portrait of the University's first African American graduate, Theodore Miller, in the 1930 edition of the *Artemisia* yearbook. Courtesy of University Archives.

the state's most populous county with 27,000 people. According to *The African American Civil Rights Experience in Nevada, 1900–1979*, Nevada's African American citizens in the state's early history had faced "blatant racial discrimination," where racism grew "more common and overt . . . in the years following the end of Reconstruction through the Great Depression. The creation of Ku Klux Klan branches throughout the state during the 1920s and aggressive efforts by city officials to segregate Las Vegas beginning in the 1930s are two obvious examples. African Americans in Nevada actively worked to combat these growing patterns of racism through advocacy and legislative reform, but their efforts during the early twentieth century were largely unsuccessful."[22]

THE UNIVERSITY TAKES HOLD, 1909–1938

Miller, born in Kansas City on January 27, 1905, enrolled at the University in August 1928. He transferred from Kansas State University. "During this entire time," he wrote in a letter to longtime University anthropology professor Warren L. d'Azevedo in 1977, "I was the only black student on the campus. I remember the University in just one way, with regards to students, faculty and everyone connected to the University, I was treated like a King." Miller went on to reminisce about being an extremely focused student who had worked full-time to make his academic ends meet the financial needs of a young minority who otherwise had no obvious support system. "My sole purpose of attending the University was to get a BS Scholarship—never heard of one (we are backtracking about fifty years). I earned every nickel of my expenses before and while attending the University." Miller worked at Donner Lake during the summer of 1929, and later, as his money ran out, washed cars at a Reno garage until one or two in the morning. A talented musician and dancer, Miller would make extra money playing piano at fraternity and sorority parties. "I had a 'piano act' that I performed onstage with a grand piano," he wrote. "The University drama group put on a show in Fallon, Nevada and took me with them to do my number as a special feature. I was in the Nevada Follies in either 1929 or 1930." Miller noted, too, that he enjoyed having some of his "wild ideas" from Kansas State University used during the engineering department's annual open house. "[I] was practically put in charge of the electrical engineering exhibition," he wrote. "When I visited the University some twenty years later, Professor Irving Sandorf called the electrical group together to have me explain some of the way-out electrical stunts I had for open house when I was a student."[23]

Following graduation on May 12, 1930, Miller went on to have a distinguished career. He married Grace Eubank, and the couple had two children. He was the chief electrical engineer of the Ninth Region of the US General Services Administration for more than two decades. He was also the assistant head of engineering for the Veterans Administration in San Francisco, and he was the supervisor of the Electrical Design Department for Mare Island US Naval Shipyard. He taught radiological defense at Stanford University and was the president of the board of directors of the Booker T. Washington Community Center in San Francisco. He died on January 3, 2000, in Houston at age ninety-four.

By the late 1930s, the University had already developed notable philanthropic relationships with several key donors. Clarence Mackay and his family had financed the $415,000 Mackay Science Hall in 1930, and in 1936 they had helped the University double in size with the purchase of the nearby Evans Estate. When Clarence Hungerford Mackay died in November 1938 at age sixty-four, Maxwell Adams, a one-time acting president of the University and dean of Arts and Science, said of the financier and chairman of the Postal Telegraph Company, "We've lost the greatest friend we've ever had at the University of Nevada. . . . Mr. Mackay was kind to us in every way and was, indeed, a great benefactor."[24] The Clark family (not related to President Walter Clark) also provided the campus with a key new building. William Clark, the son of a US senator from Montana, donated $250,000 for a new campus library in honor of his late wife, Alice McManus, who was a northern Nevadan. The Clark Library, as it became known, opened in fall 1927. Today it is home to the Office of the President, the Office of the Provost, and the Office of the Vice President of Administration and Finance.

The emergence of another key philanthropic figure in 1938, Max Fleischmann, would continue to grow the campus's infrastructure and help the University turn its attention to student scholarships—affirming that its reach could go far beyond its hillside perch above Reno. Fleischmann was first and foremost a businessman. He had made his fortune in his family's yeast business. "In the 1930s," James Hulse wrote, "Nevada boasted that it was a storm cellar for the tax-weary, and Fleischmann was one of several wealthy men who established Nevada residence to avoid state income and inheritance taxes. He contributed generously to the Nevada State Museum, and in 1938 he began to provide securities to establish a scholarship fund. By the 1940s, he had increased the gift to about $160,000, the income from which provided a number of scholarships for freshman and returning students."[25] Fleischmann also gifted a 258-acre farm in the southern part of the valley to the University. He provided philanthropic gifts for the College of Agriculture's laboratories. His foundation, the Max C. Fleischmann Foundation, contributed the funding for the 1954 construction of two buildings, the College of Agriculture Building (the Max C. Fleischmann College of Agriculture Building) and the School of Home Economics (the Sarah Fleischmann Building). The Atmospherium Planetarium, the Water Resources Building, and the

The Reverend Michael Ahern gives the commencement address at the 1936 ceremony in the gymnasium. Courtesy of University Archives.

Judicial College Building were all built later with the Fleischmann Foundation's support.

As war in Europe loomed large, the 1938 spring commencement was held on the morning of Monday, May 9. The processional met at the south end of the Quad at 10:15 a.m. and spiritedly marched to the University gymnasium. The *Nevada State Journal* reported that the graduating class of 155 students boasted the largest number of graduates ever from the Mackay School of Mines, including a grandmother, Mrs. Irma Loforth, and a married couple, Mr. and Mrs. Milton P. Parker. Walter Clark, who had resigned as president earlier that year, returned to lead the graduates in the civic oath. In a surprise, Silas Ross, chairman of the

Board of Regents, gave Clark an honorary degree.[26] It was an emotional day for Clark, who in 1920 and still early in his presidency had written the words to the civic oath, which also became known as the "Book of the Oath." More than 1,900 graduates had signed the oath, pledging to live a life of service and high ideals, since it began to be used. The book, too, unfortunately carried with it strong implications regarding the supposed burdens white individuals carried with them as they lived a life of service while acknowledging a great debt to the white race.[27] Eventually, the names of the graduates who would dutifully drop by the President's Office in the days leading up to commencement to sign the book would fill all its pages. In the 1960s, President Charles Armstrong would call for an end of the tradition of the signing of the book. These were changes that were needed. Very soon, the world, Nevada, and the University would experience abrupt and far-reaching challenges and transformations. The University, which had grown tremendously for two decades, would need to grow up in a hurry to meet the challenges it would soon face.

The University Comes to Life: Campus Life from the Past

Two students pose wearing Nevada "N" sweaters and top hats in 1904. Courtesy of University Archives.

The music of any institution of higher learning is provided by the activity of its people, and the University of Nevada, Reno, was no different. The life of the campus included "learning by doing" activities that dotted the campus's open spaces and classrooms. Student traditions such as "Painting the N" and athletic competitions brought the campus community together. The University's green, idyllic setting wasn't lost on Hollywood, either, which came to Reno to film several movies on what was considered a classic university setting.

Two boys play on University Pond, which preceded Manzanita Lake, in 1905. Manzanita Lake was created by damming up Orr Ditch, the irrigation system that still runs through parts of the University today. Originally a man-made ranchers' pond as seen in this photograph, the lake was created with the help of donor Clarence Mackay in 1911 as part of the University's beautification. Courtesy of University Archives.

Students participate in a class in the commercial department in 1894. President LeRoy Brown oversaw the establishment of the Business Department, also known as the Commercial School, focusing on commercial arithmetic, bookkeeping, and commercial law. Courtesy of University Archives.

Students sew during a 1920 dressmaking class as part of the School of Home Economics in the Agriculture Building (today's Frandsen Humanities). Courtesy of University Archives.

Two students paint along Orr Ditch in 1905. The ditch, which still exists today around campus and in surrounding neighborhoods, originally provided irrigation for Evans Ranch before the University's purchase of the area in 1884. Courtesy of University Archives.

First-year students in physical education uniforms participate in folk dancing on the Quad with the Mackay School of Mines and the Mackay statue in the background in 1920. Courtesy of University Archives.

Students on Peavine Mountain prepare to paint the "N" on September 30, 1922: (*left to right*) Alden D. Hunting, Frances Humphrey, Evalyn Nelson, Gilberta Turner, and William M. Esser. Courtesy of University Archives.

Above: Men's basketball coach John E. "Doc" Martie and unidentified students delineate the track around Mackay Field on Mackay Day in 1927. Martie coached the Wolf Pack from 1923 to 1929 and from 1931 to 1939. Hatch Hall is on the far left. Courtesy of University Archives.

Left: The original wolf head wearing a top hat after the "Wolf Pack" was chosen as the University's mascot during the early 1920s. Courtesy of University Archives.

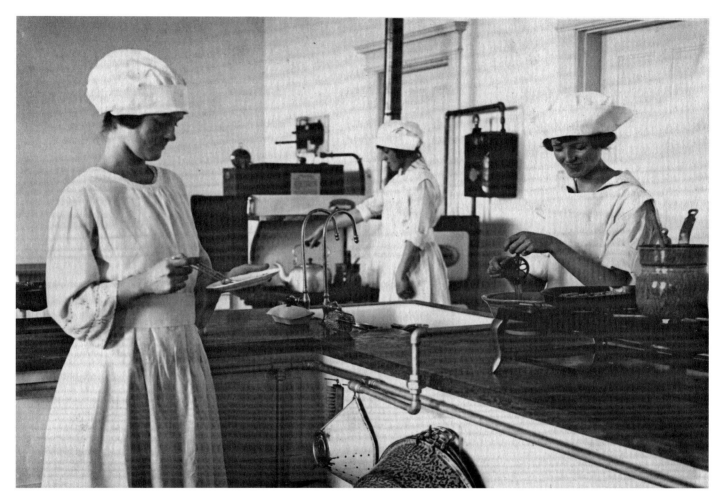
Some of the earliest courses at the University included home economics classes, offered in 1901 and later growing into the Department of Home Economics. Courtesy of University Archives.

Students sit near the Lombardi Recreation Center during a drawing class in 1979. Courtesy of University Archives.

The Fremont Cannon is fired during a University of Nevada football game against University of California, Davis, in 1979. Kennecott Copper donated the Fremont Cannon in 1970 as a replica of a howitzer cannon used by John C. Frémont's 1843 Nevada expedition. The winner of the "Battle for Nevada" football game between UNR and UNLV is given the trophy for one year. The cannon is no longer operational. Courtesy of University Archives.

Four students paddle on a concrete canoe on Manzanita Lake in 1981. Courtesy of University Archives.

During the filming of 20th Century Fox's *Mother Is a Freshman* on campus in 1944, five co-eds walk across the Tram at the edge of Manzanita Lake. Manzanita Hall (*left*), Lincoln Hall (*background*), and Frandsen Humanities (*right*) can be seen. Courtesy of University Archives.

In this still from 20th Century Fox's *Apartment for Peggy* (1948), Gene Lockhart and Henri Letondal stand in the snow near Edmund Gwenn, seated. Students skate on Manzanita Lake (*background*) with views of the Thompson Building (*left*) and Frandsen Humanities Building (*right*). Courtesy of University Archives.

Sagebrush editor Mark Curtis (*left*) checks the newspaper as it comes off the press. The *Sagebrush* can trace its award-winning history back to 1893, when it was first published as the *Student Record*. Courtesy of University Archives.

Workers build the foundation of the Jot Travis Student Union, with Lincoln Hall in the background, in 1957. It was the first student center and became the Davidson Academy's home when the Joe Crowley Student Union opened in 2007. Courtesy of University Archives.

The University Reflects the Challenges of Nevada and the Nation, 1939–1978

If you choose to do the right thing, hopefully they are going to remember who you were and why you chose to do it.

—Sherman Howard, former Nevada Wolf Pack running back

Lieutenant William Raggio returned to a far different University of Nevada after his service in the US Marine Corps during World War II than what he had experienced for a few short months after graduating from Reno High School in January 1944. Raggio had grown up not far from the campus, in a small Italian American enclave on Surprise Valley Road (today's Valley Road). As a boy, he had often wandered onto campus and used it as his own playground. Raggio was seventeen, bright and ambitious, when he graduated early from high school. He enrolled at the University as he bided his time for military service. For a semester Raggio took a full course load of logic, math, political science, trigonometry, and economics. He pledged the ATO fraternity. The campus, with the world war still raging, was in flux, Raggio remembered later. "It felt as if there weren't a lot of students like me, who were still kids essentially," he said. "All of the upperclassmen were gone fighting in the war. The classes felt small and even some of the younger professors were serving in the war. It was as if the University was in a holding pattern."[1] Raggio would leave Reno for the Naval Officers Training Program in Ruston, Louisiana, at the end of the semester in June 1944. Once the war ended and his duties in the military were complete, Raggio returned to Reno and reenrolled in January 1947. Raggio's biographer, Michael Archer, writes of what Raggio saw:

> The University of Nevada had changed considerably since Bill last attended there in 1944. Classes were larger and there were more faculty members. Though students were still coming to campus directly from high school, a large number were returning from military service. Earlier hazing traditions would have required all male freshmen to wear a small skullcap called a "dink." If a freshman were caught not wearing his "dink" he would be thrown into a pond on campus called Manzanita Lake. It soon became apparent that no one was going to insist war veterans wear "dinks." Other hazing practices, such as requiring new students repaint the big letter "N" on the side of Peavine Mountain, were also made obsolete by this new breed of lower classmen.[2]

Like thousands of other veterans, Raggio received educational benefits from the GI Bill, which created a groundswell of college students. The University reported in fall 1947 that its enrollment had reached an all-time high of 1,816 students, including 868 veterans and 521 female students. "Enrollment at the

University has climbed consistently since 1943, during the war years, when a record low of 412 students was reached," the *Reno Evening Gazette* reported. "Immediately following the close of the year in the spring of 1945 enrollment jumped to 1,100 students, almost equaling the former all-time high of 1,142 set in the fall of 1940." The surge in postwar enrollment squeezed the campus. Laboratory space was just one example of a campus bursting at the seams. Campus labs for classes in chemistry and biology were designed more for a student body of 900. They were immediately filled postwar with bottlenecks of scheduling. Men's and women's dormitories were so maxed to capacity that about one hundred students were being housed in the gymnasium during fall 1947.[3]

Even with classroom and lab space at a premium, it was a time, Raggio said, where everyone on campus seemed fueled with a determined purpose. Almost all the veterans were anxious to get on with their lives. "We enjoyed each other's company . . . and we certainly made lifelong friends and learned lifelong lessons from faculty who were some of the best minds in the world of academia," Raggio said. "I still think about the story where [famed Nevada author and University graduate Robert Laxalt, a.k.a. "French"] French Laxalt met his future wife, Joyce, on campus one day not long after he'd come back from the war. She smiled at him, and French knew that smile was forever. But for the most part, there was always a sense that we were catching back up with our lives. It was an uncluttered life in that we were all very young, but it was also a life where we knew we needed to do our work at the University and then start our next chapter."[4]

President John Moseley (1944–1949) stands next to the University's Blue Star Flag that indicates the 853 students who had entered military service during World War II by 1942. The top seven stars represent those who had lost their lives in the line of duty. Courtesy of University Archives.

Raggio would go on to graduate from the University with a degree in political science in 1948. He would marry Dorothy "Dottie" Brigman that same year. Raggio became a highly successful prosecutor, was elected Washoe County district attorney, and then served as a Nevada state senator from 1972 to 2011, during which time he often chaired the powerful Senate Finance Committee.

Numerous faculty members came to the campus with the direction of their lives also altered by World War II. Willem "Wim" Houwink joined the faculty in 1957 as a professor of economics. Born in Meppel,

Holland, in 1920, he excelled at tennis in his early years. Throughout his long life, he advocated the benefits of physical activity. Following graduation from the University of Rotterdam, he earned his doctorate from the Netherlands School of Economics in 1947. World War II interrupted Houwink's schooling. During the war, once the Germans invaded the Netherlands, he fought the Nazis as part of the Dutch underground. In 1942, Houwink was arrested by the Gestapo secret police and sent to the Dachau concentration camp in southern Germany. Houwink survived the ordeal, which lasted from 1943 to 1945. Houwink, who possessed a gentle laugh and was always a welcoming and kind presence in all interactions, was not afraid to share what he had experienced during World War II. He felt it was important to learn from the past. He once said, "On the day I arrived, I had to decide whether to give up and die or fight every single moment of every day to survive."[5] Houwink was intensely devoted to the concepts of personal and intellectual freedom. Throughout his teaching and his interactions with his students, he made the horrors of war something that was tangible and not ever to be minimized or forgotten. During a 2011 presentation he made about his experiences in Dachau, Houwink brought the same garments that he had worn during his time as a prisoner in a concentration camp to the talk. He had the audience hold his camp clothes in their own hands. Throughout his life, Houwink never wanted people to forget the war and its inhumanity.

Houwink, who retired from the University in 1983 and lived until 2016, when he was ninety-five, played a leading role in launching the *Nevada Business Review*

Air Force College detachment cadet trainees from flights 43, 44, and 45 are pictured with Mackay Training Quarters in the background in 1944. During World War II, more than five hundred US Army pre-flight cadets came to train and live at the University. They would often be part of classes, many of which became special war courses. Courtesy of University Archives.

publication; served on the Economic Education in Public Schools Committee; presided as chair of the Economics Department; established the UNR Honors Program; and was a visiting professor in Turkey, the Netherlands, Germany, Italy, England, Egypt, and Mexico. He traveled throughout the United States and the world, giving entertaining and timely lectures on the world's economies and the concept of free enterprise. In 1983, he became one of the first professors from a Western university to teach free market economics in China.

Above it all, though, were the deep and lasting friendships Houwink established with his students.

The Virginia Street Gymnasium was completed for athletics use in 1945. Designed by Reno architect Frederic DeLongchamps, the building housed visiting aircrew cadets training for World War II. The building became the main physical training and recreation center until the 1970s. Courtesy of University Archives.

Larry Struve was one of twenty-eight other University students who accompanied Houwink on a trip to Germany and Dachau in 1962. "When we arrived at Dachau, Wim gave the introductory speech of what it was like to live in a concentration camp, and what one did to survive," Struve said. "By the time the tour that day was over, there was not a sound on the bus ride back. Everyone was contemplating what they had heard and seen, what it had meant and what a sobering moment it was to hear a man like Wim share his experience with us all." But here was the thing, said Struve, who graduated in 1964 and later became commerce director for Governor Richard Bryan, a 1959 University graduate. "Wim loved life," Struve said. "He loved his students and he wanted us all to understand that in order to love life, you must always be on guard against hatred and inhumanity. As a professor, and as a mentor, he wanted all of his students to be guardians of human rights. To love and respect everyone. He understood what being a good human being meant, and that it is our duty throughout our lives, to help others always do the right thing, better than any other professor I ever had at the University."[6]

Stella Mason Parson was born on November 18, 1929, in Lake, Mississippi. Her parents, Fred and Matilda Parson, were sharecroppers on a plantation. Fred Parson made the decision that his family needed a new place to start a new life. "He stole [his family] off the plantation and hid them on a plantation in Arizona before working to pay to move them to Las Vegas," a family friend, Tara Trass, told the Associated Press in 2016.[7] Stella Parson graduated from Las Vegas High School, becoming the first person in her family to ever graduate from high school. As part of a UNLV oral history project in 1978, she remembered her neighborhood, located west of Las Vegas where there were "no paved streets" and "almost no homes for blacks at all."[8] Following graduation, she began work as a maid. Parson was an extremely hard worker. Her employer, Rosemary Ruymann, took notice of the young woman's industriousness and care for the work she did, and arranged for her to get a scholarship. Parson was able to attend the state's only university, the University of Nevada, thanks to that $150 scholarship provided by the American Association for University Women. "She said she saw something in me and thought I could do better, and I'll never forget her," she said of Ruymann.[9]

Reno in the late 1940s was still segregated. "Nevada encouraged separation of the races," historian Michael Archer wrote. "Casinos, businesses, and even churches

Stella Mason Parson's senior portrait in the 1952 edition of the *Artemisia* yearbook. She was the first African American woman to graduate from the University. Courtesy of University Archives.

were segregated. The Reno train station had a separate waiting area for blacks."[10] By 1950, Washoe County's African American population was still low at 0.96 percent (483 people) of the county's total population, though the number was on the rise because of several factors. Longtime University history professor Michael Coray, who directed the institution's first ethnic studies program, wrote, "First, the lure of available jobs ensured continuous population growth. Second, racial discrimination in the marketplace limited African-American employment prospects to the most menial and poorly paid jobs. Such practices were a constant threat to the economic viability of members of the African-American community, be they employees or small business owners. Third, and perhaps most crucial, the dismantling of segregation, and the economic, social, and residential discrimination that it sanctioned, would require the active involvement of Nevada's African-American community."[11]

Parson found work as a domestic and also manned the steam tables in the University cafeteria while she was enrolled. Her first semester was spent living in a room in Manzanita Hall, the women's dormitory. She did not have a roommate. Her time at the University was both enriching and also highly indicative of the challenges a young Black person would find in a city where segregation was still prevalent. Very few other Black students were at the University when she first arrived in Reno. The majority served in World War II and were members of the Wolf Pack's nationally ranked football teams. The campus, she remembered later, was still small enough where "everybody knew everybody else back then." Her fellow students and her instructors were "extra special nice to me." She added, "Since I was the first black female student here, I felt like everybody at the University was pulling for me."[12]

Yet in the community, Parson often faced discrimination. Certain Reno restaurants refused to seat her. She remembered feeling "confined" to the opportunities where she could socialize, in class or at church. "I guess you can accept anything if you have to," she said. "Looking back on segregation in those days, it all seems so senseless. It was frustrating to sit down in a restaurant with a bunch of friends and be told 'coloreds' weren't allowed. It was equally embarrassing to my friends. They'd all get up and leave too, but it was humiliating." Originally a business major, she had been advised by a professor to think about switching to teaching. "He told me he didn't think it was wise," Parson said. "Even if I could get a degree in business, there would be no place in Nevada or California that would hire me. While I don't think that is good advice for a black person now (to switch from business to education), it was good advice for me, the individual."[13]

When she graduated from the University in 1952 with a degree in English with minors in education and psychology, Stella Mason became the first Black woman to graduate from a university in Nevada. Her first teaching job, to complete her education requirement, was for a year as a student teacher at Orvis Ring Elementary School in Reno. "We had to get special permission for me to work as a student teacher," she said. "They had never had a black teacher in the district before. There was quite a hassle over that, but once I started, everything worked out."[14]

Stella Mason Parson would go on to have a notable and successful teaching career. She taught elementary school in Clark County for thirty-three years. She would also earn a master's degree in marriage and family counseling from UNLV. The Claude and Stella Parson Elementary School in Las Vegas was named in honor of her and her late husband, Pastor Claude H. Parson Jr. She was honored numerous times for her teaching and was listed in *Outstanding Elementary School Teachers of America*. In 2001, the University awarded her with its President's Medal—a rare distinction that honors individuals for their outstanding achievements—and the Distinguished Nevadan Award from the Nevada System of Higher Education.

Her family's bonds with the University remained strong. Her two daughters, Naida and Jacqueline, are both University graduates, as is her granddaughter, LaToyshia Parson, who graduated with a degree in psychology in 2002. Proud grandmother Stella was in the crowd on the Quad that day. Earlier that week she had met the first recipient of the Stella Mason Scholarship. LaToyshia had proudly carried her family's University history with her throughout her time as a student on campus in the late 1990s and into the early 2000s. At one point, she and some of her classmates lobbied the Nevada Legislature for more funding for academic offerings dealing with the African American experience.

Stella Mason Parson died on July 29, 2016, at age eighty-six.

Although minoritized people such as Stella Mason Parson faced discriminatory practices in Northern Nevada during the late 1940s, the University's football team during that time would play several important games that inched intercollegiate athletics in the country closer to integration. The presence of African American student-players on the Wolf Pack, including the great Marion Motley, Bill Bass, Horace Gillom, Sherman Howard, and Alva Tabor, would repudiate existing Jim Crow segregation laws still prevalent throughout the country in the mid- to late-1940s.

Marion Motley was born in 1920 and grew up in Canton, Ohio. Coach Jim Aiken recruited him to Nevada in 1940. When Motley arrived in Reno, his teammates and coach were supportive. But players and coaches from other universities were a different story. Motley later told the University's Oral History Program, "They called us names and everything, and I just wouldn't even talk to them. If I caught one in my way, I ran over him. I ran smack over him . . . we got a

Marion Motley, who starred for the Wolf Pack in the early 1940s, helped break professional football's color barrier when he became a member of the Cleveland Browns. Courtesy of University Archives.

Nevada football players Sherman Howard and Alva Tabor. Howard was a running back for the Wolf Pack from 1947 to 1948. Tabor was a fullback and quarterback for the Wolf Pack in 1948. In 1948, Howard and Tabor became the first two African Americans to play in a college football game in Oklahoma when the University of Nevada faced the University of Tulsa. Courtesy of University Archives.

lot of respect that way." In a game against Idaho, Idaho's coach wouldn't let Motley play. Aiken grew incensed. "When [the Idaho coach] told Jim I couldn't play, I had to grab Jim and pick him up around his waist and hold him off the ground.... He was going to punch this guy in the mouth," Motley said.[15] Message received. Motley played in that game. And in many more.

When he left the University in 1942, eventually for military service in 1944, Motley was the Wolf Pack's greatest player. Motley, along with Bill Willis of the Cleveland Browns and Kenny Washington and Woody Strode of the Los Angeles Rams, would go on to break professional football's color barrier in 1946 . . . a full year before Jackie Robinson broke Major League Baseball's color barrier. He was later named to the NFL 75th Anniversary All-Time Team and elected to the NFL Hall of Fame, located in Motley's hometown of Canton.

During the 1946 season, the Wolf Pack was scheduled to play in Starkville, Mississippi, against Mississippi State University. C. R. Noble, its athletics director, wrote the University of Nevada that "it is not custom in the South for members of the Negro race to compete in athletics with or against members of the white race nor members of the white race to compete against the Negro race in athletic contests. I am sure that you understand this traditional custom which Mississippi State college cannot under any circumstances violate." Mississippi State had made it clear the Wolf Pack's two

Eleven University of Nevada football players and assistant coach Glenn "Jake" Lawlor kneel in front of a Pacific Intermountain Express truck during the team's heyday in 1948: (*left to right*) Stan Heath, Tom Kalmanir, Frank Sanchez, Ken Sinofsky, Tom Reinhardt, Sherman Howard, Fred Leon, Bob Corley, Richard "Dick" Trachok, Dan Orlich, Carl Robinson, and Lawlor. Courtesy of University Archives.

Black players, Bill Bass and Horace Gillom, were not welcome in the state. William "Billy" Bass, who was born in Greensboro, North Carolina, was a running back who would go on to become one of the first Black players to break the color barrier in the Canadian Football League in 1949 with the Toronto Argonauts. Bass would become a CFL all-star and in 1951 earn a nomination for Jeff Russel Memorial Trophy, awarded at that time to the CFL player who best demonstrated skill, sportsmanship, and courage. He would later be a player-coach in Canada. Like Motley, Gillom had grown up in Ohio. In high school he was coached by Paul Brown, who would become a legendary NFL figure as coach of the Cleveland Browns. It was Brown, in fact, with the Browns, who would sign Motley in 1946 to a professional contract. A year later, Brown signed his former Massillon (Ohio) High School standout, Gillom, to a professional contract. Before coming to Nevada, Gillom fought in the Battle of the Bulge during World War II, earning three bronze stars. Gillom played on the defensive line, was a sure-handed receiver for the Wolf Pack during the 1946 season, and was the team's punter. He led the nation in punting that season.

Faced with Mississippi State's ultimatum, Aiken gathered his players. The team agreed that if Bass and Gillom weren't allowed to play, the Pack wouldn't play. Dick Trachok, a Wolf Pack player and later athletics director at the University, told the *Reno Gazette-Journal* in 2015 that the team's players, coaches, and administration were equally adamant. They voted to cancel the game. The contract between the University and Mississippi State stated that if one school were to cancel the game, it would have to pay the other $3,000—a significant amount of money for the era. No matter. The $3,000 was worth it. George Ross, a University journalism graduate who would become an influential Bay Area sports journalist, wrote in the *Reno Evening Gazette* in 1946 that "most Nevadans believe that Nevada is above the need for a caste system which demands hooded riders, peonage and two standards of opportunity. In the world of sports, where individual prowess and team play are better measures of equality than the color of skin, most of the nation is as proud of the feats of one race as of those of another."[16]

Bass and Gillom were respected Wolf Pack players, well-known and well-liked on campus. Charles Martin wrote in his 2010 book, *Benching Jim Crow: The Rise and Fall of the Color Line in Southern College Sports*,

1890–1980, that "the University of Nevada refused to leave at home its two black starters, both military veterans, and instead called off its match against Mississippi State in Starkville. Nevada students, led by white veterans, had opposed any concessions to Mississippi State."[17] For perhaps the first time in history, a predominantly white school had canceled a major college football game rather than travel to and abide by the Jim Crow laws of the post-Confederate South.

In the fall of 1948, the Wolf Pack once again stared down Jim Crow in collegiate athletics. Oklahoma's Tulsa University warned against bringing the Wolf Pack's Black players, Alva Tabor and Sherman Howard, to their state. Again, it was a telegram to campus, this time from C. I. Pontius, the president of Tulsa University, that brought what was at stake into focus. Pontius wrote that although there were no explicit rules against "Nevada Negroes playing" in the game, "Nevada is aware of the traditional background of athletics in the state of Oklahoma . . . and the decision is the prerogative of Nevada."[18]

Tabor, from Savannah, Georgia, was a jack-of-all-trades type of player, who not only could run with the ball but could throw it just as well. He also played tennis for the Wolf Pack. Before the war, while a student at Tuskegee Institute, he had won a national tennis championship. Tabor would go on to teach and coach at several Historically Black Colleges and Universities, be on the first coaching staff of the expansion New Orleans Saints in 1967, and become the first full-time Black assistant coach for the Cleveland Browns in 1972. Howard, born in New Orleans, moved to Chicago at age ten. In 1938, when he was just thirteen, his mother and father died two weeks apart, his mother from cancer and his father from a heart attack. The youngster, living with his relatives, turned to all sorts of activities, excelling at games such as ping pong and marbles, then graduating to volleyball, baseball, basketball, track, and of course, football. After World War II, Howard attended the University of Iowa on the GI Bill. He encountered prejudice in Iowa City almost from the beginning of his time there. He quickly realized, however, that he still had options regarding his education. "If you were on scholarship, the coach had you," Howard said. "But I wasn't on scholarship. I was on the GI Bill. If I wanted to change schools, and go to another school, I could. And, after my experience at Iowa, I did."[19]

Howard, after transferring from Iowa to Nevada, found the campus to be friendly and welcoming. "When I got out to Nevada, it was different than Iowa," he said. "Marion Motley had been there. I knew Bill Bass and Horace Gillom had played there, too. I thought to myself that if Motley, Gillom, and Bass had played at Nevada, maybe it was the type of university that welcomed black students. They paved the way for guys like me. The people on campus, the professors, the students, they all treated me very well. It was a good environment, compared to others. The University of Iowa wasn't a very pleasant experience for me; the University of Nevada was."[20]

Howard and Tabor both found their teammates to be especially supportive. In a book about her father, Sherman Howard's daughter Vietta Robinson writes about the progressive backgrounds of many of the Wolf Pack's players, and how the shared experience of serving in the war created close bonds for Howard and his teammates. Howard said to Vietta, "Most of my white teammates came from New Jersey, Pennsylvania, or California. Many were veterans of World War II and several of them grew up and played with Blacks in their neighborhoods. We were like a big, and close family." Lineman Bill "Wildcat" Morris, who grew up in Las Vegas, later said: "Alva and Sherman were our classmates, our friends, our brothers. We weren't going to let them down and cancel the game. If we had to, we would've played the game in a goddamned parking lot."[21]

"We knew we had the support of the team," Howard said. "That meant a lot."[22]

The Wolf Pack traveled to Oklahoma with Howard and Tabor. And the Tulsa Golden Hurricane never stood a chance. Howard, at 197 pounds and with sprinter's speed, started the game at fullback. He was the first Black player to ever play in a college football game between two predominantly white universities in Oklahoma. Howard had his jersey ripped at one point. He kept his composure and scored two touchdowns. Tabor, the team's backup quarterback, threw a fifty-five-yard touchdown pass. Howard, who served in a transportation unit that unloaded guns, trucks, tanks, and other cargo from ships in the European theater during World War II, said the threats from Oklahoma didn't deter him. "I had been through a war. I had seen devastation. I had fought for our country," he said. "Those threats from the Tulsa game? That hadn't bothered me. There wasn't any fear."[23]

The Wolf Pack won, 65–14. It was Tulsa's worst loss in thirty-one years.

"There were only two blacks on the team," Vietta said. "My father said he always knew he had the respect of his teammates. He said those young men on the Nevada team were like family to him."[24]

Looking back on his participation in the Tulsa game, Howard said he was proud that his teammates chose to do the right thing. "Whenever you do anything in life," he said, pausing for a moment as the years of his life stretched out, neatly unfurling in his mind, "you need to always think, 'When everything is gone, and years later someone hears your name, what are they going to remember?' If you choose to do the right thing, hopefully they are going to remember who you were and why you chose to do it."[25]

During the 1950s and 1960s, the University gained stature throughout the country. The attention reflected an institution that was slowly maturing. The faculty was talented and industrious. Newcomers to the faculty discovered that Reno was a great place to live. It featured a relaxing, informal, and smallish-town vibe; surprisingly pleasant and sunny weather; and access to a variety of outdoor recreation. Their time at the University often became not a stepping stone for their academic careers but more of an unexpected destination. Robert Gorrell was among the faculty members who found what he liked and stayed. He joined the English Department in 1945 from Indiana University in his home state. Over the next thirty-five years, until his retirement, Gorrell was an English professor, department chairperson in English, dean of the College of Arts and Sciences, and vice president for academic affairs. His honors included the National Council of Teachers of English Distinguished Lecturer; Nevada Humanities Committee Distinguished

Scholar; and the University's Distinguished Faculty Award. In 2001, he was inducted into the Nevada Writers Hall of Fame.

Gorrell was perhaps best known for his enduring collaboration with fellow University English professor Charlton Laird, *The Modern English Handbook*, which first appeared in 1953. Over the next several decades, it became one of the most successful textbooks about the language ever written and was used on college campuses throughout the country. *The Modern English Handbook* caught on because of its ability to unravel the mysteries of grammar, usage, and effective rhetoric, doing so in uncomplicated, easy-to-digest lessons. The writing was often wry, the lessons always important. What made a complete sentence? Easy, according to Gorrell and Laird: "A complete sentence says something about something." They noted in the book's preface, "We have had innumerable helpful suggestions from our colleagues at the University of Nevada, especially from some of the teaching assistants. From several generations of students we have gained good as well as horrible examples, but, more important, we have had evidence that teaching English is not entirely futile."[26]

Gorrell would be a resident of Reno until he died in 2011. He stayed at the University so long and loved the work so much because the work that he did was, somewhat whimsically and somewhat seriously, a reflection of the community that the University served, he said in a University oral history. Early on, Gorrell couldn't help but smile at what he considered an ironic pairing of roles when Silas Ross, the chairman of the Board of Regents who was also the local undertaker, visited with the English Department's faculty. Yet the faculty was coming to understand its role in the success of the institution, and it was doing work that was earning national acclaim. "One of the kinds of things that developed fairly quickly with the faculty in those days was a growing faculty awareness of the faculty as a growing force, as a power," Gorrell said.[27] Gorrell and other faculty would famously tangle with University President Minard W. Stout during the 1950s over issues of academic freedom that included lawsuits. An American Association of University Professors investigation of Stout's retaliatory policies toward faculty eventually led to Stout's dismissal. The faculty had slowly and steadily developed a sense of strength and purpose. Gorrell fondly remembered the lesson that his coauthor of *The Modern English Handbook* had shared with him and many other colleagues. On Laird's eightieth birthday, Gorrell recalled, "Larry is a genuine scholar of the old school—he believes that—and he believed while he was teaching—that his knowledge and his scholarship and his dedication were all that he needed. And it worked, and the students respected him, and still do. And his concern was not whether he was a good showman or anything else—although he was, actually!—but his concern was, was he finding out new things and was he conveying them to students? And he did that."[28]

While Laird and Gorrell had a tight hold of almost every English 101 student in the country through their monumentally successful textbook, at least four other individuals would help raise the University's national profile in the 1960s. Robert Laxalt had grown up in a Basque sheepherder's family that also included his brother, Paul, who would go on to become a governor

University of Nevada Press founder Robert Laxalt holds his novel of Basque life in Nevada, *Baskische Heimkehr* (Basque Homecoming) in 1959. Originally titled *Sweet Promised Land*, it was published in England by Secker and Warburg of London as *Dominigue* and was the choice of the Book Society of England. Courtesy of University Archives.

and US senator from Nevada. Following World War II, Robert Laxalt graduated from the University in 1948. He became a journalist for United Press International, often covered the state's executions of convicted murderers, and served as director of the University's news service for several years. In 1957 Laxalt wrote *Sweet Promised Land*, the story of his sheepherder father Dominique's return to his homeland in the Basque Pyrenees. The book earned international acclaim, tracing the path of an immigrant who had come to America as a young man fully expecting to quickly return to his homeland. That the return came when Dominique was an old man, in the company of Robert, was a reminder of how fleeting time was, how precious life was, and how America, for better and for worse, often did not easily let go of its immigrant population. Dominique, ironically, felt the bittersweet pull to return "home" to America at the book's conclusion. Robert Laxalt would go on to write more than a dozen books and numerous articles for some of the most successful magazines in the world. In 1961, Laxalt founded the University of Nevada Press, an important step in the development of the institution's academic life, producing general interest books, titles related to Nevada and the West, and a Basque book series that was the first of its kind in the United States.

Walter Van Tilburg Clark, the son of University President Walter Clark, made his own name as one of the country's most well-known novelists. His novel *The Ox-Bow Incident* (1940) is still considered by many to be one of the finest Western novels ever published and led to a Hollywood film starring Academy Award–winning actor Henry Fonda. His other novels included the Reno-centric *The City of Trembling Leaves* (1945) and *The Track of the Cat* (1949). Clark would serve as the University's writer-in-residence beginning in 1962 until he died in 1971.

University researchers Allen and Beatrix Gardner began a revolutionary experiment in 1966 to raise chimpanzees as human children and teach them to communicate using American Sign Language. The Gardners' cross-fostering work with Washoe the chimpanzee was done at their research laboratory in their Reno home, which came to be known as "The Ranch." After adopting ten-month-old Washoe, the two psychology

Writing professor Walter Van Tilburg Clark reviews Alfred Doten's journals in the Getchell Library in 1962. The first inductee into the Nevada Writers Hall of Fame in 1988, Clark was a professor and writer-in-residence at the University from 1962 to 1971. Courtesy of University Archives.

Basque scholar and author Eloy Placer (*left*) and Basque Studies founder and longtime University professor William Douglass on the bus to Ustaritz in the Basque Country during the 1970 summer session. Under Douglass's direction, the program brought the University worldwide renown, which continues today. Courtesy of University Archives.

professors began teaching Washoe American Sign Language. In 1967, when Washoe was about fifteen months old, the Gardners reported early results that Washoe had learned signs for numerous words at a meeting of the American Association for the Advancement of Science in New York. *The New York Times* wrote that "the Gardners reported that the chimpanzee created expressions like 'water birds' for a pair of swans and 'open flower' to gain admittance to a flower garden." The news of Washoe signing the words "water" and "bird" was akin to "getting an SOS from outer space," Harvard University psychologist Roger Brown said in 2007.[29] The couple's research findings set off a torrent of cognitive research over the next decade. Invitations to lecture about the signing chimpanzees arrived from around the world, including Brazil, South Africa, Italy, and France. Famed primatologist and anthropologist Jane Goodall even invited them to visit Gombe Stream in Tanzania, giving the couple their first opportunity to see chimpanzees in the wild.

Washoe, who learned about 130 signs in American Sign Language, died in Washington in 2007 at the age of forty-two. For many years she had lived on Central Washington University's Ellensburg campus as part of the Chimpanzee and Human Communications Institute. Washoe was the first of five chimpanzees to acquire language. Allen and Beatrix, known as "Trixie," replicated their success between 1972 and 1981 with four additional infant chimpanzees—Moja, Pili, Tatu, and Dar.

A "Two-Directional" Impact: How the Basque Studies Program at the University Gained International Renown

by William A. Douglass

The University of Nevada, Reno, currently has the most elaborate Basque studies center outside the homeland. It teaches a variety of undergraduate classes in Basque history, language, and culture, while offering a PhD in Basque studies. The Jon Bilbao Basque Library houses more than fifty-five thousand books, journals, and manuscripts, making it one of the world's largest collections of Basque documentation, including the best regarding the Basque emigrant diasporas that encompass every continent. Both by virtue of interlibrary loan and personal stays at UNR, scholars from around the world use this magnificent collection.

Why and how did it all begin? The why stems from the University's central location vis-à-vis Basque settlement throughout the American West. According to the 2000 US census, there were about fifty-eight thousand Basque Americans in the country. Every state had some, but the largest contingent (more than twenty thousand) was in California. The six thousand Basques in Idaho and Nevada each were much more visible given their state's overall population. The most conspicuous urban concentration was in Boise, but Reno, too, had many Basques and its own Zazpiak Basque Club, founded in the mid-1950s.

Western Nevada could boast of three other prominent Basque features. In 1957, Robert Laxalt, raised in Carson City, published his novel *Sweet Promised Land*. It recounted the story of his father's history as an immigrant sheepherder and rancher, and his eventual return decades later to the Basque homeland (accompanied by Robert). The book became an American classic and established Laxalt as the literary spokesman of the Basque American experience. Then, in 1959, the first ever National Basque Festival was held over a weekend at the Sparks Nugget hotel-casino, bringing together for the first time Basque Americans from throughout the American West.

Robert's brother would serve eventually as Nevada governor (1967–1971) and US senator (1974–1987), making Paul Laxalt the most accomplished Basque American politician to date.

The Center for Basque Studies began in 1961 when the nascent Desert Research Institute (DRI) contracted three social anthropologists from other universities to advise it about its Western North American Studies division. Omer Stewart of the University of Colorado suggested a Basque studies program—arguing that the Basques, as the region's sheepmen, were the least-understood architects of the history of the American West. They were also the "mystery people" of Europe—so investigating Old World Basque culture and language would provide the DRI with another initiative. The two other consultants seconded the suggestion, and Wendall Mordy, the first director of the institute, accepted it.

The challenge was how to proceed. Mordy was fully aware of the impact of Robert Laxalt's book and the recent first National Basque Festival. In 1963, Robert, then director of the fledgling University of Nevada Press, was scheduled for a year's sabbatical leave that he intended to spend in the Basque Country writing his second book. Mordy hired Bob and his wife, Joyce, to be his consultants to determine how Old World Basques would react to the prospect of a Basque studies program at the University. If they received a positive reaction, Mordy envisioned hiring Laxalt as the program's director.

At that time, I was conducting field research in two Spanish Basque villages for my PhD dissertation in social anthropology at the University of Chicago. I visited Bob for a day in St. Jean de Luz in the French Basque area where he was ensconced with his family. He had befriended noted Basque scholar Philippe Veyrin, and that gravely ill scholar had given the University of Nevada the right to purchase his personal library of 750 Basque books from his estate. Bob had no intention of becoming director of the Basque Studies Program, and he asked if I would be interested in the position.

In the summer of 1967, after graduating from University of Chicago, I moved to Reno to initiate the program. The following year, I recruited noted Basque bibliographer Jon Bilbao to join me at the DRI. Meanwhile, the Veyrin collection arrived in Reno, giving Nevada instant recognition as a serious center for Basque research. The Desert Research Institute was neither a teaching nor archival institution, so the books were housed in two rooms in the basement of Getchell Library. The University now had a Basque library and continued to add to it. Jon Bilbao, a DRI employee, became the de facto Basque librarian, spending afternoons and evenings organizing the collection and accommodating the occasional patron. Virginia Jacobsen, wife of William H. Jacobsen, a linguist in the English Department and coordinator of Basque linguistics, volunteered for several years to assist Jon. Jon began teaching the Basque language at the University, and I offered the occasional course on Old World Basque culture there and in Elko and Winnemucca through the extension program. I also became editor of a Basque book series within the University of Nevada Press that continues to publish books on the Basques to this day. Under my aegis we published more than forty.

Eventually, it became apparent that the Basque Studies Program was incapable of surviving at DRI. The Desert Research Institute had no interest in the bibliophilic and pedagogic activities that were making increasing demands on our time, and we were unable to secure sufficient grants to be self-supporting as researchers at a research institute where positions and other resources were funded primarily from grants. So, in 1972, Bob Laxalt was instrumental in securing funding for a professional position for Jon Bilbao at the University, and the Basque Studies Program moved to the University and was placed under the library's responsibility. In 1977, Getchell Library was expanded and the Basque Studies Program space more than doubled in size. While I continued to coordinate it, I remained at DRI until 1979 when my ten-year National Institute of Mental Health Research Scientist Award grant ran out. Again, Bob was instrumental in securing a professional position for me at UNR, the Basque Studies Program's second.

Another notable development was when we hosted the first exploratory meeting in 1973 of what eventually became the North American Basque Organizations. It was inspired

Jose Ramon Zengotitabengoa, political science professor Joe Crowley (before his University presidency 1978–2001), Basque Studies director William Douglass, and author Robert Laxalt stand near two Basque sculptures in 1962. This statue is still on campus, now outside the Rotunda in the Mathewson-IGT Knowledge Center. Courtesy of University Archives.

when Jon and I visited Argentina to research our book, *Amerikanuak: Basques in the New World.* While there we witnessed the operation of the Argentine Federation of Basque Entities, an association overseeing that country's thirty-odd Basque clubs while fomenting common projects among them.

In 1982, I hired Carmelo Urza to launch a University Studies in the Basque Country Consortium that began with an academic year abroad for American students. It was housed in part of the Basque Studies Program's office space. It quickly transcended its original Basque focus. When Urza retired recently, the University Studies Abroad Consortium had its own building and operated programs in twenty-eight countries around the world. More than one hundred American universities were sending students abroad through the consortium, a total of about sixty-one thousand American students, of whom fourteen thousand studied in the Basque Country.

The impact was, of course, two-directional. The American students both affected the local economy and the thinking of their youthful counterparts who were raised with the censorship and narrow vision of the Franco dictatorship. In this vein, another UNR project merits mention. In 1983, Gorka Aulestia and Linda White began collaborating on creating the first English-Basque, Basque-English dictionary. It took no fewer than six years, and the two volumes were published in the Basque book series. Intended as a tool to help Basque Americans and other interested English speakers to learn Basque, it actually had its biggest impact in the Basque Country. In 1992 a shortened, combined paperback edition was published there and became the key reference work for Basque schoolchildren in their English classes.

Through the combination of producing the iconic book *Amerikanuak,* facilitating North American Basque Organizations, and creating the University Studies Abroad Consortium, the Basque Studies Program had become a major factor in the maintenance of the Basque American identity. That is commemorated in the abstract National Monument to the Basque Sheepherder in nearby Rancho San Rafael Park, a project in which Carmelo Urza, Robert Laxalt, and I played a prominent role. It is also commemorated in the recently inaugurated figurative sculpture, *The Basque Herder,* located next to the University's Knowledge Center. Indeed, a seedling of Gernika's oak tree, the prime symbol of Basque culture, is growing nearby.

In 2000, my successor, Joseba Zulaika, formed an advisory board of prominent Basque Americans and Old World Basques whose primary function was to secure private funds. To date, it has raised more than $2 million for a Center for Basque Studies endowment that provides the center the funds to launch initiatives in both its research and undergraduate/graduate teaching activities. Today, it has four professional positions (currently Sandra Ott, Larraitz Ariznabarreta, Mariann Vaczi, and director Xabier Irujo, plus administrative assistant Kate Camino). There is also an ambitious publications program that, to date, has produced more than two hundred titles on Basque subjects.

In 2015, the Basque Library was named for Jon Bilbao, and it is now headed by Iñaki Arrieta Baro. I was honored as well at that time when the Basque Studies Program/Center was rechristened the William A. Douglass Center for Basque Studies.

Finally, a 2007 book published by the Oral History Program (Pedro Oiarzabal, *A Candle in the Night: Basque Studies at the University of Nevada 1967–2007*) discusses the history of Basque studies at UNR in considerably greater detail. Its title reflects the words of Basque president José Luis Ardanza on his visit to UNR in 1988. In his emotional tribute, he thanked this university for keeping the flame alive during the Franco dictatorship when Basques were prohibited from expressing their culture and language in their homeland.

The idea that the University would one day have its own medical school, particularly as the 1950s concluded, would've seemed preposterous to most Nevadans. James Hulse wrote that the University at that time "had been able to support some research work in agriculture and in fields related to mining, but there had been little money to add scholars in other fields. Research in most areas of engineering, the sciences, and the humanities had been undertaken by individual faculty members on their own initiative, with little outside help."[30]

Several things happened during the coming decade that eventually led to the creation of a School of Medicine at the University of Nevada, Reno. First, Charles Armstrong was named president in 1958. The University's tenth president previously served as chief executive at Pacific University in Oregon. He was a patient, thoughtful, and welcome presence following the turmoil and recriminations of the Stout administration. In his inaugural address, Armstrong spoke of a new beginning for the campus:

> I conceive that it must be my most urgent and continuing responsibility to do all within my power to maintain a certain atmosphere both within and without the University. Within the University this means an atmosphere of freedom, and of the responsibility inherent in freedom; an atmosphere in which all members of the University community, students, faculty, and administration, may work toward our common goals in mutual confidence and respect . . . an atmosphere, in sum, wherein the concept of human dignity and worth is practiced as well as preached.[31]

The Noble H. Getchell Library opened in early 1962 for the expanding student body and its resource needs. It was situated where the University Hospital/Infirmary had been located. The library's early occupants included the Oral History Program, the Basque Studies Program (after the Basque Studies Program was initiated as part of the Desert Research Institute), and Government Publications. Courtesy of University Archives.

Armstrong also believed in the value of research, which included the creation of the Desert Research Institute (DRI), an emphasis on attracting doctoral students, and his support of the University of Nevada Press. Armstrong's efforts created a foundation for research and scientific inquiry that positioned the University for an important next step in the creation of a medical

Students helped move books into the newly built Getchell Library in 1961's "Bookwalk." Courtesy of University Archives.

Dean George Smith, Rueben Zucker, Karen Arcotta (being hooded), and Dr. Thomas Scully at the Medical School's hooding ceremony in 1980. Nelson Neff and Dr. George Smith designed the logo on the flag. Courtesy of University Archives.

school, which included garnering statewide support for such an endeavor. A study from the Western Interstate Compact on Higher Education had indicated that even with its relatively small population, Nevada, along with Montana, Idaho, and Wyoming—states that had no medical schools—would need such a school soon. It was a request that would soon be met. Leading the effort was Nevada physician Fred Anderson, a longtime member of the Board of Regents. Anderson, who was born on a ranch in Secret Pass in eastern Nevada, graduated from the University in 1928. A Rhodes Scholar, Anderson completed his medical degree at Harvard University. Elected to the Board of Regents in 1956, he would serve as a regent for more than two decades. Anderson's advocacy for the medical school and his keen understanding of Nevada politics would prove crucial in the school's creation.

Anderson recalled in a University oral history that efforts were slow and tedious in creating a medical school:

> At this time, which would have been about 1967, and with the state's population going up rather rapidly—but still not being anywhere near the 800,000 to a million that I felt we should have before we had a medical school—we did not seem to be getting much nearer to solving our medical problems than we had been before. The main problems were getting our own students into medical school and getting the rural counties supplied with doctors and making up the doctor shortage—particularly in Las Vegas, which was growing so fast. Doctors were coming in proportionately at a slower rate than the population was increasing.[32]

The Fleischmann Atmospherium Planetarium groundbreaking ceremony shows President Charles J. Armstrong holding a shovel in 1961. Courtesy of University Archives.

The Fleischmann Atmospherium Planetarium, later known as Fleischmann Planetarium and Science Center, was built in 1963. It was one of the first to use the Spitz SciDome digital projector to produce high-quality 3-D movies and is still at the cutting edge of planetary science technology. Courtesy of University Archives.

The plan initially was to create a two-year medical program rather than a four-year program, Anderson said, "because a four-year one would cost a great deal more and because at the time, there were, amongst the medical schools throughout the country, anywhere from 5 to 10 or more percent dropping out after the first two years, making 1,000 or more vacant places available in the third year of those schools. So at that time you could transfer students quite readily from a two-year school."[33] On February 11, 1967, Anderson made the following motion during a Board of Regents meeting: that long-range planning would be instituted for a health sciences center associated with the University of Nevada in Reno. Planning and development would proceed as financially and otherwise feasible with the goal of admission of the first class to medical school in about 1971 or 1972. The board's formal financial commitment of up to $300,000 was to match a like amount committed by the trustees of Washoe Medical Center. The total was to be used with the federal matching funds for the development of a new teaching research facility for environmental pathophysiology—including animal research, as set forth by the College of Agriculture.

The Board approved the motion, 6–2.

A great deal of statewide haggling followed. Some physicians in Las Vegas opposed the medical school. The Nevada Taxpayers Association wondered about the fiscal prudence of what it felt was an overly generous state contribution. State legislators' support varied on whether they represented the southern or northern portion of the state. Finally, though, there was a major breakthrough. "Perhaps the thing that affected the legislature more than anything we did was that Howard Hughes—who had not long before that moved to Las Vegas, bought the Desert Inn, and occupied the entire top floor—communicated with our governor, Paul Laxalt, by letter, offering us a sum of $6 million [for the new medical school]," Anderson said.[34] It was a gift that changed everything:

Paul Laxalt, our governor, and Bob Maheu, who was director of Hughes's operations in Nevada, between them conceived the idea that Hughes's would make these gifts—one of $250,000 toward the study for the community colleges and some support for the Elko college; the other, $6 million for the Medical School. As to his exact motives in doing that, I don't know whether this was really public relations or whether he had a deep interest in medicine. The fact that he had had some previous interest in medicine is shown by the fact that he had many years earlier established the Hughes Medical Foundation, with its headquarters in Florida. Although I was never able to get exact details on that, it was my understanding that most of the earnings of Hughes Aircraft Company were to go toward that.[35]

Hughes's philanthropy was an offer, Anderson said, "for between $200,000 and $300,000 per year after the school was built and the first students accepted, each year for a period of 20 years, carrying over into his own personal will and not in Summa Corporation, the main business venture, which was bound to be involved in legal disputes if there should be death or other disaster. No matter what happened, we were fairly certain of getting our money as being given to us from his own personal will if he died before the gift terminated."[36]

A 1969 legislative bill was enacted, authorizing the development of the health science program. It was also called for operating funds for renovation and remodeling of the Mackay Science Hall and the Mechanical Arts Building, the first two buildings that the medical school used. The future site of the School of Medicine was on land that was once a Valley Road farm that had previously belonged to the College of Agriculture.

The first class of thirty-two medical students met on campus in September 1971. By 1977, the Nevada Legislature authorized the University of Nevada to extend the School of Medicine to a four-year school that would award doctorates of medicine. The University of Nevada School of Medicine's first building, home to a library, teaching facilities, anatomical dissection room, research units and laboratories, and offices, was dedicated as the Fred M. Anderson Health Sciences Building in 1972.

Student activism on campus reached a peak during the late 1960s and early 1970s. The events of Governor's Day 1970 speak to the tenor of what was being felt on many college campuses in the US during the spring of 1970. In late April, President Richard Nixon revealed to the nation that he was sending US troops into Cambodia. Many saw the invasion of Cambodia as an escalation, rather than a de-escalation, of a war in Vietnam that seemingly had no end in sight. In reaction, protests were held on college campuses throughout the country. On May 4, 1970, four unarmed students were shot and killed by members of the Ohio National Guard at Kent State University. Governor's Day, an annual event honoring the Nevada governor at the University, was scheduled for May 5. In addition to a reception for Governor Paul Laxalt in the Jot Travis Student Union Lounge scheduled for that morning, the annual Military Department awards ceremony and review of the Reserve Officers' Training Corps (ROTC) brigade would follow at Mackay Stadium. English professor Robert Harvey, history professor James Hulse, and a few other faculty members, including art professor Ben Hazard—who had joined the faculty the year before, becoming the first African American faculty member—played

Kathryn H. Duffy, associate professor of Business Administration, teaches a real estate law class in 1962. Courtesy of University Archives.

roles in trying to stem passions and frustrations of student protestors. The students felt their perspective on the escalation in Cambodia plus the senseless killing of four students at Kent State at the hands of fellow Americans hadn't been acknowledged. Hulse wrote:

> Several students who opposed the war and the military policies of the federal government announced a "peace rally" for the same day [as Governor's Day] on the south lawn [Manzanita Bowl] of the campus. Without sufficient prior planning, the rally became a march toward the stadium, and part of the governor's motorcade—with automobiles carrying military officers and University personnel—was temporarily interrupted by a few marchers. Two or three hundred students poured into the stadium, walked around the field where military exercises were to be held, and later filled the stands, shouting anti-war slogans. They delayed the ceremony for several minutes, and some of the demonstrators went onto the field and threatened to disrupt the ROTC cadet drill.[37]

Hazard, who had driven back from the Bay Area to Reno with young son Mark the day before, said in his oral history some students had reached out to him in advance of the counter-protest. He hadn't had time to speak directly to them. But, sensing something bigger was on tap, Hazard felt it was important to be on hand that morning: "We were trying to make ourselves very visible to students and constantly talking with different students, and saying, 'Let's keep it cool. Let's keep it cool.'"[38] Hazard, who had served in the military earlier in his life, added:

> When I saw the crowd jump up and get ready to move out [inside the stadium, where the ROTC cadet program was about to commence], then I knew I had to do something, and I better do it fast. So I took on a leadership role, knowing [the protesting students] would be looking, knowing that they would be misinterpreting and misunderstanding. But my decision was I had to do something to prevent those kids from going through the same hell that I've seen take place in Berkeley and Oakland and across the country. So I got out there, took a leadership position, and helped direct the crowd in the most contained manner as possible—the most un-mob-like.

Hazard said he could understand the protesting students' roiling frustration. Yet he also realized his role at that moment was to make sure no one got hurt:

> It's almost as if you're standing next to a friend and being held underwater, and you see how long you could hold your breath.... But no. These kids got so hot and frustrated, they're starving for air. They're

drowning. No one is giving them consideration.... Not President (N. Edd) Miller, nor anyone else, got up and said, "I think it's a tragedy about what happened at Kent State. Let's take a moment of silent prayer" and then proceed on with the ceremonies.

No, they act as if Kent State, which was less than twenty-four hours old, had never existed. They act as if there was *nothing* happening across the country. Business as usual.[39]

Still, it was the quick thinking and calm actions of faculty members such as Hazard and Harvey that led to a de-escalation of passions that day. Hulse noted the key role that Hazard and others played, writing:

Some faculty members and moderate students joined the ranks of the protestors for the purpose of urging restraint. Knowledgeable about violent confrontations that had occurred elsewhere, several faculty members and students decided the best way to deal with a potentially dangerous crowd was to join it with voices of moderation and responsibility, in the hope of reducing the influence of the hate-mongers and rabble-rousers. By this process, the most emotional members of the crowd were prevented from turning the situation into a riot.[40]

The demonstration ended without violence, and the University acknowledged the Kent State tragedy. But

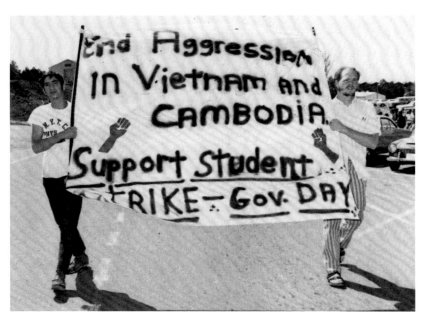

Two University students protest the Vietnam War on Governor's Day in 1970, the day after the fatal shootings at Kent State University. Students at the University of Nevada blocked motor vehicles and advanced onto Mackay Field. Courtesy of University Archives.

Given "a minute" to get up, graduate student William Copren sits for his full sixty seconds in front of a police car in front of Lincoln Hall, blocking the progress of the Governor's Day motorcade during a Vietnam War protest in 1970. Courtesy of University Archives.

two violent acts soon rocked the campus. The next day, Wednesday, May 6, President Miller announced that classes on Friday—the day that national memorials for the Kent State students who had been killed would be held throughout the country—would not be mandatory and that no action would be taken against faculty or students who failed to attend class that day. In the early morning hours of Thursday, May 7, while the building was unoccupied, Hartman Hall, the University's ROTC building, was firebombed. A second firebombing occurred on the morning of Monday, May 11, against the Hobbit Hole, the house located at 1035 North Virginia Street that was used as a meeting area by protestors before the Governor's Day demonstration the week

Students surround an Army tank that was part of a military exhibit in front of the Getchell Library during a war protest on Governor's Day 1970. Courtesy of University Archives.

Peace signs are displayed during an ROTC awards ceremony in Mackay Stadium during a Vietnam War protest in 1970. Courtesy of University Archives.

ROTC cadets stand with bayonets unsheathed while war protestors advance toward them. Courtesy of University Archives.

before. The Hobbit Hole had been a coffee shop until the previous semester. Two students who were inside the home at the time of the firebombing escaped injury.

Governor's Day was a flashpoint that would have short-term repercussions for the University and long-term effects for many who were involved. Miller, in a University oral history recorded in 1972–1973, said that "the scars are still there" from what had happened during the demonstration. "I can't reconstruct it maybe even any other way, because I fully sympathize with the desire to protest on that day," said Miller, who left the University in 1973 to become president of the University of Maine at Portland-Gorham. "That's fine. It should have happened; if I'd been a student I would have wanted to express myself, too. And I also understand the temptation brought about by the ROTC review that day. So I'm not sure what should have happened, but it was an enormously disappointing kind of way for the thing to turn out."[41]

The student activism also led to steps toward change for representation of underrepresented groups, both in student and faculty composition as well as programs. The effort began on campus following the events of 1970. In October 1971, sixteen people, including thirteen students, several of whom belonged to the campus' Black Student Union organization, were arrested following their occupation of the activities office of the Associated Students of the University of Nevada (ASUN) in the Jot Travis Student Union. The protestors staged their sit-in to call attention to their request for equal campus space for their organization. In 1972, the University hired Michael Coray to teach African and Afro-American history. He would also coordinate a new ethnic studies program that would include not only the Black experience but also what newspaper accounts referred to as academic offerings for members from the "Indian, Asian American and Mexican American" groups.

Ben Hazard was no longer a faculty member when efforts to bring more diversity to the campus and its curriculum were being made. His arrival in Reno during the summer of 1969 had been historic. He was twenty-nine years old at the time, born in 1940 in Rhode Island and raised by his aunt in Harlem, New York. While serving in the air force, Hazard became a sign painter. He earned his bachelor of fine arts degree from the California College of Arts and Crafts (now the California College of the Arts) and his master of fine arts degree in art practice from the University of California, Berkeley. His paintings and sculptures today are considered important contributions to the creative and progressive period of Black art and expression—the Black arts movement of the 1960s.

Several ugly incidents marred Hazard's introduction to the Reno-Sparks area. Upon learning Hazard was Black, prospective landlords came up with a series of flimsy excuses not to rent to him. He had started his search for a place to live earlier that summer, and the excuses from landlords who did not want to rent to a Black person piled up for three months. Two properties accepted Hazard's rent check but then told him their properties had been sold when they learned about his race. One landlord said he changed his mind and that he rented the space to a friend instead of Hazard. Another accepted Hazard's check. But then, after Hazard had gone to his home in Oakland, California, to get two-year-old son Mark and his furniture, the landlord left a note on the door of the property for Hazard, saying it was no longer available.

Hazard said at the time that he wasn't going to let any of the housing obstacles deter him. "I want to make sure that by being the first black professor that I also will not be the last," he said. "It makes my reason for being here all the more important. . . . It is an honor to be at the University. I want to do what I have been hired to do, and at the same time, I want to be aware of who I am and what I can do to help my people.

"A long time ago I decided I would never leave a place because I couldn't take the pressure. I will leave only when I have accomplished what I came to do. I can't leave now and let someone else carry the ball."[42] After a newspaper account of Hazard's search for housing, Faculty Senate passed a resolution asking that the University implement an "active, aggressive housing program" for new faculty members, particularly those who might face discrimination.

On September 19, it was reported that a white landlord had "reconsidered" and rented a house to Hazard. In the wake of Hazard's story, the State Equal Rights Commission urged Black people throughout Nevada to file complaints of housing discrimination so that federal investigators could be called into the area. At the time, Nevada did not have an open housing law. Because, in part, of examples such as the one faced by Hazard during the summer of 1969, the Nevada Legislature approved the state's first law in spring 1971.[43]

Hazard increasingly found himself in the middle of a campus debate regarding several important issues. News accounts described an "emotion-filled" three-hour meeting on April 7, 1970, in which many of the

THE UNIVERSITY REFLECTS THE CHALLENGES OF NEVADA AND THE NATION, 1939–1978 campus's Black students expressed their frustration with the administration's failure to address conditions at the University. Otis Burrell, a Black athlete who won the 1966 National Collegiate Athletics Association (NCAA) championship in the high jump and who was one of the top-ranked track and field competitors in the world, shared how he experienced difficulties getting into the graduate program and finding a job on campus because of the color of his skin.[44]

Members of the Black Student Union asked that the University provide more meaningful tutoring for minorities; hire more Black faculty counselors; offer more Black studies; and grow Black enrollment from the current 1.3 percent to 15 percent, which would raise the number of Black students to about nine hundred. In 1970, there were fewer than 100 Black students on campus. Over the next several days, Hazard joined prominent University figures such as the Rev. John Dodson and John Marschall of the Center of Religion and Life (now the Newman Center), and James Hardesty, the student body president who would go on to become chief justice of the Nevada Supreme Court, to organize a series of meetings to discuss issues that were on the minds of not only Black students but white students, faculty, and staff as well. President Miller participated in many of the meetings. He noted, "We can agree that there are problems and express a willingness to do something about them."[45]

Hazard announced that he was leaving the University of Nevada on July 18, 1970. He was joining the Oakland Museum as curator of education and special exhibits for a salary of $1,400 per month. In an interview with the *Reno Evening Gazette*, Hazard cited his frustration with the Nevada Board of Regents because the board was "cheating the state and the community" and not seriously addressing many of the issues, particularly for minority students. "They aren't working with the university, but playing a political game and appeasing the community rather than presenting the facts," he said. There was no denying that the events after the Governor's Day demonstration had been deflating for many students and certain faculty members. In the July 18, 1970, newspaper story relating Hazard's announcement that he would be leaving the University, Hazard said, "The community is becoming more interested in humanly related things, its interest is moving away from just gambling. I hope the people in the community will continue and resolve the problems that are facing them—not just acting like they don't exist." Added his son Mark Hazard years later: "Dad referred to his time in Reno a lot. He said that Reno experience really got his momentum going."[46]

Hazard accomplished a lot after his time in Reno. He was the first Black person to be curator, Special Exhibits and Education, for the Oakland Museum and served in that role from 1970 to 1981. During this time Hazard received national recognition for involving diverse communities in the museum as active partners, producing more than three hundred programs and exhibitions that increased visitor attendance to more than one hundred thousand annually. He was appointed by President Jimmy Carter to the Institute of Museum Service Board in Washington, DC, and he sat on panels for the National Science Foundation and the National Endowment for the Arts and Humanities. He was often commissioned as an artist. During his tenure on the faculty at the University of New Mexico he completed monuments to the Tuskegee Airmen,

Navajo Code Talkers, and the Buffalo Soldiers at the New Mexico Veterans Memorial in Albuquerque. He was also commissioned to create a portrait of President Barack Obama and his family. When it was completed, it was displayed in the family quarters of the White House. "Dad was like a lot of artists—he didn't die a millionaire," Mark Hazard said. "He had humble means to start and humble means at the end. But the things he did . . . the art he did and the projects he completed . . . sometimes money doesn't mean nearly as much when you look at how Dad lived his life and what he felt was important."[47]

In February 1977, Rebecca Stafford, the chair of the Department of Sociology, was named dean of the College of Arts and Sciences. Stafford's appointment was historic: she was the institution's first female appointed dean of a college other than the traditionally female colleges of Nursing and Home Economics. Her selection was also a vivid example of the forces female faculty members faced as they worked to gain traction on campus. Stafford's résumé and accomplishments were impeccable. Growing up in Topeka, Kansas, she edited her high school's newspaper, was on the debate team, and worked nights at the city's newspaper writing obituaries. She was a 1958 graduate of Radcliffe College, and she received her MA and PhD in sociology at Harvard University. She was a rising scholar in the field of marriage and family relationships.

Robert Gorrell, who by then was the University's academic vice president and advising President Max Milam on the selection of the dean, remembered in a 1983 University oral history what happened next: "There was quite a lot of controversy over choosing Becky Stafford [as the] dean of arts and sciences. Becky

Rebecca Stafford made University history in 1977 when she was appointed dean of the College of Arts and Sciences. She was the first woman to be appointed a dean of a college other than the traditionally female colleges of Nursing and Home Economics. Courtesy of University Archives.

had been chairman of sociology while I was dean of arts and sciences, and I thought a very good chairman and a very good administrator. . . . And on the basis of the national search, the (search) committee did come up with two candidates—Becky and a man. The arts and sciences chairmen very strongly recommended the man rather than Becky, and in talking with the arts and sciences chairmen, it was apparent that quite a lot of it was not wanting a woman dean." Gorrell remembered that such thought wasn't uncommon on campus at the time. "Well, I can remember a couple of instances; I remember one department chairman pounding the table and saying there would be no women in his department and he'd see to it and there weren't," he said. "They didn't think they could work with a woman dean." Gorrell and Milam both knew Stafford.[48] They respected her highly. They knew there was little doubt she would make an excellent dean.

In a 1978 oral history, Milam recalled that Stafford had done an outstanding job during the interview process. "And I was impressed," he said. "She'd done a very good job preparing." Both Milam and Gorrell agreed that Stafford was the best choice. She was appointed dean.[49]

"I think a large part of it is just plain old male chauvinism by some of the department chairmen that just can't see themselves working for a female dean," said Milam, who served as the University's twelfth president from 1974 to 1978. "I'm not going to name names, but I think there was some element of that in the reaction."[50]

Stafford, as she demonstrated throughout a distinguished career in higher education that would include serving as president of three universities until her retirement as president of Monmouth University in New Jersey in 2003, proved to be progressive, ambitious, and effective. Stafford organized an advisory board for the college, which included several prominent northern Nevadans. In an April 1977 interview, she said her priorities for the college included growing an honors program, implementing more interdisciplinary courses "which are issue-oriented," and developing more faculty interest in the newly developed interdisciplinary courses.[51]

"The dean is the spokesman for the faculty," Stafford said. "I don't make decisions in a vacuum but work with others." Stafford, a dog lover who ran two and a half miles each day with her dogs, was also driven. "I also see myself as a sheepdog barking at the faculty's heels," she added.[52]

With "issue-oriented" and "interdisciplinary" among the watchwords at the College of Arts and Sciences, women's studies was approved as an interdisciplinary program in 1978. The University offered what is credited as being its first official women's studies course during the fall 1979 semester.

The Women's Studies effort grew quickly on campus. This Women in Transition Class lecture from 1979 was very popular. Courtesy of University Archives.

"Eventually we ended up with women who were deans," Anne Howard, an English professor who joined the faculty in 1963, remembered. "You knew when that happened, we were going to be able to offer courses, and eventually to have the head of women's studies be an actual position. We had very little budget. But that didn't matter so much. We would adjust things and make them fit."[53]

Howard joined a Department of English that had no other full-time female faculty. It was housed in Frandsen Humanities, at that time indicative in some ways of the entire University. Although it was the 1960s and the building was striving for modernity, it still harkened to an earlier time. Rough edges still abounded.

Frankie Sue Del Papa served as ASUN president during her senior year, 1970–1971. She would go on to be the first woman elected as Nevada secretary of state and Nevada attorney general. Courtesy of University Archives.

This image near the Schulich Lecture Hall is part of a collection, "Women in Transition," as the Women's Studies Program began to take hold. Courtesy of University Archives.

Howard once wrote of Frandsen, "The atmosphere was very male. Upstairs in Foreign Languages, a few women taught; downstairs, only emergency fill-ins were women—'housewife help' in Dr. Robert Gorrell's term. I found it hard to believe I was the only regular staff member who was a female in a discipline that granted a healthy portion of its doctorates to women. By 1970, the department doubled its female faculty by hiring a second woman, Ann Ronald, confusing many a student, since by that time first names became acceptable practice when addressing faculty."[54] Howard, who would chair several key committees related to campus life, including the President's Ad Hoc Committee on Women's Studies as well as the Committee on the Status of Women, came to realize that she and her female colleagues often needed to "work around" the status quo. "I learned very early on that it could be very complicated to go around things in order to get things done," she said. "You had to go to people who were very influential on campus. We had some good presidents . . . some who were supportive and some who were not as supportive. You just had to work a little harder in order to get things done."[55]

An example was the Women's Studies 101 class that was offered in fall 1979. It was as interdisciplinary as a course could be. It was taught by five instructors: Howard, Stafford, Frank Hartigan of history, Amal Kawar of political science, and Larry Larsen of business. The course combined history with contemporary and future issues women faced. The five instructors each had offered to teach the course. In a 1979 interview, Howard, who taught the language portion of the course, said, "In a way, it's an effort to remedy the omissions of the past. . . . I think women need to be informed about their own past and their own characters." Twenty-five students, all women, were enrolled in the class that semester. But, Howard added, "If a man wants to minor in women's studies, we're perfectly happy to have him."[56]

By 1997, women's studies had become a major, and it is considered the forerunner to today's Gender, Race, and Identity (GRI) Department. GRI features a BA in gender, race, and identity as well as undergraduate minors in Black studies; ethnic studies; holocaust, genocide, and peace studies; Indigenous studies; Latinx studies; LGBTQ studies; religious studies; social justice; and women's, gender, and sexuality studies. And at the graduate level, it offers both an MA and a graduate certificate in gender, race, and identity.

In 1966, while still completing his PhD, Joe Crowley was hired as a one-semester temporary appointment for $3,500 at the University of Nevada. His temporary appointment led to a full-time contract the following academic year for $7,000 in the Department of Political Science. Crowley's profile on the campus rose steadily, including a two-year stint in Washington, DC, with the Environmental Protection Agency and the National Commission on Water Quality. Returning from Washington in 1975, he soon became chair of the Department of Political Science and chair of the Faculty Senate.

In 1977–78, the campus and the entire state system for higher education were in tumult. The state system's chancellor had resigned; a community college division president had lost his job; and University President Max Milam, on February 10, 1978, had been ousted in a 5–1 vote by the Board of Regents (three board members had missed the meeting at the campus's Center for Religion and Life because of a snowstorm). Crowley, well-respected as a youngish (forty-four years old) professor and faculty leader, was named interim president on February 24, 1978. His first official act as president: On February 25, Crowley, working on a Saturday in his new office on the second floor of Clark Administration, received a call from a student organization in renewable natural resources that was holding an event on campus. They'd neglected to obtain the proper permit. The University's food services called to see if anyone in the President's Office could sign it at the last minute.

Joe Crowley, a future University president, joined the Department of Political Science faculty in 1966. Courtesy of University Archives.

Joe Crowley did not hide from the fact that he was born and raised in Iowa, and he often proved to be a good sport in illustrating his roots. Courtesy of University Archives.

President Joe Crowley, who listed his home phone number in the phone book, always made sure to laugh (or have others laugh along with him). Courtesy of University Archives.

THE UNIVERSITY REFLECTS THE CHALLENGES OF NEVADA AND THE NATION, 1939–1978

Campus in 1977. Courtesy of University Archives.

"Well," Crowley said calmly, "bring it on up and I'll sign it." Although he was calm about it, Crowley later admitted he had a lot to learn in his new position.[57] "I was just overwhelmed," he said of those early days. "I knew a fair number of people and had a fairly good working knowledge of campus. But the hardest thing I had to learn was how much I needed to know about the institution."[58]

Following a tumultuous and somewhat controversial selection process that included a brief period where Crowley's name was omitted from the group of finalists for the full-time position, Crowley was appointed president on March 23, 1979. Not all of northern Nevada was certain of the wisdom of the choice. But it was apparent very early on that the calm, reasoned, and convivial manner of Crowley resonated as an inspired choice for the University's thirteenth president. An example could be seen in the efforts of some members of the University's Buildings and Grounds Department who wanted to signal to the campus that a new and exciting era was now dawning. As the regents still huddled in a closed session to determine if Crowley was the right choice, welders Lee Mayo and Steve Arellano, at the request of Buildings and Grounds Department chief John Sala, were already working to bring the long-dormant Morrill Hall bell back to life.

Ed Pine, the University's chief financial officer, called Sala at one point.

"Is the Morrill Hall bell working yet?" Pine asked.

"No, not yet," Sala said.

Mayo and Arellano, according to newspaper reports of the time, "hoisted the 250-pound bell in place, positioned the 18-inch-long clapper and while electricians Dave Davis and Mike Stone stood by, the welders, panting and puffing from exertion, got the word that Dr. Joe [Crowley] had been elected on a 7–2 vote. Mayo and Arellano [then] manually rang the venerable bell."[59]

Ushered in by the clanging atop the campus's oldest building, the Joe Crowley era had begun.

Crowley would serve as president for more than two decades, longer than any other person in University history. He would continue to learn how much he needed to know about the institution. He would also be surprised many times by the lengths the people of the University would go to propel it to perform at its highest level—like welders Mayo and Arellano did that day when they rang a bell that hadn't been heard from in more than fifteen years.

What Crowley would learn, and put into practice, and share with the people of Nevada would bring about the University's most sustained period of growth.

Lawlor Events Center, under construction in 1983. Courtesy of University Archives.

The University Finds Its Purpose and Place, 1979–Present

We do have a mandate to do a better job of explaining ourselves to our publics. We ought to do a better job of explaining ourselves to ourselves. People—decision-makers and the general public—are interested in understanding what, specifically, we do here; why we are doing it; and whether we're doing it well. We need to provide answers and the answers need to be immediate and practical.

—Joe Crowley, thirteenth president of the University of Nevada, Reno

Morrill Hall, which had originally housed the entire University when it opened in 1886, was rededicated in the fall of 1979 after an extensive renovation. The first and oldest building on campus had been feeling its age for some time, its third floor condemned in 1964. The renovation was the result of a fourteen-year effort by hundreds of donors throughout the community, augmented by city, state, and federal funds. Virginia Phillips had originally approached President N. Edd Miller in 1965 to ask for his support to start a fundraising campaign to save Morrill. With about $800,000 by 1978 to start work, restoration began on the basement and the first two floors. When Morrill was rededicated on September 12, 1979, with Phillips and many others present, all that was left to do was to add an elevator, finish a third-floor museum and place some window coverings.[1] It was the beginning of a renaissance for the building and its surrounding grounds. Morrill Hall, the Mackay School of Mines, and the Quad, all on the National Register of Historic Places as a "Jeffersonian Academic Village," were honored during the country's National Landmarks of Democracy celebration in the spring of 1987.

Anthropology professor Don Fowler, the director of the University's Historic Preservation Program, said, "The nice thing about being on the National Register is that it says to the world at large, 'Here's a place where significant things happened.'"[2]

Just about three weeks later, on October 5, 1979, Joe Crowley was inaugurated as the University's thirteenth president. From the outset of his address, before an assembled crowd of about one thousand on the Quad, it was clear that Crowley was intent on reminding the University of what its mission needed to be. It wasn't just enough to be inward-facing, content to occupy a spot on a hill that overlooked Reno but holding little connection to it. The University of Nevada, Reno, he said, needed to be an institution integral to Reno's future—and the future of Nevada. It needed to constantly reach out, to build lasting connections with the community and the state that it was serving. "We do have a mandate to do a better job of explaining ourselves to our publics," he said. "We ought to do a better job of explaining ourselves to ourselves. People—decision-makers and the general public—are interested in understanding what, specifically, we do

Morrill Hall (ink drawing by Tom Summers). Courtesy of University Archives.

here; why we are doing it; and whether we're doing it well. We need to provide answers and the answers need to be immediate and practical." Crowley, importantly, saw the flow of information and collaboration between campus and community as a "two-way street. The traffic moves in both directions."

"The many people, the several constituencies who comprise the University community and those from the larger community as well, must be involved if the decisions the president ultimately makes are to be correct ones," Crowley said. As the ceremony began, he was presented with a three-inch silver medallion, a symbol of the promise and energy of the University and its president. Created by art professor Jim McCormick, it is known today as the President's Medal. Near the end of his speech, Crowley also did something for which he would become widely known. Although it was often dry, Crowley's sense of humor—his humble ability to often not mind being the butt of a joke—was an aspect that he hoped many would see in the University as well.

"On the day the laughter stops, when the sense of humor is gone, and that day I hope will never arrive, it will be time for another inauguration," he said.[3] A few years later, when the University was recrafting its mission statement, it included these simple words that not many universities would ever have in a mission statement: "A sense of humor."

President Joe Crowley presents the Distinguished Nevadan Award to activist Maya Miller in 1981. Courtesy of University Archives.

Fraternity members from Omega Xi and Phi Delta Theta race tricycles near the Quad during a Mackay Day activity in 1979. Courtesy of University Archives.

Joe Crowley: One of a Kind

by James Richardson

Joe Crowley was one of a kind. A University president who set records for longevity in office (1978–2001). An administrator who even after retirement returned for another year to assist with another time of turmoil at the University. A man so loved by students that they voted to name the impressive new Student Union building in his honor. And a professor so well-respected by the faculty that he was selected as one of the youngest department chairs ever (in political science) and also one of the youngest Faculty Senate chairs as well (1972–73). Joe ("just call me Joe") also brought great honor to the University nationally. He served as president of the NCAA in 1993–1995—a signal honor. While serving in that role, he promoted many worthy causes, including support for increased participation of women in intercollegiate athletics and more minority representation in NCAA activities. Joe was involved in many other activities on the national scene, and he performed them with dignity, good humor, and honor. He also was a great family man who loved his dear wife, Joy, their four children, and an ever-growing number of grandchildren and great-grandchildren.

Joe and I served together over many sessions of the Nevada Legislature. He served as a senior representative for the entire system, and I represented the Nevada Faculty Alliance. His entrée to the halls of power in the legislature and with various governors was legendary, contributing greatly to rising respect for the University and higher education in general, as well as dramatically increased resources from the state. Indeed, during one session in the 1980s, Bob Maxson, the popular president of UNLV, stated that he saw little need to come to Carson City because Joe was taking care of things for all institutions. Joe was always welcomed by Senator Bill Raggio, then majority leader and head of the Senate Finance Committee, and Joe Dini, Speaker of the Assembly. Joe worked with them over many sessions to increase support for all higher education institutions in Nevada. His quiet way of working with those two gentlemen was impressive and effective; I learned much from his mentorship.

I will never forget that first session in 1985 when I joined Joe working with the legislature. Richard Bryan was governor, and Raggio and Dini were in charge across the mall in the legislature. Governor Bryan had recommended strong support for higher education, along with a brand-new "merit pool" to reward outstanding achievements of faculty members. When the session was over, after four years of meager support, budget cuts, and no raises for faculty (there had been a recession in Nevada), the work of these elected leaders and Nevada's higher education system resulted in a very significant cost-of-living allowance raise for faculty, the new merit pool of 5 percent established as a separate budget item, a one-time 5 percent bonus for all faculty, and significant overall funding increases for all institutions. It was a very good session for UNR and the entire system. Establishment of the annual merit pool (which lasted until the 2008 Great Recession) enabled the University to become competitive in national hiring efforts and facilitated the hiring and retention of excellent faculty in all fields of study.

To celebrate the good results of the 1985 session, Joe and I shared a drink at Jack's Bar with some other higher education representatives, including Ron Sparks, who was then the very effective budget and finance person for the entire system. Until Joe retired, we had many other such celebrations (and occasional lamentations), working with chancellors such as Dan Klaich and Jane Nichols and other higher education officials such as Robert Dickens, a former student of Joe's who became director of government relations at UNR, serving for many years under Joe's leadership.

I was quite accidentally but happily positioned to have been involved in Joe's rapid elevation to interim president and then to the permanent presidency. (I was a member of the Faculty Senate's executive board and also was selected to serve on the search committee for a permanent president.) When the previous president was summarily relieved of duty by the regents, the chancellor at the time, Don Beapler, was well aware of the disquiet this unexpected development might have on the faculty and others in the university community. He gained a commitment from the regents that if the Faculty Senate and the Council of Deans could agree on a candidate, then that person would be appointed. The Faculty Senate, led by Senate Chair Joan Chambers (from Library), acted quickly, soliciting nominations from the faculty, and after due consideration, recommended Joe as the preferred candidate. The deans, after a bit of carping about his being so young and "only an associate professor," finally saw the wisdom of our recommendation, and agreed to support Joe, who was named interim president.

Then a national search was established to find a permanent president for the University. Joe decided, after serious discussions with Joy, to submit his name as a candidate. Deliberations of the search committee were at times quite contentious, with some wanting a more senior and nationally known person to assume the helm. However, calls and letters from faculty and others inundated the committee, urging that Joe be appointed permanent president. After much deliberation (and encouragement from the chair of the regents, Bob Cashell), the committee finally agreed to include Joe's name on the list of finalists. And, as the saying goes, "The rest is history."

Joe Crowley was a terrific choice as UNR president, and he served the University, and indeed the state and the nation, well for many years. He made his mark in many arenas and on many people, including myself and many leaders of the University and in our state. He is sorely missed. We need more leaders with the qualities and effectiveness that Joe demonstrated throughout his meaningful life.

Joe Crowley was the president of a university that had undergone a name change during the late 1960s. The name change would have far-reaching implications for how the University was known and recognized not only in northern Nevada but throughout the state and beyond. Some marketing sleight of hand in the use of a comma rather than a dash in the University's name during the 1990s would further add either clarity or confusion, depending on one's perspective. The first major change occurred in 1967–68 when the University System of Nevada implemented a reorganization. Neil D. Humphrey became chancellor of a higher education system that included the four-year institutions of the University of Nevada in Reno, and the fast-growing Nevada Southern University in Las Vegas (now UNLV). A more independent Desert Research Institute came about, and community colleges were more firmly established throughout Nevada. James Hulse wrote, "Humphrey [who had served as Governor Grant Sawyer's budget director in the early 1960s and who at one point had served as acting president at the University of Nevada] established the chancellor's office in downtown Reno to dispel the notion that it was part of the Reno campus, and it became the practice to refer to the Reno and Las Vegas divisions [UNR and UNLV] as equal institutions."[4]

By the mid- to late-1970s, it was common to call the University on first reference the "University of Nevada-Reno" and on second reference "UNR." That all changed when the University, using Reno's Curtis and Rogers advertising firm, began an awareness campaign in fall 1989 that touted the University's successes in teaching and research. Newspaper, magazine, television, and radio ads suddenly featured the faces, voices, and stories of some of the University's most effective and well-known faculty as well as its highest achieving and most notable students. Included in the advertisements was the subtle substitution of a comma, rather than a dash, in referring to the University as the "University of Nevada, Reno." Paul Page, vice president for development, noted at the time that he didn't mind if people continued to refer to the University as "UNR." If they wished to quibble about the loss of a dash and the addition of a comma to the University's name, that was okay, too. "That's not what the advertisements are all about," Page said of the conversations that people were having about the comma. "We're talking about $250,000 for a yearlong advertising campaign featuring our outstanding faculty and students. No money was used (for the name change)."[5]

Bourne Morris, who became one of the Donald W. Reynolds School of Journalism's most respected professors and chair of the Faculty Senate, had come to Reno not long before the name change. The veteran advertising professional who was widely considered an industry leader said there was nothing sinister about the University going with a comma rather than a hyphen. Rather, she said at the time, it was an effort by the University, using modern advertising and marketing methods, to raise its profile and tell its story of teaching and research. "A lot of colleges and universities are doing a lot of heavy marketing right now because it's simply becoming part of the way in which institutions keep themselves healthy and growing," she said.[6]

Several radio talk show hosts and editorial page writers in Reno and in Southern Nevada had fun at the University's expense about the use of a comma rather than a hyphen in the institution's name. But what was much more substantive were the stories of success occurring on campus during the 1980s and into the 1990s. There was nothing gimmicky about the faculty's work. As the University advertisements demonstrated by the mid-1990s, something special was happening in the effort in "Building the Best Small State University in America."[7] A concerted effort throughout

The groundbreaking ceremony for Lawlor Events Center in 1981 included Dick Trachok, athletics director; Bob Cashell, Board of Regents president; Mike O'Callaghan, former Nevada governor; Robert List, Nevada governor; Erma Lawlor, wife of the late Jake Lawlor; Joe Crowley, University president; John Tom Ross, regent; Bob Barengo, a state legislator; and Robert Bersi, chancellor. The Lawlor Events Center, which opened in 1983, was named in honor of Glenn "Jake" Lawlor, an alumnus of the university who returned in 1942 to coach multiple sports and became director of athletics in 1959. Courtesy of University Archives.

the University built upon areas of strength while also developing and enhancing programs that could meet the needs of the future.

Just one example of how the University could grow stronger was the Department of Civil and Environmental Engineering's large-scale structures research in the College of Engineering. Manos Maragakis, who joined the faculty in 1984 and would rise to become dean of the college 2008–2022, recounted what happened: "This is more than a bullet point of excellence for the University. This has demonstrated that we can do it. We have one of the best earthquake engineering programs in the world, and in Reno we have the biggest earthquake facility in the country and one of the biggest in the world. When given the chance, this University is capable of great achievement. Nearly thirty years ago, this college took something from zero and made it a ten."[8]

It started with the work of a group of Engineering faculty who were determined to make the most of what they had. And then grow it to a national if not international level. Over the next three decades, the Center for Civil Engineering would publish almost two hundred technical reports that provided the basis for seismic retrofits of large-scale structures throughout Nevada, the West, and the country, saving local, regional, state, and federal agencies millions of dollars. Earthquake research facilities developed through federal funds and

Nye Hall residents Cassandra Dreighton (*left*) and Denise Rawson hang out in their room in 1987, an image that was used for the University's "Residential Living Brochure." Courtesy of University Archives.

A celebration of International Women's Day, such as this International Women's Day Parade in front of the Joe Crowley Student Union in 2008, has become a regular campus event throughout the 2000s. Courtesy of University Archives.

private donations, and they have come to be recognized as some of the largest and most sophisticated in the country. The faculty featured some of the world's finest civil engineering researchers, including Ian Buckle, whose work expanded the earthquake engineering research capabilities at the University.[9]

During this period of immense productivity, engineering was growing in other areas as well. Indira Chatterjee, associate dean of the College of Engineering, joined the faculty in 1988 focusing on electrical and biomedical engineering. Federal agencies such as the National Institutes of Health and the Department of Defense supported her productive research portfolio. She also won the F. Donald Tibbitts Distinguished Teaching Award in 1995. Chatterjee constantly advocated for and mentored female faculty and female students. She was an advisor for more than three decades for the Society of Women Engineers. Through the CREATE (Creating Retention and Engagement for Academically Talented Engineers) program, which provides exceptional engineering students with scholarship funding, Chatterjee's influence helped the University take goals of diversity and inclusivity more seriously. The program helped female students build a stronger sense of belonging in the college and the University at large.

In 1989, mezzo-soprano Dolora Zajick performed in Reno during her extraordinary ascent in the world of opera. In early March, Zajick performed as part of *Dolora Zajick and Friends* in Nightingale Hall. Zajick, a 1975 graduate of the University, was fresh off her Metropolitan Opera debut in New York City. Her performance in Reno reflected her friendship and collaboration with Ted Puffer, the longtime University voice, opera, and vocal repertory professor. For almost thirty years Puffer influenced the performing arts at the University and in northern Nevada. He and his wife, Deena, founded the Nevada Opera in the late 1960s. Zajick said of Puffer, "Ted is among the best. His knowledge of opera is unsurpassed."[10] Zajick's return to Reno was an opportunity, she said, to be accompanied by her teacher, Puffer, on piano. "Ted plays very strong, like an orchestra," Zajick said. "It carries." She also shared that she still applied Puffer's lessons in world-class opera performances. "That's why I like to sing with Ted," she said. "He doesn't just say, 'Sing like you have champagne bubbles up your nose.' He tells you to do specific things, like dropping your jaw. If you're having trouble loosening up your jaw, he has specific exercise you can do."[11]

Zajick, who was born in Oregon but grew up in Las Vegas and graduated from high school in South Lake Tahoe, had originally come to the University to study medicine. She quickly switched to music and graduated with bachelor's and master's degrees. She kept a home in Reno and often found time to perform in northern Nevada to benefit the arts community despite an increasingly packed professional schedule. After her Met debut in 1988, her career never slowed. Throughout the 1990s and into the new century, she earned critical acclaim as one of the finest opera singers in the world. *The New York Times* wrote that Zajick's voice was "the only one existing today without any competition in the world."[12] She performed with opera greats Luciano Pavarotti and Placido Domingo, with famed conductors such as Riccardo Muti and Mstislav Rostropovich. Yet, throughout it all, Zajick said she always felt a strong sense of connection to Reno and people such as Puffer who played instrumental roles in her success. "It's important," she once said during an interview in her southwest Reno home, "to keep in touch with who I am and where I came from."[13]

Of all the appointments Joe Crowley made as the longest-serving president in University history (1978–2000), few exceeded the importance of 49-year-old Michael Coray, named the school's first special assistant to the president for diversity on June 7, 1994.[14] It was a historic position, one that would challenge the University's comfort regarding the accessibility and inclusivity it had always said it offered students and faculty.

Coray arrived on campus during the summer of 1972 as the University's first Black professor of history. He had been a standout athlete in South Central Los Angeles, growing up in a single-parent household where his mother, Harriet, had worked as a maid in Beverly Hills. After earning a basketball scholarship at the University of California, Santa Barbara, he floundered academically and was placed on academic probation. His experience, which he eventually righted as he embarked on a career in academia, was humbling but important. "Only after I flunked out was it then that I found out that there was more to this academic stuff

Michael Coray, who joined the faculty in 1972 to lead the Ethnic Studies Program, was the University's first Black professor of history. He later made history again as the institution's first special assistant to the president for diversity. Courtesy of the Coray family.

Michael Coray, history professor and special assistant to the president for diversity, with his wife, Suzi, always had a simple motto: bring voices to the table that might otherwise not have been heard. Courtesy of the Coray family.

THE UNIVERSITY FINDS ITS PURPOSE AND PLACE, 1979–PRESENT

than met the eye," he said.[15] Upon arriving on campus, Coray's charge was to lead the University's new ethnic studies program. He enjoyed his history faculty members and earned a reputation among his students for his impassioned lectures. Coray, however, often found the experience of being one of the "first" on campus to be isolating and difficult. "Hell yes, I felt lonely," he said in 1995. "I felt marooned, intellectually marooned."[16] By 1986, Coray was one of five Black professors at the University. Eighteen faculty members were Asian, five Hispanic, and one Native American. Female faculty comprised about 20 percent of all faculty members. It wasn't enough, he said in a 1986 interview.

"The affirmative action on this campus has nothing to do with good intentions," he said. "It can be measured, just like a faculty evaluation. What's the bottom line? Don't tell me what you want to do. What have you done? I've been around too long. I've heard the rhetoric too long." Coray defined in 1995 what he was hoping to do: "We need to be more mindful of building stronger relationships with ethnic minority communities. What I want is for the University of Nevada to become a better place. And obviously I define what better is in my terms. I want it more accessible to women and minorities, but also warmer toward women and minorities."[17]

Coray was echoing frustration that had existed on campus for many years. Anthropology professor Warren L. d'Azevedo compiled a highly detailed 1975 study, *American Indian and Black Students at the University of Nevada, Reno: 1874–1974*, only a few months after James Hulse's *The University of Nevada: A Centennial History* had been published. D'Azevedo, a renowned ethnographer, studied the Native people of the Great Basin, among others, and strongly advocated for Indigenous people throughout the world during his time at the University from 1963 to 1988. His 1975 report developed lists and personal information of ethnic groups on campus at the time; it included painstaking research about Native American and Black students and their graduations throughout the University's history. He found that for several prolonged periods, 1922–1930 and 1935–1952 for Black students, and 1928–1934 and 1935–1952 for Native American students, there was scant evidence that representatives from either group had attended the University. "During the first one hundred years of the University of Nevada's existence, approximately 277 American Indians and 303 Black students have attended regular sessions on the Reno campus," he wrote. "More than 90 percent of these students attended the University after 1960. Fewer than 20 percent of the undergraduates have received degrees, and the total number of advanced degrees for both groups is eleven. Over 60 percent of each of these groups of students have withdrawn from the University before completion of their studies. Despite this situation, the University of Nevada has been slow to react to the pressures for change."[18] In advocating for change, d'Azevedo implored the University to offer fee waivers for "qualified disadvantaged students" as well as boost "serious efforts to recruit American Indian, black and other minority persons to the teaching faculties as well as top level professional and administrative positions throughout the University."[19]

In 1994, the University had a 10.8 percent "non-white enrollment." The year 1995 was a turning point. A watershed moment occurred when Paul Mitchell, the recruitment and retention coordinator for the Donald W. Reynolds School of Journalism, successfully recruited Kristen Go to attend the University. Go, an Asian American student from Stockton, California, was considered the nation's top high school journalism prospect. Go would go on to become the school's sixth Pulitzer Prize winner as part of the *Denver Post* newsroom's coverage of the Columbine High School massacre and is today considered one of the leaders in the ever-changing journalism industry. Mitchell's selling point in his recruitment was exactly what Coray had been speaking about for years. "Diversity is most important at the college level because this is where you really get into critical thinking about exploring the world view," Mitchell said. "That's the bottom line: more diversity translates into actually bringing in more top academic students."[20] By 1995, the number of Hispanic students at the University had risen to 459, a 9.8 percent increase over the previous year.

"One of the things we're trying to do is make sure Hispanic students are aware of the importance of higher education," Coray said. "It's part of the whole emphasis on outreach." In October 1997, the University's 12,442 student enrollment reached 1,614 minority students—about 13 percent of the campus population.[21]

Coray had no idea, however, what would happen next in the University's growth of its minority and first-generation student body. It would change the campus forever.

Journalism professor Paul Mitchell speaks to an incoming freshman in 2010. Courtesy of University Archives.

Above: The American Indian Organization continued to grow on campus throughout the 1970s. The 1976 membership of the organization included Elaine Allen, Ken Bender, Dixie Brady, Leah Brady, Shelley Christensen, Beatrice Cortez, Jean Eben, Cheryl Foreman, Franic Gonzales, Pam Harris, Dian Jackson, Basil Jimmy, Carmen Lopez, Jaen Luhrs, Susan McDade, Vickie McDade, Cathy Melendez, Randy Melendez, Elroy Mike, Rhonda Mills, Dan Mosley, Cheryl Pete, Renay Peters, Alden Ritley, Mike Shaw, Willie Steve, Mary Thomas, Vernon Thompson, John Wassn, Gwen Wilson, and (advisor) Morris Buckheart. Courtesy of University Archives.

Left: Members of the American Indian Organization, pictured in 1970: (*standing*) Ray Marjo, President Damon Wainscoat, and Karen Wells; (*seated*) Tim Brown, Judy Harris, and Vicki Voorhees. Courtesy of University Archives.

Native American Perspective: The Road to Reconciliation and Meaningful Engagement

by Daphne Emm-Hooper

The University of Nevada, Reno, has a complex history from the Native American perspective. Native Americans have a long and rich history in the Great Basin region, what is now known as Nevada, with diverse Indigenous communities residing in the area for thousands of years before European colonization. This includes the Northern Paiute, Southern Paiute, Western Shoshone, and Washoe people.

When European settlers arrived in Nevada in the mid-nineteenth century, they brought with them ideas of formal education and established schools. This was a time when United States federal policy sought to assimilate Native American children into Euro-American culture, eradicating their languages, traditions, and cultural practices.

In the early twentieth century, efforts were made to educate Native American students, primarily with the goal of assimilation. Many Native American children were forcefully taken to boarding schools, where their Native languages and cultures were actively discouraged. This period represents a dark chapter in Native American history and is often referred to as the era of forced assimilation.

The University of Nevada, Reno, was founded as the State University of Nevada in 1874. Initially, it did not have a strong relationship with the Native American communities in the region. The prevailing attitude at the time was one of assimilation, and Native American cultures and perspectives were largely disregarded or suppressed.

In 1862, President Abraham Lincoln signed the Morrill Act, which distributed public domain lands to raise funds for colleges across the nation. The Morrill Act worked by turning land taken from tribal nations into seed money for higher education. It was all part of Lincoln's creed: "The right to rise." And though generations of land-grant graduates have exercised that right, few have thought to ask who actually paid for the opportunity, and how it was done. It came through the transfer or violent seizure of Indigenous land. Meanwhile, Indigenous people remain largely absent from student populations, faculty, and curriculum. According to landgrabu.org, in 2019–2020, there was less than 0.5 percent aggregate enrollment of Alaskan/Native American students at fifty-two land-grant universities.

Land-grant universities were built not just on Indigenous land, but with Indigenous land. It is a common misconception that the Morrill Act grants were used only for campuses. In fact, the grants were as big or bigger than major cities, and they were often located hundreds or even thousands of miles away from their beneficiaries. In Nevada, 81,224 acres of land were taken from Native communities and sold for the establishment of the University of Nevada.

In 1970 the University created a position, funded by the Bureau of Indian Affairs, to support the Indian students. Twenty fee waivers were available for Native American students. During this time, eighty-three Native students were enrolled at the University. The students organized the American Indian Organization. While there was support and effort to improve the belonging, American Indian enrollment at UNR began to drop steadily after 1971. This may have been, in part, by the diversion of some students to the community college system.

In recent decades, the University of Nevada, Reno, has taken steps to address the historical injustices and is working toward inclusivity and collaboration with Native American communities. Efforts have been made to establish meaningful partnerships and build relationships with tribes in the region. The University has developed programs and initiatives to promote Native American cultures, languages, and traditions, as well as support Native American students in their educational pursuits.

One notable initiative is the Native American Alumni Chapter, which serves as a network for Native American graduates and supports Native American students on campus. The University has established an Indigenous studies minor, offers Paiute language courses, and in 2024 will implement a tribal government course and add a Native American faculty member.

Furthermore, ongoing efforts have established respectful and collaborative relationships with twenty-eight Native American reservations, colonies, and communities throughout the state. In 2022, the University created the position of director of Indigenous relations and a Native American Graves Protection and Repatriation program manager, establishing the Department of Indigenous Relations. Also, the Nevada Legislature expanded the Native American Fee Waiver in 2023 to include members and descendants of federally recognized tribes, creating an opportunity for many Native American Nevada residents to access higher education.

It is important to recognize that the journey toward reconciliation and meaningful engagement with Native American communities is ongoing. Universities such as UNR continue to work toward addressing the historical injustices and fostering a greater understanding and application of Native American perspectives and contributions.

Students work at computer stations in the Getchell Library in 1995. Courtesy of University Archives.

Nevada Governor Kenny C. Guinn appeared before the Nevada Legislature in Carson City during the early evening of January 18, 1999, knowing full well he was not a typical Nevada governor. He was not from the political arena. He didn't particularly like the game of politics. He was a former Clark County School District superintendent and a successful chief executive officer in banking and public utilities. Guinn's own personal story had been one that spoke to the value of education. He was the son of Clifford and Virgie Guinn, who had migrated to California's Central Valley during the Great Depression from Arkansas. Guinn was an honor student and excelled in sports while attending high school in Exeter, California. When Guinn earned his undergraduate and master's degrees from Fresno State University, he became the first person in his family ever to graduate from college. As a young educator in Clark County, he would eventually earn his doctorate in education from Utah State University. Guinn had seen and experienced what education—particularly a college degree—had meant in his life. Throughout his campaign for governor in 1998–1999, he would often say, "Education is not on my agenda. It *is* my agenda."

Nevada's twenty-seventh governor had several pressing needs to be addressed in his State of the State address that evening. A $141 million state budget shortfall required a fiscal remedy over the coming biennium. There was also some hopeful news, however. Guinn proposed how Nevada would use funds from a national tobacco industry settlement the previous year. About 50 percent of the $48 million it was due that year and about $40 million per year for many years to come would fund an annual scholarship of up to $2,500 to the state's publicly funded universities and community colleges for every Nevada student who had maintained a B average during high school. At the time, the $2,500 amount covered the tuition and fees a student would need to earn a bachelor's degree.

"I believe this money can give us a once-in-a-lifetime opportunity to provide Nevada's children with the means to advance their education in a way never thought possible," he said. "It is an idea whose effects transcend party lines, regional differences, and social class. An idea that places at our door, this evening, the chance for all of us to do something truly heroic. To write a great and indelible chapter in the history of our state and in the lives of our children. . . . We will start with the class of 2000, and we will offer these 'Millennium Scholarships' in the fall of that year. I believe every Nevada student who studies hard and makes good grades should be able to continue his or her education—regardless of financial status.

"The Millennium Scholarship will make that possible."[22]

The impact on the University was felt almost from the beginning of Guinn's announcement. By April 2000, the number of students who applied for scholarships at the University almost doubled, with more than 5,000 students seeking scholarships from a pool of funding that included the Millennium Scholarship.[23] The University was expecting up to a 20 percent increase in enrollment when fall 2000 classes began. The University's seven residence halls' 1,460 beds were at 100 percent capacity and filled up a month earlier than normal, it was reported in early August. When fall semester classes began on August 28, 2000, the University welcomed more than 1,300 Millennium Scholars (later adjusted to more than 1,400 once final numbers were tallied). When coupled with an overall first-year class of about 3,000 students, it represented about a 21 percent increase in new student enrollment from the previous year. Overall enrollment exceeded 13,000 students for the first time in University history.[24]

More than 800 Millennium Scholars attended a special ceremony on the Quad two days before classes began. Before they began a long and winding march through campus to the Lawlor Events Center, the bells of Morrill Hall chimed 115 times in honor of the University's 115 years in Reno. Courtney Beadle, a freshman from Las Vegas, had been planning to attend the Colorado School of Mines. She changed her mind once she heard about the benefits of the Millennium Scholarship. "The [Millennium Scholarship] was really the deciding factor in going to school here," she said. "This pretty well takes care of my tuition and all my expenses through the rest of college."[25] In fall 2001, the growth continued. The University set another record in enrollment with more than 13,900 students and saw increases in its first-year class (up 6 percent from 2000) and sophomore class (up 18 percent from 2000).[26]

With the growth began a fundamental shift in the composition of the University's student body. In fall 2000 the University admitted its most diverse first-year class with about 25 percent of the total first-year students coming from underrepresented groups.[27] Additionally, the University reported in 2005 that from 1994 to 2004, the total number of students from underrepresented groups increased by 93 percent to 2,452 students. Native American student enrollment grew by 33 percent during that decade, with African American student enrollment rising by 75 percent and Hispanic enrollment increasing by 136 percent. Johnell Cropper, president of the University's Black Student Organization in 2005, said that the growth of students from underrepresented groups had made the University seem more accessible to students of color. "If you say, 'We have a great school,' but you bring in ten people and none of them look like me, I'm not going to make that connection," Cropper said. Mike Fernandez, the 2005 president of the Asian American Student Association, said the Millennium Scholarship had opened doors to a college education that otherwise might've been closed to students from underrepresented groups: "That $10,000 [the four-year total award of the Millennium Scholarship] is definitely a help to us," Fernandez said. "It gives us an incentive to get our degrees. Before that scholarship, a lot of minority students didn't have the money."[28]

In the coming years the tobacco settlement money dwindled. The Nevada Legislature struggled to find the funding to continue the program into the 2010s. In 2011, the Nevada Legislature approved and Governor Brian Sandoval signed into law Senate Bill 220, establishing the Kenny C. Guinn Memorial Scholarship. A trust fund administered by the Nevada treasurer awarded scholarships to college seniors majoring in elementary or secondary education.

The Millennium Scholars of the early 2000s would have a lasting impact on the state. One, Nicole Cannizzaro, came from a family in Las Vegas where her mother worked as a waitress and her father worked as a bartender. "My parents worked opposite shifts to ensure someone was always home with the kids and someone was always working," she said. With the help of a Millennium Scholarship, she graduated from the University in 2006, becoming the first person in her immediate family to graduate from college. After graduating from the William S. Boyd School of Law at UNLV, Cannizzaro became a prosecutor and was elected to the Nevada Senate in 2016. In 2019, she became the first woman to serve as majority leader. During her time in office, she has helped pass legislation that expanded the Kenny C. Guinn Millennium Scholarship, and she has supported higher education scholarships such as the Nevada Promise Scholarship and the Silver State Opportunity Grant Program. Cannizzaro mentioned once in an interview why representation—whether it was in the legislature, in education, or in life—mattered so much to her. "When the representation of a body reflects the people in the community, or when a traditionally underrepresented population is now part of the majority, those voices are better able to be heard, considered, and are therefore more impactful," she said.[29]

In spring 1992, the Nevada System of Higher Education's Committee on the Status of Women reported that sexual harassment was very high among faculty on the state's campuses. At UNR and UNLV, up to 50 percent of faculty and professional staff reported experiencing sexual harassment, the committee reported.

"The sexual harassment results were surprising to most people," sociology professor Mary White Stewart, who was a key member of the committee, told the *Reno Gazette-Journal* in April 1992. "It became clear to us . . . the university needed to become more what we call female friendly—that is, make the environment more comfortable for women overall."[30]

Because of the findings of Stewart and her colleagues, the University began revising its sexual harassment policy that spring. The Board of Regents approved a faster hearing process for all cases of sexual harassment on Nevada's university and college campuses.

Stewart's involvement in the issue went beyond being a member of the committee. She was a longtime mentor to new female faculty members throughout her career at the University, which had spanned almost thirty years. She was director of the Women's Studies Program, and she helped form the Gender, Race, and Identity Program. Colleagues admired and emulated her example of wanting to ensure the success of new female faculty.

Longtime Foundation sociology professor Marta Elliott remembered meeting Stewart for the first time in 1996:

> She took me out to dinner, and I knew that I could trust her from the very beginning. She spoke straightforwardly about the situation I would be walking into and made it clear that she cared not only about what was best for the Department of Sociology, but what was best for me.
>
> During my many years in which she was my senior colleague and mentor, Mary stood up for me when I encountered problems on the job based on my gender, my status as an individual with an intermittent disabling condition, and my struggle managing the tenure-track as a single mother of two.
>
> She was always the person I knew understood me and would defend me. The way Mary mentored and protected me over twenty years of working together shaped how I interact with the junior colleagues I now mentor as the chair of the Department of Sociology, to whom I try to apply the same degree of honesty, trustworthiness, and protective instincts.[31]

On May 31, 2000, President Joe Crowley gathered his family and several members of the campus in the Clark Room of Morrill Hall. The room was named in honor of President Walter Clark, whose term as president Crowley had eclipsed two years earlier. It was a sunny day. The Quad outside was brilliant from recently completed spring commencement exercises. Crowley was sixty-seven years old at the time. He and his family had lived for twenty-five years in a middle-class home in a middle-class neighborhood on Muir Drive not far from Peavine Elementary School, Rancho San Rafael Park, and the University. Crowley had an announcement to make. Many people assumed that the nation's longest-serving president at a single public university had many more years left in him.

Crowley told those in the room that he would be stepping down. He said he felt the time was right. "I'm an academic person, a social scientist of sorts," he said. "But I also believe in the gut. I've just had this growing feeling inside that the time [to step down] is right."[32]

Crowley's voice only broke once, as he looked at his family—his wife, Joy, was in the room, as were his sons Neil and Tim and daughters Margaret and Theresa. All four Crowley children were University graduates. A few months earlier, on a walk near Rancho San Rafael, with the family's black, six-year-old, medium-size mutt, Molly, tethered to a brown leather leash, Crowley seemed aware that his historic tenure was winding down.

He recalled something Joy had said in a conversation twenty years earlier, when he became the University's acting president. The Crowley family hadn't lived in the Muir Drive home for very long when "the children asked, 'We don't have to move, do we?'" Joy had said. "We told them, 'No, we don't have to.' Besides, what was a university president's tenure, anyway? Four or five years?"

"I'm cognizant of the fact that this can't go on forever," Crowley said as he walked Molly, the sunny winter morning still chilled with a breeze. "But I do know this: The measure at the end always has to be, 'Did it get done, and was it good?'"[33]

A Modern, Comprehensive University: Campus Buildings Today

The University underwent a construction boom of sorts throughout the first decades of the 2000s. It was a time of meeting the needs of what was to become a Carnegie R1 "Very High Research" institution in 2018. Labs were modernized. A new library and Student Union rose. An engineering building, a new math and science center, and student achievement center all added the amenities of a highly sophisticated, modern twenty-first century institution that was connected to its community like never before.

The University's reach in 2017 is seen from this aerial shot looking from the north. Courtesy of UNR Marketing / Communications.

Since the completion of the Joe Crowley Student Union and the Mathewson-IGT Knowledge Center in the late 2000s, the heartbeat of the campus increasingly has shifted to this modern enclave of student activity. Courtesy of UNR Marketing / Communications.

A panorama of the Quadrangle in 2015. Courtesy of UNR Marketing / Communications.

A panorama of the area in and around Manzanita Lake in 2015.
Courtesy of UNR Marketing / Communications.

The Davidson Mathematics and Science Center opened in 2010, the campus's first new capital project for the natural sciences in almost forty years. Courtesy of UNR Marketing / Communications.

The William N. Pennington Student Achievement Center opened in 2016, representing a "one-stop shop" for many student services. Courtesy of UNR Marketing / Communications.

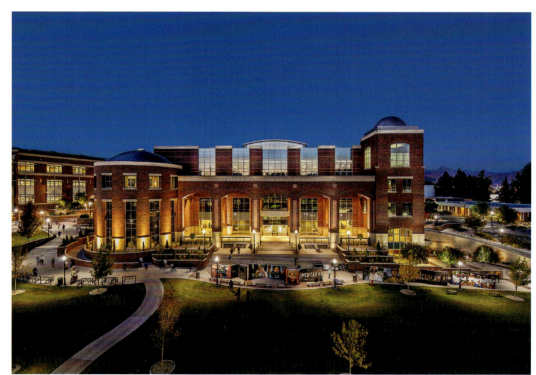

The Mathewson-IGT Knowledge Center was billed as one of the most technologically sophisticated libraries in the country when it opened in 2008. It remains such a facility to this day, combining the latest multimedia tools, library resources, and computing and information technologies. Courtesy of UNR Marketing / Communications.

Performing arts took a huge step with the opening of the University Foundation Arts Building in 2019. The building is home to world-class performances, major exhibitions, and a state-of-the-art performing and rehearsal space. Courtesy of UNR Marketing / Communications.

President Marc Johnson said the E. L. Wiegand Fitness Center's opening in 2017 heralded an important new era for the wellness of University students, calling it a center of the "mind, body and spirit," with locker rooms, fitness and strength training areas, rooms for fitness classes and an indoor running track. Courtesy of UNR Marketing / Communications.

The 100,000-square-foot William N. Pennington Engineering Building, featuring forty labs and a Class 100 cleanroom, opened in 2020. Courtesy of College of Engineering / Vance Fox.

The University of Nevada, Reno at Lake Tahoe is just a short walk from the shore. Courtesy of UNR Marketing / Communications.

The University of Nevada, Reno at Lake Tahoe offers a learning, research, and study environment, exemplified by the Prim Library, which melds with the lake's aesthetic. Courtesy of UNR Marketing / Communications.

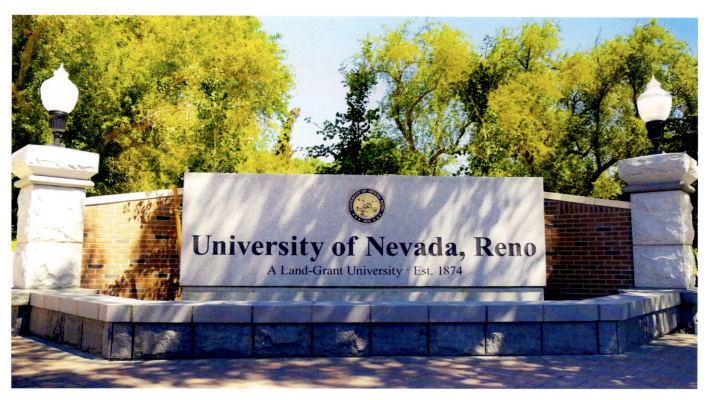

A new University monument on the corner of Ninth and Virginia Streets was dedicated in October 2022. The road at the nearby University entryway at Ninth Street became known that fall as University Way, a signal of even stronger engagement with the City of Reno. Courtesy of UNR Marketing / Communications.

As the student body became more diverse, a teaching culture that stressed experiential learning was taking hold. Throughout its history, the University had always stressed excellence in teaching as one of its major selling points. The professor for whom the University's excellence in teaching award is named, F. Donald Tibbitts, was a good example of the care, attention, and passion that characterized many of the University's finest instructors. Tibbitts, who received the University's first "Outstanding Teacher" award in 1973, was a faculty member in the Department of Biology and the School of Medicine for thirty-five years. When Tibbitts retired in 1994, as he was honored with other emeriti during that May's commencement ceremonies, he received the longest ovation of anyone. He would die, unexpectedly, about six weeks later, at age sixty-five.[34]

The University's best teachers exhibited a mastery of the subject matter, best practices and unconventional approaches in and out of the classroom, and a willingness to refine and reassess what was working and what wasn't. That last quality was particularly important as digital screens and visual learning increasingly became a part of their students' experiences.

Sarah Cummings, who started her career at the University in 2008, was given the F. Donald Tibbitts Distinguished Teaching Award in 2016. Cummings was a chemistry instructor who from the very beginning was known to have a special gift that made her teaching memorable. She attended a strong liberal arts college, Haverford College in Pennsylvania, as an undergraduate. It was there, in that somewhat unlikely liberal arts environment, that she realized something special can happen when a chemistry faculty is collaborative and nurturing not only of fellow faculty members, but of their students. "I really admired the way the chemistry faculty was always available," she said. "It was so welcoming, and such a family-type environment. . . . I loved those interactions when I was an undergraduate. I loved the feeling of being supported, of being welcomed, of being encouraged to learn new things."[35] As much as it was about the subject matter, small details helped bring Cummings's teaching to life. Even as her class sizes increased, she still knew all her students' names. Whenever possible, she worked equally as hard at helping them learn outside of the classroom. For several years, Cummings served as a faculty mentor for the Women in Science and Engineering Program, a living-learning community for thirty-six first-year female students in the science, technology, engineering, and math (STEM) fields. "That was a fabulous experience," Cummings said. "I enjoyed it so much because it was an opportunity to interact with a smaller group of students."[36] A former student, Natasha Monga, who went on to graduate from the School of Medicine and is a diagnostic radiologist, said Cummings was a perfect role model. "She was always available to talk to, and was always so helpful," Monga said. "She was very relatable. I could go into her office and talk about organic chemistry, and other things, too . . . why she chose chemistry and why she chose to pursue her PhD."[37]

Ann-Marie Vollstedt, winner of the Tibbitts Award in 2019, came to campus in 1997 as a diver on the Wolf Pack women's swimming and diving team. She was also a Western University Exchange student from Alaska. After receiving her undergraduate degree in engineering in 2002, she began working toward her master's degree. When she served as a teaching assistant for Eric Wang, an associate professor in mechanical engineering, she realized she enjoyed being in front of a class. "I remember I thought, 'Wow, this is something I should be doing,'" she said. "I really liked teaching and interacting with the students."[38] She soon became fascinated with the whole craft of teaching. With the completion of her PhD in 2009, she joined the College of Engineering faculty. Among Vollstedt's first duties was to teach the college's introductory course, Engineering 100, becoming one of the first points of contact for all engineering students. "Ann-Marie has an exceptional ability to make people enjoy the work they're doing," said Manos Maragakis, dean of the College of Engineering. "I've never known her to complain about anything. Ann-Marie is a problem-solver. She comes at everything that way. It isn't about obstacles; it's about finding ways around those obstacles. It's always about solving problems."[39] Vollstedt was known to keep things fresh and lively in her classes through a variety of methods. When the complexity of the material felt a little daunting, she and four hundred students sometimes engaged in a heated competition to see who could come up with the best paper airplane designs—and then transfer that fundamental knowledge to help solve larger problems. She said her approach was often to tap into the energy of her students, knowing full well that if they are encouraged enough while being taught with a sense of propriety and rigor, great things could happen. "One of the biggest goals is for the students to experience that energy, that excitement, that comes with when you're new to a college campus," she said.[40]

"To Say You Can't Do It Is Not the Answer": The University's Story of Success in Research and Innovation Has Defied the Odds

by Mridul Gautam

From the day I first interviewed for the job of vice president for research and innovation in April 2013, I knew the University of Nevada, Reno, was a place where big things in the areas of research and innovation could happen.

When I visited campus and met several of the outstanding researchers, it was one of those "a-ha" moments that we all have in our lives. It was astounding to learn about the breadth of the work and the impact these hard-working and highly talented faculty were having on people's lives. Even more importantly, these researchers were driven to do more. I knew immediately that all the elements for success were there. This is what I wrote about in my cover letter when I applied for my current position. We have a very productive, world-class faculty with students who are motivated to pursue excellence. When you have these elements, everything else follows.

First, though, was a very simple question: How do we measure success? What are we striving to achieve to measure our success? We wanted to be among the best while focusing on the goal of making people's lives better in the highest tradition of an American land-grant university. We moved very quickly to establish some of our milestones and baselines for success. An obvious institutional goal—and what some thought was a "stretch" goal for us—was to achieve the prestigious classification as a Carnegie R1 "Very High Research" institution. This was something our University had never achieved before—to be classified among the top 130 institutions in the country in research. The numbers spoke for themselves as we made the push to be among the best. At the time, we had about 660 faculty members. Even for the relatively small size, our University possesses some of the most productive faculty members in the country. Research expenditures of about $150,000 per faculty member characterized the work during the mid-2010s, and it continued to increase to $236,000 per faculty member by 2019 and about $287,000 today. To put these numbers in perspective, the research productivity of our faculty is among the top sixty-one universities in the entire country. This is a faculty body that has always addressed the grand challenges of our time, for the betterment of Nevada and the world. Their research work, discoveries, and creativity have helped build a high-energy innovation ecosystem in the state that is anchored by the University of Nevada, Reno. The upswing in smaller high-tech, knowledge-based, dynamic, and entrepreneurial businesses is helping to create high-paying jobs in Nevada, and these are very often connected to the University.

Not surprisingly, they've been at the center of the transformation Nevada's economy has undergone throughout the late 2010s and into this decade, which has seen advances made in emerging fields such as technology, biosciences, and advanced manufacturing. More specifically, our researchers are making impressive contributions in high-energy density plasma physics, quantum information sciences, artificial intelligence systems, robotics, cybersecurity, gastroenterology and cardiovascular systems, chemical ecology, clean energy and related materials, intelligent mobility, rare-earth mining and processing, clean water solutions, infrastructure for seismically affected regions, and climate change.

This work has led to the creation of new jobs, and it has helped retain the lion's share of the five thousand or so graduates we produce each year in Nevada. We produce the next generation of leaders for Nevada, and because of these many opportunities before them, they are choosing to stay here. The faculty's research has also continued to support legacy industries and business sectors of long-term importance to Nevada, such as agriculture, mining, health care, and tourism. And there is an employment continuum created from research that is intertwined with education and workforce development, contributing to career access and career readiness for our graduates.

Faculty research has been a remarkable story at our university. A little less than the current 670 faculty have been able to move our university forward in all areas of research and innovation for more than a decade now. We have seen our research expenditures grow from about $87 million in 2013 to more than $181 million in 2023. These numbers are impressive, particularly when you consider that our peers have about one thousand or more faculty. Credit must go back to the daily effort that our faculty, staff, and students on this campus put forward, every day. It has been a team effort, very much in the spirit of collaboration that has been one of the true hallmarks of our university throughout our history. For my colleagues in research and innovation, it's been all about what can we do to help the faculty, to excel in the work that they are doing.

And what can you say about a faculty where there are always new things to learn so that we can transform the questions that we have today into tomorrow's way of doing things? Just one example of our 670 faculty members is chemical and materials engineering professor Dev Chidambaram, who received the Regents Mid-Career Researcher Award in 2023. His work includes a $1 million National Science Foundation (NSF) award to advance the circular economy for lithium batteries in Nevada. It also includes a $1.3 million award from Advanced Research Projects Agency-Energy, an arm of the US Department of Energy, to develop stable, noncorroding oxygen evolution electrodes. His students have received three Regents Outstanding Graduate Student awards and numerous scholarships and fellowships from NSHE (Nevada System of Higher Education) and the US Department of Energy and NSF, and they have graduated with prestigious fellowships at various national laboratories across the country. Of course, Chidambaram sees his success purely in terms of electricity—the kind of creative electrical current that surges through our entire research and innovation enterprise at the University: "I consider my students as electrons in the electrochemical research. Without electrons, there is no electrochemistry." Without great researchers, there can be no great research institutions.

We learned in December 2018 that we had reached the Carnegie classification of "R1" and "Very High Research" for the first time in our history. The classification was reaffirmed in December 2021 when we were once again recognized as "R1" by the Carnegie Classification's latest update cycle. So much of achieving these milestones has to do with how our faculty approaches their work. You set high expectations to succeed as a researcher. Whenever there is a failure, you cannot be deterred. You must constantly seek solutions. This is the way the faculty on this campus has always operated. To say you can't do something is not the answer on our campus. Having become a mature, comprehensive university where all fields of academic, scholarly, and research endeavors matter, is the reason we were recognized as an R1 institution. The faculty, staff, and students of this university have come together in a unified manner and worked together and ensured that research is ingrained in our structure and culture and we are in pursuit of a common goal—enhancing the quality of life of our community and the citizens of the state.

The work of our faculty has seen the number of our National Science Foundation Faculty Early CAREER Development Career awardees grow to record levels. CAREER Awards recognize researchers who are on their way to becoming leaders in their respective areas of research. We have also seen our role in helping realize Nevada's economic future grow substantially. Through the Innevation Center, a research hub a few blocks from downtown Reno, and the Nevada Center for Applied Research, we have attracted new businesses to northern Nevada. Industry leaders, entrepreneurs, and agency officials receive access to the University's ideas, labs, equipment, and expertise through the centers. More than $240 million in venture capital has been raised by affiliated startups through these operations. The outcome: Sixty-two companies with University-based operations have been formed, with more than $163 million in grants, sponsored-research contracts, and donations received. These affiliated companies have created 735 new jobs.

And all this comes back to a faculty research culture that has stressed productivity and impact. A decade ago, we were in search of our measures of success. Today our research successes are fueling the future of Nevada. To say you cannot do something is never the answer in research. Our faculty continues to embrace the idea that we can always find the answers, and what's more, share them to make our world a better place. It is what research at our university is all about.

President Marc Johnson greets Governor Brian Sandoval, on campus to sign Assembly Bill 69 to drive autonomous vehicle technology and testing in Nevada. Courtesy of University Archives.

Philanthropy continued to play an important role as the University expanded throughout the early 2000s. Several key individuals and local philanthropic foundations provided substantial donations that capped capital campaigns, started or finished fundraising for new buildings with multimillion-dollar gifts, or met University needs in programming, scholarships, endowed professorships, and more. They included Dixie May and the Wilbur D. May Foundation, whose family could trace its time in Northern Nevada to the 1930s and the sprawling 2,600-acre Double Diamond Ranch; William Pennington, a Nevada gaming executive; Chuck Mathewson, chairman of the board of International Game Technology; the E. L. Wiegand Foundation; and the Redfield Foundation. The timing and focus of their support often spoke to the University's priorities. In the early aughts, the institution was dealing with growing enrollment and the need to find space for a faculty that also needed to grow following the budgetary challenges of the Great Recession.

Under President John Lilley, who served from 2001 to 2006, several key capital improvement projects were either completed or were almost completed. The majority were centered in one form or another on student success. Chief among them were the opening of two buildings after Lilley left to become president of Baylor University: the 2007 completion of the Joe Crowley Student Union and the 2008 opening of what was touted as one of the most technologically advanced libraries in the country, the Mathewson-IGT Knowledge Center.

Under presidents Milt Glick (2006–2011) and Marc Johnson (2011–2020), the campus's infrastructure continued to grow. The Jot Travis Building, which had been the old Student Union, was renovated in 2008 to house the Davidson Academy, a free public school for profoundly gifted young people. The William N. Pennington Health Sciences Building opened in 2011. Getchell Library, which had opened in 1961, was demolished and replaced by the William N. Pennington Student Achievement Center. During the latter half of Johnson's presidency, the University experienced one of its greatest periods of faculty growth. More tenure-track positions were created, and student enrollment topped twenty-one thousand for the first time. As state support dwindled after the Great Recession of 2008–2010, new buildings were still constructed. They included student residences Great Basin and Peavine Halls, the E. L. Wiegand Fitness Center, the University Foundation Arts Building, and the William N. Pennington Engineering Building. In addition, historic campus buildings such as Lincoln Hall and Palmer Engineering were repurposed or retrofitted. Of the almost $500 million in capital improvements that occurred during the Johnson presidency, only $71 million came from the state, further magnifying the importance of donor contributions and other creative funding methods.

Johnson's tenure was one of the longest in University history; only Joe Crowley, Walter Clark, and Joseph Stubbs served longer as president. He was the University's provost when Glick died suddenly of a stroke in 2011, and he led the campus through a period of grieving. He was appointed interim president before being selected by the Board of Regents as the University's sixteenth president in 2012. Johnson wrote in an open letter to the campus on his final day in office, September 25, 2020:

> It has been quite a journey. We have worked together to lift the University from the recessionary period of the early 2010s, to a time of profound and remarkable achievement in all aspects of our institutional mission, to today, the time of COVID-19. There have been days where we have gathered together to comfort and to mourn, when we have questioned and challenged one another, when we have stood together and when we have celebrated historic institutional milestones. Of all those days, I cannot think of an institution and a group of people that I am always more proud of than the University of Nevada, Reno and the individuals who on a daily basis make real our campus's never-ending impulse for action. Our institutional achievements have included our attainment in late 2018 of the classification of Carnegie R1 "Very High Research" institution; the attainment in 2019 of the classification as a "Carnegie Engaged" institution; eleven straight years, a streak that began with my predecessor, Milt Glick, ranked in the "top tier" of "Best National Universities" by *US News & World Report*; record-setting student achievement, including record levels of student diversity; record-setting faculty achievement, productivity and research. I mention these superlatives because they belong to all of you. It is your hard work, your belief in the value of our mission that has kept our University on this decade-long trajectory.
>
> I have been fortunate to be surrounded by so many talented, creative, determined and hard-working people. Your high institutional aspirations, strong sense of collegiality and collaboration, and the warm glow of your collective personalities and dreams, have powered our university to great heights.[41]

University presidential inaugural speeches have been something of a mixed lot throughout time. There have been clear moments of inspiration and vision. Joseph Stubbs said, "And from your University that sits upon the hill, guarded by the enduring mountains, and under the serene splendor of the eternal skies, will go out unseen and unmeasured a wave of influence and power that will raise us all in the world of living." Joe Crowley said, "We do have a mandate to do a better job of explaining ourselves to our publics. We ought to do a better job of explaining ourselves to ourselves." Other speeches have been somewhat flat and forgettable.

As he prepared for his inauguration on September 29, 2006, Glick knew people were hoping to hear words that might inspire, or at the very least give them hope. During the previous fifteen years, before being appointed to serve as the University's fifteenth president, Glick had ridden shotgun (provost) for Arizona State University's rock star president, Michael Crow. In his visits with faculty, students, staff, and the community, Glick had been struck by the passion everyone held for the University. He felt everyone was sitting on top of something that was magical and rare. It was something that didn't need a lot of complexity, or metaphorical layering or even over-explanation to share. A few months later, he would boil down the University to its essence on a 5-by-7 index card that he reduced to 3½-by-4 with scissors. His habit to use index cards printed with measurable goals began during his time in Arizona. "It's got to fit in my pocket," he said of the index cards. "If they don't, I'm not going to remember everything that's printed on them." The print was small, but his message for the University was mammoth. His "Keys to the Future" and "Measuring Success" trumpeted his vision for the state's oldest highest institution of learning. "Keys to the Future" included instilling a "culture of completion" to improve graduation and retention rates; creating a "sticky campus" with facilities and programming that keep students engaged; increasing research capacity and quality; and blurring the lines between the campus and the community. "Measuring Success" cards included specific metrics for enrollment, retention, and completion.[42] Over the five years of his presidency, Glick had thousands of these cards printed and handed them off to everyone from captains of industry to the custodial staff. He did so with a gracious spirit, an impish grin, an ever-present Diet Pepsi in his hand, and often from underneath a sweat-stained river hat that became his trademark.

But all this was in the future. For his inaugural, Glick spoke about the past, and counterpointed it with what the future held.

"The next Comstock Lode is not in the mines of Nevada," he intoned confidently, "it is in the minds of Nevadans."[43]

They were words worth remembering. The University would have to hold tightly to them as 2008–2010 brought the Great Recession, $100 million in budget cuts and the loss of hundreds of campus jobs. Asked whether the University's work still mattered

Democratic presidential nominee Barack Obama and University President Milt Glick (2006–2011) during a campaign stop on campus, September 30, 2008. Courtesy of University Archives.

during severe budget reductions and the loss of faculty and staff, Glick said, "I still believe that what we do at our University will determine the quality of life for all Nevadans" and "Nevada needs more education, not less."

It was a difficult time, but the University still made tremendous strides during the most devastating period of budget reductions. The campus, with no more than a handful of National Merit Scholars when Glick became president in 2006, had thirty-eight by 2011. Enrollment, retention, and graduation all reached all-time highs

First Lady Michelle Obama visits the Quad on October 3, 2012, as part of her husband's reelection campaign. Courtesy of UNR Marketing / Communications.

by that year. For the first time ever, the University was ranked among the Tier I schools in *US News & World Report*'s prestigious annual rankings.

When Glick died in April 2011 at age 73, he was remembered as a leader who took the time to learn students' names, their hometowns, and what their dreams were. "Do you know what Sargent Shriver's best line ever was?" he once asked, referencing the founder of the Peace Corps. "'Begin to look less at yourself and more at each other; learn more about the face of your neighbor . . . and less about your own.'"[44]

The future of Nevada was indeed in the minds of young people who came to the campus searching for their purpose. They often not only found purpose, but the beginnings of who they were to become once they graduated. One example was Colin Kaepernick, who was the greatest quarterback to ever play at the University. Following his career as a starter for the Wolf Pack from 2007 to 2010, he remains the only quarterback in college football history to pass for more than 10,000 yards and rush for more than 4,000 yards during his career. For his efforts, he was inducted into the Wolf Pack Hall of Fame.

He led the Wolf Pack to 13–1 record his senior season. It included one of the greatest upsets in NCAA history when the Wolf Pack beat the nation's third-ranked team, Boise State University, 34–31 in overtime at Mackay Stadium on a chilly November night before a national television audience on ESPN. The Wolf Pack finished with its highest Division I season-ending ranking, eleventh, and Kaepernick placed eighth in that year's Heisman Trophy balloting. He would go on to become a second-round pick by the San Francisco 49ers in the 2011 draft and led the 49ers their first Super Bowl appearance in almost two decades during the 2012 season. In 2016, Kaepernick began to speak out about social injustices in the country. His protest—taking a knee during the national anthem—during that season was controversial. It led to a national conversation about topics such as social justice, human rights, the relationship between the Black community and police departments throughout the country's history, and economic inequality.

Kaepernick's leadership skills and his innate ability to shoulder heavy responsibilities were on full display throughout his time with the Wolf Pack. Head football coach Chris Ault had revolutionized college football a few years before Kaepernick's arrival with the creation of the "Pistol" offense: the quarterback would stand not the customary seven yards from center but rather four yards, which introduced a dizzying array of run-pass-option and play-action selections that put college offenses on the attack like never before. Ault, who had transformed the program from also-ran status when he became head football coach in December 1975 at age 29, was a former Wolf Pack quarterback himself. His workdays, especially when he doubled as athletics director and football coach, would start before five o'clock in the morning and often not end until well after dinner. Ault unashamedly made it clear every day to his assistant coaches, players, support staff, and his family and friends that he bled not red, but silver and blue. Winning 234 games as head coach of the Wolf Pack, Ault would become one of the great coaches in college football history and was inducted into the College Football Hall of Fame in 2002.

In 2007, in his freshman year in Ault's cutting-edge offense, Kaepernick, who throughout his time as a student majoring in business was a member of the Dean's List, was already demonstrating immense physical skills and incredible intelligence that would trigger the pistol. His untiring work ethic and natural sense of accountability presaged how he would one day become a leader on a much larger sociological scale. John Bender, a native of Three Hills, Alberta, Canada, was a four-year starter on the Pack's offensive line 2007–2010. From the time they were redshirt freshmen together, Bender knew Kaepernick had a special affinity to be a leader: "Kap was a lead-by-example kind of guy. When it was needed, though, he had a pretty stern voice. I remember when we first met. He was a really skinny kid, tall and lanky. He always worked extremely hard. I remember watching him and thinking, 'This kid wants to play, and he wants to do well.'"[45] Luke Lippincott, from Salinas, California, was a 1,000-yard rusher when he played with Kaepernick. He said of Kaepernick:

> Colin and I were roommates for the games. We would always spend the night in the hotel room racking up the room service bill and going over all the plays. . . . I knew Kap was great, too. He was super skinny, and you didn't really know what he could do. But he had an awesome work ethic. He was always up for anything to make himself better. I really respected him for that. My thing was always to lead by example. I was always the first into the weight room and the last to leave. No one could keep up with me . . . until Kap came along. He would want to stay longer than me. I would go so hard until I puked; but Colin would always match my work ethic. That's how I knew he was a leader. That's what we all responded to, and that's why he was our leader.[46]

Added Bender in the same *Nevada Today* story: "Humble and hungry. That's always been Kap."

Years later, as a national debate played out regarding Kaepernick's social stands, his Wolf Pack teammates remained steadfast in their support. Although numerous NFL players followed Kaepernick's lead during the 2016 season and took a knee to protest the social justice environment in the country, Kaepernick wouldn't play again in the NFL after that season. Conversely, he is one of the world's most recognizable figures. *Time* magazine named him a runner-up for Person of the Year in 2017. He has received the W. E. B. Du Bois Medal from Harvard University, considered Harvard's highest honor in African and African American studies. Bender said:

> I think Colin sleeps well at night. He knows what he's doing is right. It's too bad the thing that everybody has talked about, the kneeling thing, has been hijacked by other people for their political agenda. Colin hasn't said a lot about all of this, but when he speaks, he's very eloquent. The platform he used—kneeling for the national anthem—has been challenging for him to get his larger point across, particularly for the people who really don't want to listen to what he has to say. There's no question in my mind that he's among the top thirty-two quarterbacks in the world, and is probably in the top twenty. There is no question about that. Yet he's not able to have a job. He's been prevented from going out and doing the thing he loves. That's been challenging for him, no question. But he's put his money where his mouth is. He's made and continues to make a huge difference for large groups of people who don't always have a voice.[47]

Colin Kaepernick: A Leader Who Has Shown Us a Greater Capacity for Justice and Compassion

by Paul Mitchell

It was a spring late Friday afternoon and, like most Friday afternoons, hardly anyone is on campus. "Dr. Mitchell, there's someone I'd like for you to meet," says Barry Sacks, former Nevada assistant football coach. At six feet, three inches, I look up. This kid's a good six feet, five inches–six feet, six inches, wiry, smooth brown skin, close-cropped hair, and a pleasant smile.

"How are you, young man, I'm Dr. Mitchell."

He extends his hand.

"I'm Colin, sir. Colin Kaepernick."

Pretty sure Kap doesn't remember that encounter. This was obviously an "unofficial" campus visit. There was no other family with him and no other coaches with Sacks. Not sure if there was a meeting set with a faculty member (though pretty confident I was the first Black faculty member he met on that visit). In a later conversation, Sacks said Nevada is the only school looking at him to play football while everyone expected him to play baseball.

In retrospect, our meeting reminded me of a similar brush with greatness. When I was a kid coming out of the Nixon Theater in West Philadelphia, after seeing *Mary Poppins*, there stood "The Greatest." Muhammad Ali was holding court with a group of community people.

I ran up to him.

"Can I shake your hand?" I said.

"Shake the hand of the man," he said.

When one meets a transformative individual, whether they be brash and verbose or with a quiet confidence, it leaves an indelible impression.

Every student who enters a university is trying to do several things: graduate (either for themselves and/or for their family), develop their own identity, and find their "tribe." The

Colin Kaepernick, competing in a game against UNLV in 2009, was a four-year starter at quarterback, set many school records, and was inducted into the University's Wolf Pack Hall of Fame. Courtesy of University Archives.

challenge for student-athletes is balancing classes with practice, schoolbooks with the playbook, out-of-class meetings with position meetings. There's weight training, travel, missed classes, and dealing with the media. Lastly, there are 100-point midterms, quizzes, finals, and weekly home and away (for quarterbacks) 300-yard passing tests every fall Saturday afternoons or evenings.

But on the most basic level, the five tiers of Maslow's Hierarchy of Needs for college student development come into sharper focus: physiological (students can't focus on college if their physiological needs aren't being met); safety (an unsafe student will unlikely participate in student life); belonging (students want to belong in their college or university); esteem (achieving this requires students to feel confident, strong, and self-assured; it requires them to achieve a sense of esteem); and self-actualization (the achievement of one's true potential). Couple these needs with the needs of a biracial young man raised in a predominantly white community, living in a new state (that was once dubbed "The Mississippi of the West") while seeking to understand *his* place. The writings of Du Bois, Garvey, Malcolm X, etc. were, probably, explored and debated. Kap was able to do all of this while playing the most visible position in football.

Kap began the exploration of his African American heritage in high school and that carried over into his college days. He pledged Kappa Alpha Psi. Between becoming a fraternity member and playing football, Kap found his tribes that continue to sustain him.

In retrospect, Kap caught everyone off guard. He came to the University as an unheralded football prospect. However, a brief visit to a practice revealed the promise only the Nevada football staff had hedged its bet on. It can be best described like this: a good friend who worked for a major news publication had invited me to Pebble Beach for a golf tournament. First up was Ernie Els. The ball was struck cleanly and goes a good distance. Next up is Tiger Woods. The ball was struck cleanly, but the sound was different. *Very* different. Woods won that tournament by an incredible fifteen strokes.

At a Wolf Pack football practice, the first quarterback is up and throws the ball. Then Kap is up. He retreats several steps, then turns and spots his streaking target. The ball looks like an orange in his big hands. Then he steps forward, plants his leg, and uncoils a tight spiral. The arm motion is different. The release point is different. The velocity is different. But the main thing was the sound was different. *Very* different. Imagine the ball is a high-pitched whistle that is screaming in flight. Then it lands softly in the hands of the target. As impressive as that throw was, he was only a freshman. It would take an injury to the starter and a couple years before Kap would make history.

Before Kap's arrival, the University of Nevada, Reno, was one of the nation's leaders in terms of diversity, equity, and inclusion in college football. Arthur James of Elko was the earliest documented Black player on a Nevada team, lettering in 1921. In 1946, Mississippi State University offered the University of Nevada the opportunity to go down south for a game, with one caveat: William "Billy" Bass (who became one of the first players to integrate the Canadian Football League) and Horace Gillom, Nevada's two Black players, would not be allowed to play. The team agreed that if Bass and Gillom couldn't play, the team wouldn't play. In 1948, the team was invited to play Tulsa University in Oklahoma with the same caveat. Again, the team declined, but Tulsa reneged and allowed Alva Tabor (Nevada football's first Black quarterback) and Sherman Howard to play. Tulsa ran into a Golden Hurricane: the Wolf Pack won, 65–14, Tulsa's worst loss in thirty-one years. The Jim Crow racial segregation laws were not limited to the South. Marion Motley (considered one of the NFL's 50 Greatest Players) had to hold back his coach after the Idaho coach said Motley wouldn't be allowed to play. Motley not only played, but he was also one of the first Black players to integrate the NFL. Kap's gesture highlighted the more-often-than-not negative interactions between law enforcement and African Americans in this country.

All these men, whether knowingly or unknowingly, willingly or unwillingly, have contributed to the diversity, equity, and inclusion at the University of Nevada.

Going off to school to seek higher learning lays the foundation for better critical thinking skills and also allows those in search of knowledge the ability to ponder differing viewpoints. Knowledge can be gained in the classroom. But it's also the gained knowledge in daily conversations and interactions outside of the classroom as well that makes for a more informed community. Hopefully, these interactions lead to a greater understanding of those who have differing lived and learned experiences. But most importantly, this gained knowledge provides a greater capacity of justice . . . and compassion . . . for *all*.

Faces of the Pack: The Heartbeat of the Wolf Pack Way

"Student success" became a highly used and very applicable phrase to how the University approached its educational mission throughout the 2010s and 2020s. It included a variety of approaches: ensuring students were engaged through impactful and experiential learning; taking students into learning environments where "hands-on" learning was critical to academic growth; growing the living/learning experience on campus; developing peer mentorship and networking skills that the students could use throughout their lives.

The University's marching band, also known as "The Pride of the Sierra," has always made Mackay Stadium a special place to watch a football game. Courtesy of UNR Marketing / Communications.

Homecoming 2016: A time to celebrate. Courtesy of University Advancement / The Nevada Alumni Association.

The University greenhouses allow College of Agriculture, Biotechnology, and Natural Resources labs to develop and understand new plant products to combat global warming. Courtesy of UNR Marketing / Communications.

Meeting the needs of Nevada's agricultural economies and contributing to the understanding of Nevada's rangelands are part of the mission of the College of Agriculture, Biotechnology, and Natural Resources and University Extension. Courtesy of UNR Marketing / Communications.

Connecting the student experience to student success has been a major University focus throughout the 2010s and into the 2020s. Courtesy of UNR Marketing/Communications.

Peer mentors at the Honors College. The longtime Honors Program officially became a college in summer 2020. Courtesy of UNR Marketing/Communications.

The Dean's Future Scholars Program was founded in 2000 by William Sparkman, dean of the College of Education, to empower lower-income, first-generation students to aspire to college. It started with fifty students. By 2021, more than 1,400 students in grades seven through twelve in Washoe County had participated. Courtesy of UNR Marketing / Communications.

Instructor Mark Gandolfo leads a video production class in 2011. The use of the latest, most technologically sophisticated equipment has always been part of the learning experience at the Mathewson-IGT Knowledge Center. Courtesy of University Archives.

Nevada Foundation photography professor Peter Goin teaches photography students to see in the dark in the Church Fine Arts Building in 2005. Courtesy of University Archives.

The Center in the Joe Crowley Student Union is an integral meeting spot that brings together and provides resources for the University's diverse student population. Courtesy of UNR Marketing / Communications.

Marching band members stand next to the Fremont Cannon in 1993. Since 1970, the Fremont Cannon has been awarded to the winner of the annual football game between UNR and UNLV. Courtesy of University Archives.

Students work at computers and scanners in the new high-tech work space, @One, in 2009. The Mathewson-IGT Knowledge Center, a $75.3 million, 295,000-square-foot, technology-focused library, opened in 2008. Named for its largest benefactors, the Mathewson Family and International Game Technology, the library houses five floors of resources, multimedia labs, a robotic storage center, study spaces, and administrative offices. Courtesy of University Archives.

Equipped with four dedicated virtual reality stations, @Reality in 2018 also featured a Meta2 Augmented Reality headset designed to bridge the gap between the virtual and real world. The venue also provided users with access to four VR computers, two Leap Motion finger and hand trackers, and more. Courtesy of University Archives.

The University of Nevada, Reno School of Medicine has been a "true jewel in the crown" for the University, President Brian Sandoval said in 2022. Courtesy of UNR Marketing / Communications.

The Ozmen Center for Entrepreneurship in the College of Business has become a space for moving ideas into action. Because of this synergy, entrepreneurship has become one of the College of Business's most popular academic areas. Courtesy of UNR Marketing / Communications.

The William N. Pennington Student Achievement Center opened in February 2016. For the first time ever, student engagement and retention services were all essentially housed in one place. Courtesy of UNR Marketing / Communications.

Campus gatherings, such as this movie screening on the lawn of the Joe Crowley Student Union in 2012, became the norm as the University increasingly emphasized campus-centered experiences for its students. Courtesy of UNR Marketing / Communications.

The outbreak of COVID-19 throughout Nevada in March 2020 would mirror what was happening throughout the world. Millions were becoming infected and dying from the novel coronavirus. University students who were studying abroad were asked to return to the United States and to quarantine immediately upon their return. Governor Steve Sisolak declared a state of emergency in Nevada. On March 15, Sisolak requested that all state agencies take proactive public health measures. Chancellor Thom Reilly said that all NSHE institutions were to transition to remote instruction and operations no later than March 18. As spring break ended, students were not allowed to return to their residential communities. The University purchased a Zoom Pro license, which allowed essentially unlimited classes and duration via a meeting and teaching technology few had even heard of a few months earlier. Two hundred laptop computers were distributed to local and remote students who needed them. The University's withdrawal date was extended to April 10. Students were given an option to petition for a "Satisfactory" rather than a letter grade at the end of the semester. A University message on March 16 noted that "all units should include testing remote work capabilities now and implementing flexible remote work options when applicable. Also, all units should work to emphasize the concept of social distancing in all interactions by limiting in-person meetings and avoiding close contact

The Richard Bryan statue on campus was not immune to the prevalent desire to stay safe through masking during the COVID-19 pandemic in 2020. Courtesy of University Archives.

whenever possible. These are small, but essential steps we must all take as we attempt to 'flatten' the severity and duration of the coronavirus outbreak."[48]

The steps were all intended to be temporary. During a town hall meeting via Zoom on March 27, the University's chief medical officer and director of the Student Health Center since 1988, Dr. Cheryl Hug-English, told the almost five hundred campus community members who attended that "we don't know the end of this story yet."[49]

It had taken a herculean effort to get to March 27, when the more than 3,500 students who were living on campus were now living at home and classes were being delivered via Zoom. Behind the scenes, too, extraordinary acts showed how much students, faculty, and staff cared about one another during a troubling and dangerous moment. University Honors student Jayde Powell created "Shopping Angels" to bring groceries to at-risk populations. Student volunteers picked up groceries and other shopping essentials and delivered them to those who were most vulnerable to COVID-19 and who couldn't leave their homes. Powell's work was featured nationally, including on CNN. For several weeks after students moved off campus and buildings were closed to the public, the Pack Provisions program, the on-campus pantry that had provided food for the most food-vulnerable students, found novel ways to continue delivery. It used the Campus Escort Service and its vehicles for deliveries.[50]

Members of the University's medical community helped maintain the health and safety of the campus and contributed to the overall health care effort throughout northern Nevada and the state. Hug-English and her staff at the Student Health Center—the same student-funded center founded in the influenza pandemic of the early 1920s—worked around the clock. It tested for COVID-19, administered care and provided guidance to interpret a dizzying array of self-isolation and quarantine instructions from the state. The Nevada State Public Health Laboratory, under the direction of Mark Pandori, provided full COVID-19 testing capacity for the public health needs of the entire state. Primary care and mental health practices from the medical school provided telemedicine and telepsychiatric services for patients with acute and chronic medical and prescription needs. Telephone triage protocols were developed to make decisions about COVID-19 testing; trained medical students provided telephone triage services for rural Nevada. Substantial amounts of personal protective equipment were mobilized from across the campus—basic science labs, agriculture, art—to support University health care staff in their clinical duties.[51]

COVID-19 had presented the University with extraordinary and unprecedented challenges. Steven Hayes, Nevada Foundation psychology professor, put the challenges of the pandemic into context in a blog post to the campus in late March: "This challenge is not like a winter storm, it is more like a winter season, and that season has just begun."[52]

Spring 2020 commencement, because of the prevalence of COVID-19 in the community and state directives limiting in-person gatherings, was postponed. Virtual celebrations did not replace traditional commencement ceremonies, but rather offered the graduates a way to share their accomplishments as they finished their degrees. The University conferred 3,240 degrees—including 2,576 bachelor's degrees and 601 advanced degrees (master's and doctoral degrees)

Brian Sandoval, appointed president a few weeks earlier, wore a mask per state public health guidelines on his first day on the job, October 5, 2020, during the COVID-19 pandemic. Courtesy of University Archives.

through a virtual celebration web page. The page included a list of graduates by college, school, or unit; a video message from President Marc Johnson; and video messages from deans and other faculty members. Graduates could add a photo and a note about their time at the University to their listings.[53]

It was a time memorable for its disruption and for the campus's efforts to regain a sense of normalcy, even as it became apparent no end to COVID-19 was in sight. Nevada Foundation English professor Michael Branch called it "the most challenging thing I've faced in (my) thirty-year teaching career." He worried that some of his students were not able to access the internet from home. Branch was equally concerned about the prospect of a student tuning in to class via an iPhone. Branch had always been considered one of the campus's finest lecturers and storytellers. He worked every day at re-creating the special connection that had always existed in his classroom: "There's something magical about being in the classroom. For sixteen weeks, it's a little ideal community that shows how the world could work."[54] COVID-19 had turned all of it upside down. Journalism professor Todd Felts used the opportunity to try to grow closer to his students by adjusting the subject matter to how they were feeling, and coping, with a world racked with uncertainty. "The first week after spring break, when we moved online, we had some of the most meaningful conversations that I've ever had with my students in more than twelve years of teaching at the University," he said.[55]

Twenty-two-year-old Sheridan Manfredi, a member of the 2020 graduating class with a bachelor's degree in psychology, said the adjustments that were made because of the pandemic were understandable. What was hard, however, was dealing with the human factor—how face-to-face interactions were no longer feasible. Opportunities to see students and professors who for almost four years had been daily presences were now gone.

"The biggest challenge is the uncertainty and the lack of closure," Sheridan said. "You are left without that final goodbye."[56]

On July 13, 2020, the University announced that fall semester classes would implement a "hy-flex" approach to classroom instruction. The modality featured a combination of in-person and online delivery of teaching for larger classes. Provost Kevin Carman said up to sixty-five classrooms would be "hy-flex," with no more than half of the students physically in the room at any one time. The other half would receive online instruction at the same time. Those in the classroom would observe strict social distancing protocols. He said classes of more than one hundred students would be taught remotely.[57]

Only a few weeks into the fall semester of 2020, as the University carefully welcomed students back to campus, on September 17, NSHE announced that former Nevada governor Brian Sandoval had been named the University's seventeenth president.[58] Johnson, after almost a decade as president, had announced before the pandemic that he would be stepping down and returning to the faculty. He agreed to continue to serve as president once the pandemic hit. Sandoval's selection was historic. He was a 1986 graduate of the University and became the first graduate of the University to ever serve as president. In addition, Sandoval, who was a popular and successful governor from 2011 to 2019, was the first person of Hispanic origin to ever be selected president. Sandoval, fifty-seven years old at the time of his selection, was a unanimous choice by the Board of Regents following a national search. He credited his experiences as a student at the University for all that he had accomplished throughout his career in public service. In addition to being a two-term governor, he'd also been elected Nevada attorney general, had served in the Nevada Assembly, and had been appointed a federal judge.

"As a 1986 graduate of the University of Nevada, Reno, this is a place that is very special to me," Sandoval said during his introductory press conference on September 21 in the Great Room of the Joe Crowley Student Union. He was joined there by his wife, Lauralyn, also a University graduate and who played tennis for the Wolf Pack in the 1990s, and his daughter, Marisa, a student at Reno High School. "I've always felt that everything that I've been able to accomplish in my life, and the friends that I've made and the relationships that I have, there was one North Star for all of those things—it was this campus."[59]

As Nevada's governor, Sandoval had led the state out of the Great Recession and into a period of record prosperity. Difficult budget reductions had been part of the early years of his governorship; difficult budget reductions in the wake of COVID-19 were now looming for the University. "I've been through this," he said. "In 2011 I had to encounter a budget crisis unlike any other in state history. There were devastating decisions that had to be made. At the same time, I made a commitment, then as I believe now, that we will get through this and times will get better."[60] He also said his commitment was to make the University more inclusive and more supportive of its people, particularly students. "I want this to be a place where students will feel connected and safe," he said. "Where they will know they can become whoever and whatever they want to be."[61] On his first day in office, October 5, he snapped awake at 4:00 a.m. Wearing a state-mandated face mask, Sandoval helped deliver food to students who had tested positive for COVID-19 and were in self-isolation in special sections of the residence halls. He said:

> It really reminded me how serious the disease is. I wanted to let them know that it's our goal to make sure they feel better and recover fully while they're handling a really tough situation. It became extremely evident in talking to the students that they truly do feel that "we have a responsibility to take care of each other" and that they are really taking seriously the steps the University has told them to follow in order to keep everyone safe. . . . I use the word a lot, but the sense of "family"—concern and care for others—on our campus is very strong. Everyone is trying to make the best of a difficult situation. You could feel people's strength and resilience.[62]

Sandoval was to use this feeling of "family" in all his future interactions and correspondence with the campus, starting each of his messages with "Dear Wolf Pack Family."

One year following the report of the first two cases of COVID-19 in Nevada on March 5, 2020, the state had reported more than 300,000 cases. More than 5,000 Nevadans had died of COVID-19.[63] The classes of 2020 and 2021 were honored over the course of four days in May 2021. Because of the state's social distancing requirements, a pivot was made. Ceremonies were held in Mackay Stadium for the first time in University history. In eight commencement ceremonies, with brilliant sunshine and temperatures soaring into the high eighties, 8,350 degrees were awarded. Sandoval told those assembled: "We know the past year has presented incredible challenges for all of you. You've persevered, shown resiliency, and succeeded against great odds. . . . Through your studies and experiences over the past four years—and particularly over the past year—you have come to understand a universal truth: that when you are grounded in the right values, you are always going to make a difference in the lives of everyone around you."[64]

The students themselves were aware that they had not let the pandemic put an end to their dreams. They had seen the faculty and staff rise up in ways for them that spoke to something more than a simple dedication to the University's mission. The faculty's work on their behalf had felt personal, and meaningful, in how it had been focused on a much larger picture than course or curriculum goals. It was a faculty that had given it their all when it mattered most. Elena Pravosudova, a Tibbitts Award–winning professor in the Department of Biology in the College of Science, said, "It's been

Because of Nevada health guidelines, the 2021 spring commencement exercises were held at Mackay Stadium for the first time in the University's history. Graduates and attendees wore masks throughout the ceremony. Courtesy of University Archives.

really hard emotionally for me. I feel more exhausted emotionally, more than anything else, at the end of a class."[65] And yet, she would write later, she never lost sight of her motivation to be there for her students: "My students make me happy, and (I) realized that this sentiment is what kept me going and has colored my optimism for as long as I have been in academia."[66]

Amy Fitch, another Tibbitts Award–winning professor in the School of Community Health Sciences (now the School of Public Health), added: "Above all else, I wanted to make sure my students were getting the main things they would be getting if we were in a classroom together, and not shortchange them in any way. I also wanted it to be flexible. I didn't want them, with so many things going on in the world right now, to stress. It feels like we're accomplishing what we need to accomplish."[67]

The class of 2020–2021 felt all this, and a lot more. "Unlike this time last year, when things were so uncertain, I am graduating into a world where there is renewed hope," said Jordan Nicholson, a graduate in journalism. "There is a light at the end of the tunnel, and I can't wait to get there."[68]

THE UNIVERSITY FINDS ITS PURPOSE AND PLACE, 1979–PRESENT

A Story of Revival: First Published in 1899, the *Artemisia* Yearbook Captured the University in Its Infancy; in 2023, It Was Brought Back to Life

By Dionne Stanfill

In 1899, an important tradition of recording the University's history was started. A couple of passionate Nevada students created the *Artemisia* yearbook that would develop into more than one hundred years of documenting campus history. Through two world wars, 108 Associated Students of the University of Nevada (ASUN) presidents, and a revolution in journalism, the *Artemisia* carried on, until a lack of support and interest for student publications hit from the global recession in 2008.

In 2023, another couple of passionate Nevada students set out to revive this age-old tradition. Brayden Taeubel (class of 2024) and I (class of 2023) discovered the recently digitized versions of the publication and spent countless hours getting lost in more than a century of campus history. The accurate documentation of campus successes, defeats, advancements, and shared experiences distracted us from the class assignments we probably should have been doing.

For Christmas, Brayden gifted me the 1959 copy of the *Artemisia,* which was especially meaningful. That was the year that my idol, the future governor and senator Richard Bryan, was the ASUN president. We were compelled to revive the publication after reading each volume's editor share an optimistic hope for the future of the book. In reading every publication cover to cover, we became quite familiar with campus history. What was more rewarding, perhaps, was being able to find photos of parents, grandparents, and even great-grandparents and to then show them to current Nevada student family members. Brayden and I became inspired to revive this tradition to ensure that an accurate representation of the student experience was captured. We wanted to record the journey it takes to pursue a student's passion, just as every generation of University graduates has done to create our Nevada today. In less than a month, we became obsessed with this project and spent every day and night learning how to make a book, making the book, and eventually publishing it. If you asked us a year ago, we would tell you about the record snowstorms, a car crash, a black eye, learning Adobe software, and many other challenges that almost beat us.

But the challenges meant nothing after hearing the excitement from Nevada alumni who heard about this project. What kept us going was knowing that most Nevada graduates still have their beloved *Artemisia* yearbooks. Every *Artemisia*

In 2023, a few months before the calendar turned and the University of Nevada, Reno, celebrated its 150th birthday on October 12, 2024, the work of the institution had never mattered more for the future of Reno and for all of Nevada. Sandoval's presidency saw the University reach out even more noticeably in its efforts to build lasting connection with the community it had served since its relocation to Reno in 1885–1886. For almost a decade, master and strategic planning had been under way to position the University as an attractive "front door" leading into downtown Reno. The push to link the future of the University and Reno accelerated throughout 2022–23, in moves that were sometimes tinged with symbolism and in the capturing of imagination, and others that were laden more with strategy and pragmatism. In fall 2022 the City of Reno renamed Center Street from the Truckee River to the campus "University Way." In early October, the University dedicated a monument near the University's Virginia Street entrance and celebrated the renaming is unique and has its own style. Seeing the hard copies of the publication is an experience that no level of technology could capture. Each decade seems to have a theme. The first decades of the publication are fragile but robust with content. My favorite components from the 1899–1919 years are the hand-drawn images paralleled with the photos of smileless students in their fashions of the day. Many of the yearbooks end with joshes, or funny jokes and comics about their classmates, which numbered about one hundred.

Our favorite *Artemisia* publications are from the 1920s and are full of poetry, hand-drawn art, Swifty fonts, and page borders. Our 2023 version was largely inspired by this era and included the same chapter titles as former years, symbolizing our advancements that complement our traditions.

The 1930s and 1940s were clearly focused on the military, with entire sections of the *Artemisia* dedicated to it. The Military Ball, Military Science, Military Department, etc. are very prominent in these sections. Also prevalent are patriotic themes and the uprising of women in leadership in all areas on campus—as students, faculty members, and administrators.

It is so fun to look at young Nevada students who turned into incredible figures: governors, doctors, actors, athletes, and even presidents of our very own University! Our favorite *Artemisia* is the 1986 version because it both has the greatest cover in celebrating Morrill Hall's one hundredth birthday and many pictures of future University president Brian Sandoval in his senior year.

Throughout all the changing decades of the *Artemisia,* the pride for our land-grant University has always remained the same.

The revival edition of the *Artemisia* captures the history that was made in our year: the acquisition of UNR at Lake Tahoe, the renaming of University Way, the new monument on South campus, the Mackay Bottle Sacrifice, the remodel of Mackay Stadium, and other historic moments. Pictures and information of our institution can be easily found online or on social media today; however, this can neither relate nor complete the story of this publication. The history documented in the *Artemisia* complements the advancements made on our campus. We have transformed from a cow college in an untraditional setting for higher education into the greatest institution in the world. The hope is that the *Artemisia* is supported in future years to remember and appreciate the successes, defeats, and ambitions of our beloved University of Nevada, Reno. The 2023 *Artemisia* revives tradition and makes history.

of "University Way."[69] On January 20, 2023, the University officially opened the Gateway Parking Complex, a seven-story garage that was part of the Mathewson Gateway Project, a district of innovation and collaboration that would unite the City of Reno with its land-grant University.[70] On June 9, 2023, the Board of Regents voted to approve the first academic building in the Mathewson University Gateway project, a new home for the College of Business, through a third-party development agreement with Edgemoor Infrastructure & Real Estate. Dirt began to move during the summer of 2023; completion of the 128,000-square-foot College of Business Building was expected to be during the 2025 fall semester.[71]

In addition to tightening its connection with the city, the University made its largest land-grant expansion since the days of Max C. Fleischmann's gifts to the University in the 1950s with its acquisition of the campus of the former Sierra Nevada University in Incline Village. The acquisition began during the summer of 2021 and was finalized a year later when in July 2022 the campus in Incline became known as the University of Nevada, Reno at Lake Tahoe. Just one mile from the shore at an elevation of 6,700 feet, the eighteen-acre setting included ten classrooms, two meeting rooms, event spaces, a cafeteria and catering service, two art galleries, laboratories, office spaces, eighty-eight dorm rooms, and a commons lawn. The new campus presented a myriad of possibilities for students, faculty, staff, and friends to learn, to conduct much-needed Lake Tahoe–centered research, and to engage with the Lake Tahoe community. Sandoval termed the acquisition "a gift for the ages."[72]

Although a lot of work remained, the University's recognition of the place of the Indigenous peoples and their important relationship with the land was expanded in 2019 to include language that is read before every commencement ceremony and every other major event. University faculty members that included Debra Harry, a gender, race, and identity professor and a member of the Pyramid Lake Paiute Tribe, nurtured the wording. It sought to acknowledge awareness of Indigenous peoples on campus while highlighting three local Indigenous tribes' names—the Paiute, Washoe, and Western Shoshone tribes. Through the efforts of people such as Christina Thomas, the first Paiute language course at the University was offered in 2019. Thomas, a University graduate in music and biology and a former Washoe County School District teacher, took an independent study course from Pyramid Lake Paiute Tribe elder Ralph Burns at the University. She was inspired to action: "This course continues the opportunities for language learning for students who take Paiute in high school and introduces people who might not be familiar with Nevada indigenous languages to the culture and history of the land on which the University stands," Thomas said. "I am proud to be considered a 'language warrior' and hope, through this class, others will also become language warriors along the way."[73]

The University took another important step forward in May 2022 by hiring Daphne Emm-Hooper, the former Fernley city manager, as the director of community Indigenous relations after a nationwide search. Hooper was previously executive director of Nevada Urban Indians—a respected nonprofit organization focused on improving the well-being of Native American communities. "It is critical for the University to build bridges to pave the way for Native students to attend and complete their education," Hooper said. "It is also important for the University to provide resources through training and other means to support opportunities to tribal communities. One of the biggest goals is to begin to build relationships with the tribal communities. I have started to reach out to the communities and will begin making visits throughout the state to listen and understand how the University might work with the tribal communities."[74]

In addition to finding new ways to connect with the region it served, the University continued to make gains in diversity and accessibility. The University dispersed about $182 million in financial aid for the 2022–23 academic year, with 92 percent of all first-year students receiving some kind of aid. The student body in fall 2022 was composed of 44.1 percent of students who identified as students of color, with 49.1 percent of all students in the first-year class identifying as students of color, the most diverse group in school history.

The acquisition of the University of Nevada, Reno at Lake Tahoe campus, completed during the summer of 2022, was the culmination of a complex year-long process that made it one of the largest in University history in terms of value. The Lake Tahoe site presented the University with an opportunity to enhance the student experience, augment research in the Tahoe Basin, and build a greater connection to the Lake Tahoe community. Courtesy of University Advancement / Jordan S. Buxton.

As the University neared its 150th anniversary, annual research expenditures were at record levels, reaching $180 million. An all-time high of thirteen students received prestigious National Science Foundation Fellowships in 2022. Seven faculty also received a prestigious NSF CAREER Award, which recognizes young and rising faculty members' potential to become national leaders in their respective research fields, following a record eight the previous year. Important state-funding approvals for campus infrastructure promised to keep Nevadans safer and healthier. Just one example was a $75 million appropriation announced in summer 2022 for construction of a new Nevada State Public Health Laboratory. The work of the director, Mark Pandori, and his staff throughout the pandemic included early COVID-19 testing availability for all of Nevada. It also morphed into several groundbreaking studies about the prevalence of COVID-19, illustrating yet again the importance of the University's research mission. It was expected that the new facility would help bring more research opportunities to the Schools of Medicine and Public Health.[75]

Nayelli Lara-Gutierrez, a native of Dayton who graduated from Dayton High School in 2019, became a first-generation student at the University. There were things she experienced for the first time in her life while she majored in environmental science and minored in forest ecology and management in the College of Agriculture, Biotechnology, and Natural Resources. Throughout her life, she had felt the transformative power of having someone believe in her, most notably her mother, Lilly, who worked long hours in jobs such as being an administrative assistant for the State of Nevada to support her and her younger sister. Lara-Gutierrez had always loved the mountains, particularly the mountains that surrounded Lake Tahoe. Thanks to her studies at the University, she would learn to experience the natural world in a way that would change her life forever. At one point she admittedly went outside of her comfort zone to apply for a bioassessment internship with the Nevada Division of Environmental Protection. The work itself was complex, involving water-quality monitoring techniques. But it also involved a physical aspect that was surprisingly invigorating and required Lara-Gutierrez to hike in and out of some of Nevada's most out-of-the-way wilderness areas. She immediately loved camping with a small crew of people who became her friends, people she had to learn to work with and to partner with and to trust. There were days when everything worked with a smooth efficiency, and there were others where Lara-Gutierrez and her friends, out in the wilds of Nevada with their water samples, had to adapt to circumstances they hadn't anticipated. They would work together to solve the problems of the moment, and then, later, sit back together at night under a blanket of Nevada stars with a sense of wonder and satisfaction that no problem was too difficult to be solved as long as you were always working in unison toward a finish line that all could share. The experience brought a sort of human interconnectedness that filled Lara-Gutierrez with purpose and gave new meaning to her degree program. When Lara-Gutierrez, to the cheers of her family on the Quad during a warm evening on May 19, 2023, graduated, she was motivated to continue the journey she had embarked upon in rural Nevada—to grow, to learn, to make a difference, and to keep trying new experiences.

So it should not have been too surprising that within a few days after graduating, Lara-Gutierrez was headed off to Colorado. She was to work on an all-female chainsaw crew, conducting important forest restoration work in remote locations. Her plan was to return to Nevada in the fall and then apply for a position with the Nevada Division of Environmental Protection.

Lara-Gutierrez had found a path in her life. And the University had helped her discover it.

Her story was one that the University had been telling for almost 150 years. That in the experiences that the University offered, there could be a realization that there was always something more important to do, and to give. That the University's original land-grant purposes—teaching, research, and outreach—had an uncommonly self-actualizing human aspect to them. Lara-Gutierrez saw on Nevada's backroads something that we all hope materializes our lives—recognizing who we are at a particular moment, and then, given what we learn in that moment, how we can use that self-awareness to not only help ourselves grow but somehow affect the lives of others for the better. The University, she said, was a catalyst in making such a realization a critical jumping-off point in her life.

Lara-Gutierrez was a worthy inheritor of the words and promise of another person who had helped bring the University's purposes to life. Almost 140 years after Hannah K. Clapp had become the personification of what a University that was struggling for life should be, graduates such as Nayelli Lara-Gutierrez in the twenty-first century were bringing that promise and purpose to life. The inspiring excellence of a century and a half of Nevada's first university wasn't so much in the institutional achievements and accomplishments, though they are all worth noting. It was more than that, however; the life of the University was being forever realized in people such as Hannah K. Clapp and Nayelli Lara-Gutierrez. The University had belonged to everyone. And as it approached its 150th birthday, its place in the state it served assured, its best aspirations were still somewhere up ahead of where it is today.

The University of Nevada, Reno, had come a long way in 150 years. It had nearly died before it even had a chance to see what its future might hold. Little did the University know that from the ashes of Elko and the uncertainty of having twenty acres and little else after it relocated to Reno that it would see a 150-year history develop. No one could have imagined that what Clapp spoke of during the University's tri-decennial celebration in late spring 1904 could actually happen, and today continues to happen.

"I have rejoiced in every gain, and shall as long as I live," Clapp said to those assembled that day. "I am glad to have been spared to see this day. I am proud of this magnificent university; I am proud of its triumphs and history. I rejoice in your pride and pray earnestly that when you look about you and see how much you have, you feel the inspiration of humble beginnings, remembering that faithful service and worthy work make those humble beginnings the foundation of greatness as they are the foundation of the great institution you have today.

"This is the heritage from that first faithful band of pioneers, whose spirit now rests upon you, and whose blessing I would bestow upon you also."[76]

These are words spoken by the woman who helped define the University's purposes before the University actually knew what those purposes truly needed to be. And each day, the University continues on its journey in finding and embracing these true purposes, hopeful that one day it shall reach Hannah K. Clapp's ideal.

The Silver Thread That Binds Us All: Faces of Commencement

Commencement exercises at the University have always marked the most important rite of passage for students. The campus's "endearing quiet," coined by famed Nevada writer Walter Van Tilburg Clark, is exchanged for a celebration and a conferral of degrees.

By 2024, the University's spring commencement exercises on the Quad had grown to six ceremonies over three days. And as most University graduates would attest, the journey, even with a degree in hand, was only just beginning for them.

A number of identity groups hold graduate celebration gatherings during commencement week, including the AIAN (American Indian/Alaskan Native) Graduate Celebration of 2018. Courtesy of UNR Marketing / Communications.

The 2017 Latino graduation celebration. The University's largest growing group of students throughout the 2010s were students from Hispanic/Latinx backgrounds, with about 25 percent of all students identifying as members of this group by the early 2020s. Courtesy of UNR Marketing / Communications.

The annual African Diaspora Cultural & Affinity Graduate Celebration is a time for students and their families to commemorate a joyous time leading up to that week's commencement exercises. Courtesy of UNR Marketing / Communications.

The expectation of what is to come on the Quad during spring commencement is a mix of anticipation, happiness, and excitement for all of the graduates. Courtesy of UNR Marketing / Communications.

Above: The Quad and the Mackay statue have seen this scene play out time and again throughout the years: jubilant graduates reaching the end of a journey, and then reaching for the future. Courtesy of UNR Marketing / Communications.

Overleaf: Commencement exercises, like this one from 2017, have always seen the University at its very best. The University has produced more than 125,000 graduates since its founding. Courtesy of UNR Marketing / Communications.

Epilogue

The voice on the other end of the phone was something out of history. Nothing that Sherman Howard said on that morning in January 2018 felt insignificant, trite, or even remotely suggestive of a person who was grasping for the right words. Howard had celebrated his ninety-third birthday that November. You'd expect someone that age to sometimes wrestle with their own memory. But this was a person who was still following the same daily routine and time-tested regimen that had made him a standout athlete as well as a profoundly successful educator and coach. Every morning he was still doing the push-ups, sit-ups, and stretching exercises he had used as a young athlete. There were still three Chicago newspapers being printed then. He read each one every day. The Bible was important to him. He would pore through its passages for two or three hours a day. He was a person at peace with the world, and with himself. "My father's legs are getting weak, and he has to use a cane or a walker," his daughter, Vietta Robinson, said. "But he's doing great. Mentally, he's incredibly sharp. This is a period of his life where gratitude just springs forth from him." Laughed Sherman: "I'm not going to complain. I'm able to walk with some degree of cohesiveness. But it's like they always say, 'It's always more about your attitude and how you adjust to situations that makes all the difference.'"[1]

Sherman Howard was a standout running back for the Wolf Pack in 1947–48, on teams that, at least on the playing fields of college football, had beaten back some of the segregationist laws of Jim Crow. The October 23, 1948, game at Tulsa, Oklahoma, where the Pack won, 65–14, was historic. The Pack had been warned about playing its two African American players, Howard and Alva Tabor, in the game. Yet Nevada's white coaches and players were adamant. Howard and Tabor had to play—if they weren't allowed to, the Wolf Pack wasn't going to play. Howard told his daughter years later that the decision the entire team made in support of Howard and Tabor was what good teams always do. One for all. All for one. The strength of the Wolf is the Pack.

"My teammates said they wouldn't play if I didn't play," Howard said. "We had a strong working relationship that was held together with courage, integrity, and cooperation. . . . All the guys on the Nevada team were real close. All of us looked out for one another. There was not a person on the entire team who would not do his best for you."[2]

Howard would go on to live a life that set an incredibly high standard. He wasn't far behind the first group of Black players—including Pack great Marion Motley—who broke professional football's color barrier in 1946. In addition to playing in the National Football League for five seasons, Howard was one of the first African Americans to be an NFL scout, earning a reputation for his fine-tuned and meticulous approach. He worked with coaching legends such as Vince Lombardi of the Green Bay Packers and a good friend and former teammate, Dallas Cowboys coach Tom Landry. Howard would go on to become a teacher, coach, and administrator in the Chicago public school system, at Harlan High School. He mentored and coached people

Nevada football player Sherman Howard was a running back for the Wolf Pack from 1947 to 1948 and was a sprinter on the Nevada track and field team in 1948. Howard played five seasons of professional football with the New York Yankees and the Cleveland Browns from 1949 to 1953. He was inducted into the Nevada Athletics Hall of Fame in 1995. Howard was one of the NFL's first African American scouts and was one of the Chicago school system's most respected coaches, teachers, and administrators. Courtesy of University Archives.

such as William Rhoden, who would become a famed sports columnist for *The New York Times*.

"His high school students, and his players, especially, looked at him almost like he was their father," Vietta Robinson said. "He was a person who most definitely helped break down barriers, and who did so because he wished to help others. Not only did my father break up the prejudices of his time, he helped break up the prejudices and the limitations that these young people he taught and coached might have experienced in their own homes. He treated them all the same, and they loved him for it. There are some of his former students and players who are now in their 70s and to this day, white or black . . . and they all love him because he helped integrate their lives."[3]

"As I often said to my students, your experiences prepare you for what's going to come next," Howard said. "My life has certainly been that way. My experiences, whether it was being exposed to a number of really great influences and mentors when I was young, or serving in World War II, or playing football at Nevada or in the pros, they've always helped prepare me for what I was going through."[4]

The voice on the phone didn't waver, didn't equivocate, didn't express any doubts about the life that had been led. As he talked about his life, and the quiet, understated yet firmly resolute and undisputed impact it had, it became apparent that Sherman Howard was what the University of Nevada, Reno, has always aspired to be throughout its 150-year history. A place where people look out for one another. Where experiences in classrooms and in laboratories and in residential halls and on the campus lead to moments of truth where individuals rise to the challenge and make decisions that can alter a personal or institutional history for the better. Courage, integrity, and cooperation were the watchwords that had guided his life. They were also the guideposts for an institution of higher learning that for 150 years had grown from an afterthought in Elko in 1874 to something that belonged to all of Nevada.

What would the next 150 years look like? The University was already on a course of reflecting, perhaps better than at any other time in its history, the composition and growing diversity of the state that it served, with almost half of its student body coming from underrepresented groups. This group included 140 Native American students who had applied for a fee waiver implemented by the University in July 2023. These were students who were seeking something more than just a college degree, students who strongly believed in the concept of "community" and what their various talents and dreams could do to help make these communities more tolerant and more inclusive. The faculty and staff, too, were making good on the promise that the University had always made to the people of Nevada—to provide teaching, research, and engagement that would transform lives and the future of the state. More than ever before, the University was seen not just as a storehouse for knowledge, but as a catalyst for economic diversification and revitalization. It was the place where the future of Nevada was somewhat miraculously turned into something tangible and real.

The University had grown up over the course of 150 years. As it had grown, it had seen people such as Sherman Howard and so many others reflect highly personal but also historically broad and impactful societal reasons why it was created in the first place. Institutional purpose had mattered, but so, too, had the people of the University. What the people of the University had accomplished over the institution's first 150 years had been remarkable considering how implausible the University's beginnings had been. Some could say that the University's story was not unlike any other university, in that all institutions of higher learning have had moments where their early futures were in doubt. That may be true. But what has always made the story of the University of Nevada, Reno, so compelling is that it is truly a story of its people—the belief they have for one another, the hopes that they share as individuals and for the institution, and the sense that is held in common that today's 150 years of history is simply preamble to something much, much greater in the future.

Sherman Howard wasn't wrong. Sometimes proudly and sometimes with great self-reflective difficulty, after having learned some important lessons and acknowledging its shortcomings, the University was like that Wolf Pack team he spoke of with such fond reverence. There was not a person on the entire team who would not do their best for you. This was what the University had always been all about. This was how the University of Nevada, Reno, had discovered who it was over the course of its first 150 years. As the University entered its next 150-year period, it was time to make good on that discovery.

Above: The University's Honor Court, dedicated on September 5, 1997, and constructed solely through private philanthropy, is anchored by a 45,000-pound obelisk featuring the names of the University's top benefactors. Courtesy of University Advancement / Theresa Danna.

Opposite: Each year, new inductees into the University's Honor Court are recognized for their accomplishments and support of those who contribute to excellence at the University. Courtesy of University Advancement / Erin Bernius.

Honor Court

The University's Honor Court was dedicated in 1997 and celebrates the contributions of campus and community leaders. The Honor Court is situated at the south end of campus, adjacent to the University's historic Quadrangle and Morrill Hall Alumni Center. A series of pillars carved from 200,000 pounds of white granite mined from the nearby Sierra Nevada range features the names of major donors, award-winning faculty, students, employees, and community members who have made an indelible mark on the history and future of the University.

Each year, additional names are engraved into the pillars in proud recognition of the accomplishments and support of those who contribute to excellence at the University of Nevada, Reno. President Brian Sandoval, during his remarks at the annual celebration on June 17, 2022, said: "Although the names here are etched in granite, this is not a place that stands still. This is evidenced by the new names that we add and celebrate today . . . and the names that we will add and celebrate in the years to come."

The Honor Court dedication pillar reads, in part, "To those who have left or will leave legacies at the University for our state, nation and civilization—students and staff, faculty and philanthropists—this Honor Court is dedicated." Courtesy of University Advancement / Jordan S. Buxton.

Donors are recognized in the following categories:

Philanthropist
Founder
Patron
Gold Benefactor
Silver Benefactor

Together with donors, the names of students, faculty, staff, and community members who have contributed to the University's history of exemplary scholarship, teaching, and outreach are engraved and acknowledged in the following award categories:

Paul and Judy Bible University Teaching Excellence Award *(first presented in 2018)*

Distinguished Classified Employee Award *(first presented in 1986)*

Distinguished Faculty Award *(first presented in 1991)*

Distinguished Nevadan Award *(first presented in 1959)*

Distinguished Service Award
(first presented in 1996)

Foundation Professor *(first presented in 1983)*

Herz Gold Medal for Outstanding Scholarship *(first presented in 1910)*

Honorary Degree *(first presented in 1911)*

Outstanding Researcher Award *(first presented in 1975)*

President's Medal *(first presented in 1984)*

F. Donald Tibbitts Distinguished Teacher Award *(first presented in 1973)*

In addition, names of the University presidents are engraved in the North Gazebo area of Honor Court adjacent to the dedication pillar.

The South Gazebo of the University's Honor Court commemorates the commitment of campus and community members who have contributed to the University's legacy of success. Courtesy of University Advancement/Theresa Danna.

HONOR COURT

References

Archer, Michael, *A Man of His Word: The Life & Times of Nevada's Senator William J. Raggio,* Ashland, OR: Hellgate Press, 2011.

Church, J. E., Jr., *Nevada State University Tri-decennial Celebration, May 28 to June 2, 1904*, Reno: Barndollar and Durley, 1904.

Crowley, Joseph, *The Constant Conversation: A Chronicle of Campus Life,* Reno: Black Rock Press, 2000.

Cudek, Phyllis and Sohn, Anton Paul, *Better Medicine: The History of the University of Nevada School of Medicine*, Reno: Greasewood Press, 2003.

Davies, Richard O., *The Maverick Spirit: Building the New Nevada,* Reno: University of Nevada Press, 1999.

D'Azevedo, Warren L., *American Indian and Black Students at the University of Nevada, Reno: 1874–1974,* Reno: Department of Anthropology, University of Nevada, Reno, 1975.

Doten, Samuel Bradford, *An Illustrated History of the University of Nevada,* Reno: University of Nevada, 1924.

Gorrell, Robert M. and Charlton G. Laird, *Modern English Handbook,* Englewood Cliffs, NJ: Prentice Hall, 1976.

Howard, Anne, *The Long Campaign: A Biography of Anne Martin,* Reno: University of Nevada Press, 1985.

Hulse, James, *Forty Years in the Wilderness: Impressions of Nevada, 1940–1980,* Reno: University of Nevada Press, 1986.

Hulse, James, *Reinventing the System: Higher Education in Nevada, 1968–2000*, Reno: University of Nevada Press, 2002.

Hulse, James, *The University of Nevada: A Centennial History,* Reno: University of Nevada Press, 1974.

Hunsaker, Amy Jo and Betty J. Glass, *A Pictorial History of the University of Nevada, Reno,* Reno: University Libraries, 2016.

Laxalt, Robert, *Sweet Promised Land,* New York: Harper and Brothers, 1957.

Martin, Charles H., *Benching Jim Crow: The Rise and Fall of the Color Line in Southern College Sports, 1890–1980,* Urbana: University of Illinois Press, 2010.

Contributors

JOHN TRENT, a 1985 and 1987 graduate of the University, has served at the University for more than twenty years as a writer and editor in marketing and communications. A two-time Nevada Sportswriter of the Year, he earned his master's degree in journalism from the University in 2000.

BRIAN SANDOVAL, a 1986 graduate of the University, is the first alumni and first person of Hispanic descent to serve as president of the University of Nevada, Reno. He was appointed seventeenth president of the University in September 2020.

GUY CLIFTON is an award-winning journalist, author of Nevada history, and former editor of the student campus newspaper, *The Nevada Sagebrush*.

MRIDUL GAUTAM has served as vice president for research and innovation at the University of Nevada, Reno, since 2013.

WILLIAM A. DOUGLASS, a member of the Nevada Writers Hall of Fame, is the founder of the Basque Studies Program at the University of Nevada, Reno.

DAPHNE EMM-HOOPER is director of Indigenous relations at the University of Nevada, Reno. She is a former Fernley city manager and co-founder of the Nevada Tribal Leadership Development Program at the University.

PAUL MITCHELL is an award-winning professor and recruitment and retention coordinator in the Donald W. Reynolds School of Journalism at the University of Nevada, Reno.

JAMES RICHARDSON is an emeritus professor of sociology and judicial studies who began his career at the University in 1968.

DIONNE STANFILL served as president of the Associated Students of the University of Nevada during the 2022–2023 school year and is a member of the class of 2023.

JACQUELYN K. SUNDSTRAND is an emerita manuscripts and archives librarian at the University of Nevada, Reno, who has extensively studied the career of Professor James Church.

This book also owes a debt of gratitude to the faculty and staff members of University Libraries. In the University's best spirit of collaboration and partnership, these incredible professionals gladly shared numerous University assets, including historical photography, while also going the extra mile in embarking on additional painstaking research about the University's history. Libraries Dean Catherine Cardwell, Community and University Archivist Laura Rocke, and Director of Access Services Maggie Ressel were all instrumental in not only providing assets from Libraries' Special Collections and Archives but in sharing the joy, enthusiasm, and genuine sense of collaboration that they carry with them for their very important work.

Notes

PREFACE

1. James Hulse, "University of Nevada: A Centennial History, James W. Hulse Author," oral history interview, University of Nevada Oral History Collection, 1973–74, 180.
2. Hulse, "University of Nevada: A Centennial History, James W. Hulse Author," oral history interview, University of Nevada Oral History Collection, 1973–74, 180.
3. James Hulse, *The University of Nevada: A Centennial History* (Reno: University of Nevada Press, 1974), ix.
4. Hulse, *The University of Nevada: A Centennial History*, ix.
5. James Hulse, "University of Nevada: A Centennial History, James W. Hulse Author," oral history interview, University of Nevada Oral History Collection, 1973–74, 190–191.
6. James Hulse, "University of Nevada: A Centennial History, James W. Hulse Author," oral history interview, University of Nevada Oral History Collection, 1973–74, 191.
7. James Hulse, "University of Nevada: A Centennial History, James W. Hulse Author," oral history interview, University of Nevada Oral History Collection, 1973–74, 197.

INTRODUCTION

1. "The Sierras shut us in on the Pacific side . . .": J. E. Church Jr., *Nevada State University Tri-decennial Celebration, May 28 to June 2, 1904* (Reno: Barndollar and Durley, 1904), 71.
2. *Reno Evening Gazette,* January 4, 1879, 2.
3. Hulse, *The University of Nevada: A Centennial History,* 29.
4. Chris Enns, "Wild of the West: Hannah Clapp," *Cowgirl Magazine,* September 20, 2017.
5. Church, *Nevada State University Tri-decennial Celebration, May 28 to June 2, 1904,* 70–71.
6. "Miss Hannah Clapp answers call of death," *Reno Evening Gazette,* October 9, 1908, 2.
7. "A constant conversation: The legacy of President Joe Crowley, 1933–2017" *Nevada Today,* November 29, 2017.

THE BEGINNING, 1864–1908

1. Hulse, *The University of Nevada: A Centennial History,* 16.
2. Hulse, *The University of Nevada: A Centennial History,* 16.
3. *Nevada State Journal,* October 10, 1874, 2.
4. Hulse, *The University of Nevada: A Centennial History,* 20.
5. Elko campus description: *Pioche Record,* February 8, 1874, 2.
6. *The Daily Appeal,* June 22, 1875, 2.
7. Hulse, *The University of Nevada: A Centennial History,* 24.
8. *Reno Evening Gazette,* August 3, 1885, 2.
9. "Land-Grab Universities," *High Country News,* March 30, 2020.
10. "Proponents of Free College for Nevada Native Students Say It Will Right Historical Wrongs," *The Nevada Independent,* March 28, 2021.
11. *Nevada State Journal,* August 18, 1885, 2.
12. *Reno Evening Gazette,* April 13, 1886, 2.
13. *Nevada State Journal,* March 31, 1886, 3.
14. *Reno Evening Gazette,* April 13, 1886, 2.
15. *Reno Evening Gazette,* April 15, 1886, 3.
16. "The New University. Formal Opening Exercises Yesterday," *Nevada State Journal,* April 23, 1886, 3.
17. Regent Henry Shaw remarks: *Nevada State Journal,* April 24, 1886, 3.
18. Morrill Hall description: *Nevada State Journal,* April 25, 1886, 2.
19. Church, *Nevada State University Tri-decennial Celebration, May 28 to June 2, 1904,* 69.
20. Church, *Nevada State University Tri-decennial Celebration, May 28 to June 2, 1904,* 63.
21. *Reno Evening Gazette,* August 14, 1888, 3.

22 Church, *Nevada State University Tri-decennial Celebration, May 28 to June 2, 1904*, 69.

23 Church, *Nevada State University Tri-decennial Celebration, May 28 to June 2, 1904*, 68–72.

24 Samuel Bradford Doten, *An Illustrated History of the University of Nevada* (Reno: University of Nevada, 1924), 55.

25 Church, *Nevada State University Tri-decennial Celebration, May 28 to June 2, 1904*, 69.

26 Doten, *An Illustrated History of the University of Nevada*, 54.

27 *Reno Evening Gazette*, November 21, 1893, 3.

28 Church, *Nevada State University Tri-decennial Celebration, May 28 to June 2, 1904*, 73.

29 *Reno Evening Gazette*, June 12, 1891, 1.

30 *Reno Evening Gazette*, September 11, 1894, 3.

31 Hulse, *The University of Nevada: A Centennial History*, 35.

32 Mackay's "magnificent gift": *Reno Evening Gazette*, May 8, 1907, 5.

33 *Reno Evening Gazette*, June 9, 1908, 1.

34 *Reno Evening Gazette*, June 10, 1908, 1–2.

35 *Reno Evening Gazette*, June 10, 1908, 1–2.

36 *Reno Evening Gazette*, June 10, 1908, 1–2.

37 *Reno Evening Gazette*, June 10, 1908, 1–2.

38 Matthew Shaer, "The Sordid History of Mount Rushmore," *Smithsonian Magazine*, October 2016.

39 Hulse, *The University of Nevada: A Centennial History*, 102.

40 Hulse, *The University of Nevada: A Centennial History*, 102.

THE UNIVERSITY TAKES HOLD, 1909–1938

1 *Reno Evening Gazette*, May 27, 1914, 1.

2 Hulse, *The University of Nevada: A Centennial History*, 39.

3 *Reno Evening Gazette*, September 11, 1914, 8.

4 *Reno Evening Gazette*, October 11, 1918, 1.

5 *Nevada State Journal*, August 1, 1922, 5.

6 *Reno Evening Gazette*, September 18, 1922, 8.

7 *Kansas City Star*, May 10, 1967, 4.

8 Hulse, *The University of Nevada: A Centennial History*, 42.

9 *Reno Evening Gazette*, May 24, 1924, 1–2.

10 Kimberly Roberts, "1899 Women's Basketball: A Story of the University's First Intercollegiate Sports Win," *Nevada Today*, December 11, 2018.

11 Kimberly Roberts, "1899 Women's Basketball: A Story of the University's First Intercollegiate Sports Win," *Nevada Today*, December 11, 2018.

12 *Reno Evening Gazette*, August 19, 1908, 5.

13 *Reno Evening Gazette*, October 4, 1957, 14.

14 *Nevada State Journal*, May 24, 1964, 15.

15 "Dickie Jack" student file, Carlisle Indian School, Carlisle Indian School Digital Resource Center, https://carlisleindian.dickinson.edu/student_files/dickie-jack-student-file.

16 "Richard Edward Barrington," *Sierra County Historical Society Newsletter*, Winter 2020.

17 "Richard Edward Barrington," *Sierra County Historical Society Newsletter*, Winter 2020.

18 *Plumas Independent*, December 24, 1942, 8.

19 "Sierra Valley Lumberman Dies," *Reno Evening Gazette*, July 16, 1959, 11.

20 "Lloyd Harold Barrington," *Sierra Booster*, July 17, 1959, 9.

21 Robert Bruce Slater, "First Black Graduates of the Nation's 50 Flagship State Universities," *Journal of Blacks in Higher Education*, Autumn 1996.

22 Kate Hovanes and Anne Oliver, *The African American Civil Rights Experience in Nevada, 1900–1979*, Nevada State Historic Preservation Office, August 2020.

23 Theodore Miller's 1976–77 letters to University anthropology professor Warren L. d'Azevedo, University of Nevada, Reno, Archives.

24 *Nevada State Journal*, November 13, 1938, 1.

25 Hulse, *The University of Nevada: A Centennial History*, 233.

26 1938 commencement and Walter Clark honored: *Nevada State Journal*, May 9, 1938, 1.

27 Samuel Bradford Doten, *An Illustrated History of the University of Nevada* (Reno: University of Nevada, 1924), 199.

THE UNIVERSITY REFLECTS THE CHALLENGES OF NEVADA AND THE NATION, 1939–1978

1. William Raggio, author interview, March 1998.
2. Michael Archer, *A Man of His Word: The Life & Times of Nevada's Senator William J. Raggio* (Ashland, OR: Hellgate Press, 2011), 45.
3. *Reno Evening Gazette*, October 20, 1947, 7.
4. William Raggio, author interview, March 1998.
5. Willem Houwink obituary, *Reno Gazette-Journal*, March 25, 2016.
6. Larry Struve, author interview, April 2017.
7. *San Francisco Chronicle/SF Gate*, August 5, 2016.
8. "Stella Parson, First Black Woman to Earn Nevada Degree, Has Died," *Reno Gazette-Journal* (online), August 5, 2016.
9. "In Memoriam: Stella Mason Parson: 1929–2016," *The Journal of Blacks in Higher Education*, August 12, 2016.
10. Archer, *A Man Of His Word: The Life & Times of Nevada's Senator William J. Raggio*, 42.
11. "First, the lure of available jobs ensured continuous population growth," Michael Coray, "African Americans in Nevada," *Nevada Historical Society Quarterly*, 1992, 239–257.
12. *Reno Gazette-Journal*, May 18, 2002, 1.
13. *Reno Evening Gazette*, February 14, 1977, 25.
14. *Reno Evening Gazette*, February 14, 1977, 25.
15. "Legacy of the Greats: How the Wolf Pack Teams of the 1940s Beat Jim Crow," *Nevada Today*, February 8, 2018.
16. "Legacy of the Greats: How the Wolf Pack Teams of the 1940s Beat Jim Crow," *Nevada Today*, February 8, 2018.
17. "Legacy of the Greats: How the Wolf Pack Teams of the 1940s Beat Jim Crow," *Nevada Today*, February 8, 2018.
18. "Legacy of the Greats: How the Wolf Pack Teams of the 1940s Beat Jim Crow," *Nevada Today*, February 8, 2018.
19. "Legacy of the Greats: How the Wolf Pack Teams of the 1940s Beat Jim Crow," *Nevada Today*, February 8, 2018.
20. "Legacy of the Greats: How the Wolf Pack Teams of the 1940s Beat Jim Crow," *Nevada Today*, February 8, 2018.
21. "Legacy of the Greats: How the Wolf Pack Teams of the 1940s Beat Jim Crow," *Nevada Today*, February 8, 2018.
22. "Legacy of the Greats: How the Wolf Pack Teams of the 1940s Beat Jim Crow," *Nevada Today*, February 8, 2018.
23. "Legacy of the Greats: How the Wolf Pack Teams of the 1940s Beat Jim Crow," *Nevada Today*, February 8, 2018.
24. "Legacy of the Greats: How the Wolf Pack Teams of the 1940s Beat Jim Crow," *Nevada Today*, February 8, 2018.
25. "Legacy of the Greats: How the Wolf Pack Teams of the 1940s Beat Jim Crow," *Nevada Today*, February 8, 2018.
26. "Robert Gorrell, 1914–2011: An Appreciation," *Nevada Today*, January 12, 2012.
27. Robert Gorrell, "Robert M. Gorrell: University Growing Up: Rambling Reminiscences of an English Professor and Administrator, 1945–1980," oral history interview, University of Nevada Oral History Collection, 1983, 3.
28. Robert Gorrell, "Robert M. Gorrell: University Growing Up: Rambling Reminiscences of an English Professor and Administrator, 1945–1980," oral history interview, University of Nevada Oral History Collection, 1983, 175.
29. "Groundbreaking Researcher Gardner Dies at Age 91," *Nevada Today*, September 1, 2021.
30. The University "had been able to support some research work," Hulse, *The University of Nevada: A Centennial History*, 61.
31. Hulse, *The University of Nevada: A Centennial History*, 59–60.
32. Frederick Anderson, "Frederick M. Anderson, M.D.: Surgeon, Regent and Dabbler in Politics, University of Nevada Oral History Collection, 1985," oral history interview, University of Nevada Oral History Collection, 203–227.
33. Frederick Anderson, "Frederick M. Anderson, M.D.: Surgeon, Regent and Dabbler in Politics, University of Nevada Oral History Collection, 1985," oral history interview, University of Nevada Oral History Collection, 203–227.
34. Frederick Anderson, "Frederick M. Anderson, M.D.: Surgeon, Regent and Dabbler in Politics, University of Nevada Oral History Collection, 1985," oral history interview, University of Nevada Oral History Collection, 203–227.
35. Frederick Anderson, "Frederick M. Anderson, M.D.: Surgeon, Regent and Dabbler in Politics, University of Nevada Oral History Collection, 1985," oral history interview, University of Nevada Oral History Collection, 203–227.

36 Frederick Anderson, "Frederick M. Anderson, M.D.: Surgeon, Regent and Dabbler in Politics, University of Nevada Oral History Collection, 1985," oral history interview, University of Nevada Oral History Collection, 203–227.

37 Hulse, *The University of Nevada: A Centennial History*, 73–74.

38 "Ben Hazard, the First Black Professor at the University of Nevada, Reno," *Nevada Today*, March 1, 2022.

39 "Ben Hazard, the First Black Professor at the University of Nevada, Reno," *Nevada Today*, March 1, 2022.

40 Hulse, *The University of Nevada: A Centennial History*, 73.

41 N. Edd Miller, "N. Edd Miller: Presidential Memoir University of Nevada, Reno, 1965–1973, 1989," oral history interview, University of Nevada Oral History Collection.

42 "Ben Hazard, the First Black Professor at the University of Nevada, Reno," *Nevada Today*, March 1, 2022.

43 "Ben Hazard, the First Black Professor at the University of Nevada, Reno," *Nevada Today*, March 1, 2022.

44 "Ben Hazard, the First Black Professor at the University of Nevada, Reno," *Nevada Today*, March 1, 2022.

45 "Ben Hazard, the First Black Professor at the University of Nevada, Reno," *Nevada Today*, March 1, 2022.

46 "Ben Hazard, the First Black Professor at the University of Nevada, Reno," *Nevada Today*, March 1, 2022.

47 "Ben Hazard, the First Black Professor at the University of Nevada, Reno," *Nevada Today*, March 1, 2022.

48 "The Long Campaign: How the Work of Anne Howard and Her Colleagues Led to Women's Studies at the University," *Nevada Today*, March 25, 2021.

49 "The Long Campaign: How the Work of Anne Howard and Her Colleagues Led to Women's Studies at the University," *Nevada Today*, March 25, 2021.

50 "The Long Campaign: How the Work of Anne Howard and Her Colleagues Led to Women's Studies at the University," *Nevada Today*, March 25, 2021.

51 "The Long Campaign: How the Work of Anne Howard and Her Colleagues Led to Women's Studies at the University," *Nevada Today*, March 25, 2021.

52 "The Long Campaign: How the Work of Anne Howard and Her Colleagues Led to Women's Studies at the University," *Nevada Today*, March 25, 2021.

53 "The Long Campaign: How the Work of Anne Howard and Her Colleagues Led to Women's Studies at the University," *Nevada Today*, March 25, 2021.

54 "The Long Campaign: How the Work of Anne Howard and Her Colleagues Led to Women's Studies at the University," *Nevada Today*, March 25, 2021.

55 "The Long Campaign: How the Work of Anne Howard and Her Colleagues Led to Women's Studies at the University," *Nevada Today*, March 25, 2021.

56 "The Long Campaign: How the Work of Anne Howard and Her Colleagues Led to Women's Studies at the University," *Nevada Today*, March 25, 2021.

57 "A Constant Conversation: The Legacy of President Joe Crowley, 1933–2017," *Nevada Today*, November 29, 2017.

58 Joe Crowley, author interview, March 1998.

59 *Reno Evening Gazette*, April 1, 1979, 28.

THE UNIVERSITY FINDS ITS PURPOSE AND PLACE, 1979–PRESENT

1 *Reno Evening Gazette*, September 13, 1979, 25.

2 Morrill Hall on the National Register, *Reno Gazette-Journal*, May 12, 1987, 31.

3 *Reno Evening Gazette*, October 6, 1978, 28.

4 Hulse, *The University of Nevada: A Centennial History*, 71.

5 *Reno Gazette-Journal*, September 8, 1989, 31.

6 *Reno Gazette-Journal*, September 6, 1989, 16.

7 *Reno Gazette-Journal*, September 12, 1995, 13.

8 "Engineering in the Room for Economic Development," *Nevada Today*, March 13, 2012.

9 "College of Engineering Dean Manos Maragakis: A Retrospective on a Distinguished Tenure," *Nevada Today*, May 2, 2022.

10 *Reno Gazette-Journal*, February 26, 1989, 53.

11 *Reno Gazette-Journal*, August 27, 1994, 49.

12 *Reno Gazette-Journal*, April 8, 2004, 54.

13 *Reno Gazette-Journal*, May 14, 1994, 41.

14 "Michael Coray: 'Bringing Voices to the Table That Otherwise Might Not Have Been Heard,'" *Nevada Today*, February 28, 2023.

15 "Michael Coray: 'Bringing Voices to the Table That Otherwise Might Not Have Been Heard,'" *Nevada Today*, February 28, 2023.

16 "Michael Coray: 'Bringing Voices to the Table That Otherwise Might Not Have Been Heard,'" *Nevada Today*, February 28, 2023.

17 "Michael Coray: 'Bringing Voices to the Table That Otherwise Might Not Have Been Heard,'" *Nevada Today*, February 28, 2023.

18 Warren L. d'Azevedo, *American Indian and Black Students at the University of Nevada, Reno: 1874–1974* (Department of Anthropology: University of Nevada, Reno, 1975), 1, 81.

19 Warren L. d'Azevedo, *American Indian and Black Students at the University of Nevada, Reno: 1874–1974* (Department of Anthropology: University of Nevada, Reno, 1975), 1, 81.

20 "Michael Coray: 'Bringing Voices to the Table That Otherwise Might Not Have Been Heard,'" *Nevada Today*, February 28, 2023.

21 "Michael Coray: 'Bringing Voices to the Table That Otherwise Might Not Have Been Heard,'" *Nevada Today*, February 28, 2023.

22 "Governor Kenny C. Guinn State of the State Address, January 18, 1999," Legislative Counsel Bureau Research Library, Nevada State Legislature, www.leg.state.nv.us/Division/Research/Library/Documents/HistDocs/Sos/1999.pdf.

23 *Reno Gazette-Journal*, April 21, 2000, 23.

24 *Reno Gazette-Journal*, August 24, 2000, 23.

25 "The (Millennium Scholarship) Was Really the Deciding Factor in Going to School Here," *Reno Gazette-Journal*, August 27, 2000, 29.

26 *Reno Gazette-Journal*, August 28, 2001, 3.

27 *Reno Gazette-Journal*, March 12, 2001, 11.

28 *Reno Gazette-Journal*, February 16, 2005, 1.

29 "Representation Matters: An Interview with Nicole Cannizzaro," Points of Light (blog), August 17, 2021.

30 "Mary White Stewart: A University Career That Changed Lives for the Better," *Nevada Today*, April 29, 2021.

31 "Mary White Stewart: A University Career That Changed Lives for the Better," *Nevada Today*, April 29, 2021.

32 "A constant conversation: The legacy of President Joe Crowley, 1933–2017," *Nevada Today*, November 29, 2017.

33 "A constant conversation: The legacy of President Joe Crowley, 1933–2017," *Nevada Today*, November 29, 2017.

34 *Reno Gazette-Journal*, August 14, 1994, 53.

35 "Tibbitts 2016 Award Winners: Two Disciplines, Two Human-Based Approaches," *Nevada Today*, June 8, 2016.

36 "Tibbitts 2016 Award Winners: Two Disciplines, Two Human-Based Approaches," *Nevada Today*, June 8, 2016.

37 "Tibbitts 2016 Award Winners: Two Disciplines, Two Human-Based Approaches," *Nevada Today*, June 8, 2016.

38 "Tibbitts winners share love of teaching . . . and of long, hard-working summers," *Nevada Today*, May 14, 2019.

39 "Tibbitts winners share love of teaching . . . and of long, hard-working summers," *Nevada Today*, May 14, 2019.

40 "Tibbitts winners share love of teaching . . . and of long, hard-working summers," *Nevada Today*, May 14, 2019.

41 "The Honor of Being Your President," *Nevada Today*, September 25, 2020.

42 "Milton D. Glick: 1937–2011, an Appreciation," *Nevada Today*, April 18, 2011, and "Glick Memorial: There Is Not Another Person like Milt Glick," *Nevada Today*, April 22, 2011.

43 "Milton D. Glick: 1937–2011, an Appreciation," *Nevada Today*, April 18, 2011, and "Glick Memorial: There is not another person like Milt Glick," *Nevada Today*, April 22, 2011.

44 "Milton D. Glick: 1937–2011, an Appreciation," *Nevada Today*, April 18, 2011.

45 "69–67: Prelude to a Miracle," *Nevada Today*, October 11, 2018.

46 "69–67: Prelude to a Miracle," *Nevada Today*, October 11, 2018.

47 "69–67: Prelude to a Miracle," *Nevada Today*, October 11, 2018.

48 Office of the President Marc Johnson campus messages: "Campus Community Update," March 16, 2020; "University Implementing New Procedures," March 18, 2020; "Campus Community Message," March 20, 2020; "Experiencing Change and Uncertainty: We Build Resiliency," March 23, 2020.

49 "Everyone on Campus Has Done Extraordinary Things in an Extraordinary Circumstance," *Nevada Today*, March 27, 2020.

50 "University Honors Student Jayde Powell Creates Shopping Angels to Deliver Groceries to COVID-19 at-Risk Populations," *Nevada Today*, March 23, 2020.

51 "NSHE Institutions Lending Help to State during Pandemic," *Nevada Today*, April 2, 2020.

52 Steven Hayes, "The Ordinary Coronavirus Hero: You," *Nevada Today*, March 24, 2020.

53 "Extraordinary Circumstances: Celebrating the Class of 2020," *Nevada Today*, May 13, 2020.

54 "Best Laid Plans: How COVID-19 Upended Life on Campus and Changed Everything," *Nevada Today*, August 19, 2020.

55 "Best Laid Plans: How COVID-19 Upended Life on Campus and Changed Everything," *Nevada Today*, August 19, 2020.

56 "Best Laid Plans: How COVID-19 Upended Life on Campus and Changed Everything," *Nevada Today*, August 19, 2020.

57 "Online Town Hall: How the Campus Will Return Safely and Strategically," *Nevada Today*, May 19, 2020.

58 "Board of Regents Appoints Sandoval New President," *Nevada Today*, September 17, 2020.

59 "The Sandoval Presidency: What Will It Look Like?" *Nevada Today*, September 21, 2020.

60 "The Sandoval Presidency: What Will It Look Like?" *Nevada Today*, September 21, 2020.

61 "The Sandoval Presidency: What Will It Look Like?" *Nevada Today*, September 21, 2020.

62 "Sandoval's First Day: You Can Come Home Again," *Nevada Today*, October 8, 2020.

63 "A Year in the Pandemic: Nevada Timeline," *KUNR*, March 5, 2021.

64 "Commencement History Made in Mackay Stadium," *Nevada Today*, May 20, 2021.

65 "In Classroom or on Zoom, Tibbitts Winners Impacting Students' Lives," *Nevada Today*, May 5, 2020.

66 "My students make me happy": "The Optimism Series: My Students Make Me Happy," *Nevada Today*, May 9, 2023.

67 "In Classroom or on Zoom, Tibbitts Winners Impacting Students' Lives," *Nevada Today*, May 5, 2020.

68 "Not Your Typical Senior Year," *Nevada Today*, May 11, 2021.

69 "University to Celebrate University Way and Monument Dedication," *Nevada Today*, October 17, 2022.

70 "University of Nevada, Reno Celebrates the Completion of the Gateway Parking Complex," *Nevada Today*, January 20, 2023.

71 "Nevada System of Higher Education Board of Regents Approves University of Nevada, Reno Mathewson University Gateway Project," *Nevada Today*, June 12, 2023.

72 "The University of Nevada, Reno at Lake Tahoe Is Uniquely Designed with Students in Mind," *Nevada Today*, February 22, 2023.

73 "University Offers First-Ever Paiute Language Course," *Nevada Today*, August 8, 2019.

74 "Daphne Hooper: New Director of Community Indigenous Relations," *Nevada Today*, July 14, 2022.

75 "State of the University: 'We Are a University That Is Rising,'" *Nevada Today*, September 30, 2022.

76 Church, *Nevada State University Tri-decennial Celebration, May 28 to June 2, 1904*, 73.

EPILOGUE

1 "Legacy of the Greats: How the Wolf Pack Teams of the 1940s Beat Jim Crow," *Nevada Today*, February 8, 2018.

2 "Legacy of the Greats: How the Wolf Pack Teams of the 1940s Beat Jim Crow," *Nevada Today*, February 8, 2018.

3 "Legacy of the Greats: How the Wolf Pack Teams of the 1940s Beat Jim Crow," *Nevada Today*, February 8, 2018.

4 "Legacy of the Greats: How the Wolf Pack Teams of the 1940s Beat Jim Crow," *Nevada Today*, February 8, 2018.

Index

Page numbers in *italics* refer to figures.

Academic Department, 9
accessibility, 152–54
accreditations, classifications, and rankings, xx, xxi, xxv, 2, 106, 120, 121, 123
activism, xxiii, 74–81, *76*, 125–27
Adamian, Paul, xxiii
Adams, Jewett, xix
Adams, Maxwell, 40
admissions, 6, 8
advanced degrees, xx, 30, 98, 145
advertising, 93–94, *95*
affirmative action, 98
African Americans. *See* Black people
African Diaspora Cultural & Affinity Graduate Celebration, *157*
Afro-American history, 79
Agriculture, College of, xx, 17, 26, 74, 132, 133; building, *26*, 41, *45*; Experiment Station, xix, xxiv, *21*, *23*; as School of, xix; as School of Agriculture, 9
Ahern, Michael, *41*
AIAN (American Indian/Alaskan Native) Graduate Celebration, *156*
aid, financial, 152
Aiken, Jim, 60–61, 62
Air Force College, *57*
Ali, Muhammad, 127
All-American (football), xxi
All-Time Team, 61
alumni, xix, 32, 101, 150, 167
Ambler, Laura Louise, xxi, 30–31
American Association for the Advancement of Science, 67
American Association for University Women, 58
American Association of University Professors, 65
American Indian/Alaskan (AIAN) Native Graduate Celebration, *156*
American Indian Organization, xxii, *100*, 101
American Sign Language, xiii, 66–67
Anderson, Fred M., 72–74
Anderson Health Sciences Building, Fred M., 74
Andes Mountains, 18
Andrews, Christine Harriet, *3*
anniversaries, University, viii, *xviii*, xxiii, xxv, 32, 155
Ansari, Nazir, xxiii
Ansari Business Building, 21
Apartment for Peggy (film), xxi, *53*
arboretum, xxiii
Archer, Michael, 55
Arcotta, Karen, *72*
Ardanza, José Luis, 70
Arellano, Steve, 87
Argentine Federation of Basque Entities, 70
Argentum, xxiv
Ariznabarreta, Larraitz, 70
Armstrong, Charles J., xi, xxii, 42, 71, *73*
Arnot, Mary Eugenia, 36
art, 18, *50*, 79, 80–81, 114
Artemisia yearbook, *viii*, xix, xx, xxiv, xxv, *59*, 150–51
arts. *See* music
Arts and Sciences, College of, xxiv, 81, 82; Church Fine Arts Building, 17, 18, *136*; as Department of, xxiii
Ashton, Henry, 8
assimilation, 100–101
Associated Students of the University of Nevada (ASUN), xxv, 30, 78, 150
Atherton, Blanch, *11*
athletics, xxiv, 19, 34–36, *36*, 61, 63, 80, 92, 128–29, 147, 163–64; halls of fame, 37, 61, 126, 164; women and, xxiv, xxv, 34–36, *36*, 92, 118. *See also* football; gymnasiums
@One, 138
@Reality, *139*
Aulestia, Gorka, 70
Ault, Chris, 126
Australia, xxv
autonomous vehicles, 121

Barengo, Bob, *94*
Baro, Iñaki Arrieta, 70
Barrington, Jessie, 37
Barrington, Lloyd Harold "Dickie Jack," xxi, 37–39, *38*
Barrington, Richard, 37–38
baseball, 61
basketball, 34–36, *36*
Basques, xxii, 65–71, *67*
Bass, William "Billy," 60, 62–63, 129
"Battle for Nevada" (football game), *50*
Battle of the Bulge, 62
Beadle, Courtney, 103
Beapler, Don, 92–93
Beckman, Julia, 36
bells, Morrill Hall, 87, 103
Bender, John, 126
Bersi, Robert, *94*
Bilbao, Jon, 68–69, 70
Bilbao Basque Library, Jon, 68
BioFit, xxv
Bishop Manogue High School, xxiv
Black people, 13, 58–64, 84; activism, 78–81, 125; faculty, xxiii, 78–81, 97–98, 127–28; students, xxi, 39–40, 58–64, *61*, 98, 125, 129, 163; women, xxii, 58–60
Black Rock Press, xxii, xxiv
Black Student Union, xxii, 78, 80, 103

181

Blakeslee, Zena, *36*
Blue Star Flag, *56*
boarding schools, 37–38, 101
Boardman, Horace P., 18
Board of Regents, Nevada, xxii, 1, 5, 9, 72, 80
"Book of the Oath," xx, 42
Borglum, Gutzon, xx, 13, 15
Boyd, Delle, 32, *36*
Boyd School of Law, William S., 104
Boyle, Emmet D., 32
Bradley, Lewis R., xix, 5
Bradshaw, James "Rabbit," xxi, 36–37, *37*
Branch, Michael, 146
Brigman, Dorothy "Dottie," 56
Bristol, Frederick Amos, xix, 11, *12*
Brown, LeRoy D., xix, 1, 9, 45
Brown, Paul, 62
Brown, Richard, 10
Brown, Roger, 67
Brown, Thomas, 9
Brown, Tim, *100*
Brownsill, Edith, 36
Bryan, Richard, 58, 92, *144*, 150
Buckle, Ian, 96
Buildings and Grounds Department, 87
Bureau of Indian Affairs, 101
Bureau of Mines, Nevada, xxi
Burns, Ralph, 152
Burrell, Otis, 80
Business, College of, xxiii, 141, 151; as Department, 9, 45

California, 7, 38–39, 68; state fair, *30*
Cambodia, 74, 75
Camino, Kate, 70
Camp, Walter, 37
campus, University, *xxviii*, 19, *19*, 23, *31*, 43, *86*, 106, *106*, 122. *See also individual buildings*
Campus Escort Service, 145
Campus Transportation Service, xxiii
Cannizzaro, Nicole, 104
canoes, xxiv, *51*
Carlisle Industrial Indian School, 37–38

Carman, Kevin, 147
Carnegie Foundation for the Advancement of Higher Education, xxv, 2, 106, 120, 121, 123
Carpenter, Kenneth J., xxii
Carson City, 1, 5, 37
Carter, Jimmy, 80
Cashell, Bob, *94*
Central Pacific Railroad, 6
Central Washington University, 67
Chambers, Joan, 93
Chatterjee, Indira, 96
chemistry, *22*, *23*, 118
Chidambaram, Dev, 120–21
chimpanzees, xiii, 66–67
Chism, Calder, 35
Chism, David, 35
Chism, John, 35
Church, Florence, 16, 32
Church, James Edward, xx, 15–18, *16*, 17–18
Church Fine Arts Building, James Edward, 17, 18, *136*
Civil and Environmental Engineering, Department of, 95–96
Civil Engineering, Center for, 95–96
Civil War, 15
Clapp, Hannah K., xix, 1–3, *1*, 9–11, 155
Clark, David, 35
Clark, Euphemia, 35
Clark, Miriam, 35
Clark, Walter Ernest, xx, 29, 31–32, *33*, 34–35, 41–42, 66, 105
Clark, Walter Van Tilburg, 35, 66, *67*
Clark, William, 40
Clark, William A., Jr., xxi
Clark County School District, xxv
Clark Library, 41
Cleveland Browns, 61, 62, 164
Clow, Mary, *11*
College Football Hall of Fame, 126
colonization, 7. *See also* pioneers
Colorado School of Mines, 103
colors, school, xix
Columbia School of Journalism, 31
comma vs. hyphen, University name, 93–94

commencement ceremonies, viii–ix, xix, xxi, xxv, *12*, 13–14, 41–42, 145, *149*, 156, *156–61*
Commercial School, xix, 45
Committee on the Status of Women, xxiii, 83, 104
Community College Division, xxiii
computers and technology, xxv, *102*, 113, 118, *136*, *138*, *139*, 144
Comstock Lode, xx, 7, 124
concentration camps, 57, 58
Coolidge, Calvin, 32
Cooperative Extension program, xx
Copper, Kennecott, 50
Copren, William, *76*
Coray, Harriet, 97
Coray, Michael, xxiii, 59, 78, 97–98, *97*
Coray, Suzi, *97*
Corley, Bob, 62
Courtright, Raymond "Corky," 36
COVID-19, viii–ix, xxv, 123, 144–50, 154
Creel, Cecil, *15*
Cropper, Johnell, 103
Crow, Michael, 123
Crowley, Joseph N., vii, xxiii, 3, *69*, 84–89, *84*, *85*, *91*, 92–93, *94*, 105, 123
Crowley, Joy, 92, 93, 105
Crowley, Margaret, 105
Crowley, Neil, 105
Crowley, Theresa, 105
Crowley, Tim, 105
Cummings, Sarah, 118
Curtis, Mark, *53*
Cutting, Henry Colman, xix, 11, *12*

Dachau concentration camp, 57, 58
dancing, *47*
Davidson Academy, xxiv, 54, 122
Davidson Mathematics and Science Center, xxiv, *112*
Davis, Blanche, xix
Davis, Dave, 87
d'Azevedo, Warren L., 40, 98
Dean's Future Scholars Program, *135*
Dean's List, 126

DeLongchamps, Frederic, 33, *33*, 58
Del Papa, Frankie Sue, *83*
Desert Research Institute (DRI), xxii, xxiii, xxiv, 68–69, 71, 93
Dickens, Robert, 92
Dickerson, Denver, 13–14
dictionaries, 70
Digital Wolf Pack Initiative, xxv
Dini, Joe, 92
dinks, 55
Distinguished Nevadan Award, 38, 60, *91*
diversity, xxiii, 79, 96–99, 103, 118, 152–54, 156, 165
Dodson, John, 80
dogs, 82, 105
Domingo, Placido, 96
Donner Lake, 40
dormitories, xix, xx, *20, 24*, 56, *95*. See also *individual halls*
Doten, Alfred, 67
Doten, Samuel B., xxi, 10, 17, 32, 33
Double Diamond Ranch, 122
Douglass, William A., xxii, *67*, 68–69, *69*
Douglass Center for Basque Studies, William A., 70
Dreighton, Cassandra, *95*
DRI (Desert Research Institute), xxii, xxiii, xxiv, 68–69, 71, 93
Du Bois, W. E. B., 39; medal, 127
Ducat, Arthur, 10
Duffy, Kathryn H., *75*

earthquakes, xxv, 95–96
Economics Department, 57
Edgemoor Infrastructure & Real Estate, 151
education, xxiv, 60; Native Americans and, 37, 100–101; power of, 1, 97–98, 102–3
Education, College of, 135; as School of, xx
ElderCollege, xxiii, xxiv
electrical engineering, xx, 40, 96
electricity, xix
Elko, NV, 1, 2, *4*; University relocation from, xix, xxiii, 1, 6–7, 155
Elliott, Marta, 105
Elliott, Russell, xi

Els, Ernie, 129
Emm-Hooper, Daphne, xxv, 152
endowment. See funding; philanthropy
Engineering, College of, 95–96, 118, 119; buildings, xx, xxi, xxiii, xxv, *27, 115*, 122; as Department of Civil and Environmental Engineering, 95–96; as Mackay School of Earth Sciences and Engineering, xxiv; as School of Mines and Mining Engineering, 9
engineering, electrical, xx, 40, 96
English Department, 64–65, 82
enrollment, xix, xxi, xxii, xxiii, xxiv, xxv, 2, 55–56, 103, 122; minority, 80, 98–99, 101, 103
environmentalism, 84, 132, 154
Esser, William M., *47*
ethnic studies, 59, 79, 84, 97, 98, 101
Eubank, Grace, 40
Evans Estate, 40
Evans Ranch, 46
Exline, Chris, viii

faculty, 9, 12, *27*, 64–67, 74–81, 118–22, 148–49; minority, 97–99, 127–28; senate, 79, 92–93; women, xxiii, 81–84, 96, 98, 104–5, 155
Farm, University, xx
fee waivers, 98, 101, 165
Felts, Todd, 146–47
Fergusson, S. P., 18
Fernandez, Mike, 103–4
films, xxi, 43, *52, 53*, 66, 73, *142–43*
fire, 21, 30, 77
first-years, vii, 119
Fitch, Amy, 149
Fitzgerald Student Services Building, xxiv
flags, 56, *72*
Fleischmann, Max C., xxi, 41, 151
Fleischmann Building, Sarah, 41
Fleischmann Foundation, Max C., 41
Fleischmann Planetarium and Science Center, xxii, *73*
flu, Spanish, xx, 29–30
Folsom, Ernest, *15*

Fonda, Henry, 66
football, xxi, 125–26; professional leagues, 61, 62, 129, 163, 164
football, University team, xix, xx, xxiii, 35–37, 50, *61, 62, 130, 138, 164*; discrimination and, xxi, 59–64, 125–30, 163
Foundation, University, xxiii
Foundation Arts Building, University, xxv, *114*, 122
Fowler, Don, 89
Frandsen, Peter "Bugs," 26, 32
Frandsen Humanities Building, 45, *52, 53*, 82–83
fraternities, *91*, 129
Frazier, Robert, *36*
Fredericksen, Paul, *31*
freedom, academic, 57, 65, 71
Frémont, John C., 50
Fremont Cannon, xxiii, *50, 138*
Frey, Frances, *11*
funding, xiii, 1, 5–15, 73–74, 92, 102, 124, 147–48. See also philanthropy

Gandolfo, Mark, *136*
Gardner, Allen, xiii, 66–67
Gardner, Beatrix "Trixie," xiii, 66–67
Gateway Parking Complex, 151
Gautam, Mridul, 119–21
Gender, Race, and Identity (GRI), 84, 104. See also ethnic studies; women's studies
Geological Survey, US, xxiv
Getchell, Nobel H., xxii
Getchell Library, Nobel H., xxii, xxv, *67*, 69, 71, *72*, 77, *102*, 122
GI Bill, 55, 63
Gignoux, J. E., 6
Gillom, Horace, 60, 62, 63, 129
Glick, Milton D., xxiv, 122, 123–25, *124*
Go, Kristen, 99
Goin, Peter, *136*
Gorrell, Robert, xii, 64, 81–82, 83
Governor's Day, xxiii, 74–78, *76*
graduation. See commencement ceremonies
Grayson, M., *36*
Great Basin Hall, 122

Great Basin region, 100
Great Recession, 122, 123, 124, 147, 150
Great Room, 147
greenhouses, *132*
Greenland, 18
GRI (Gender, Race, and Identity), 84, 104
Guinn, Clifford, 102
Guinn, Kenny C., 102
Guinn, Virgie, 102
Guinn Memorial Scholarship, Kenny C., 104
Gwenn, Edmund, *53*
gymnasiums, xxi, 19, *21*, *22*, *23*, 36, *41*; Mackay Athletic Field and Training Quarters, xx, *15*, *57*; Marguerite Wattis Petersen Foundation Athletics Academic Center, xxiv; Virginia Street Gymnasium, *58*; Wiegand Fitness Center, xxv, *114*, 122

halls of fame, 61, 126; Nevada Athletics Hall of Fame, 37, 164; Nevada Writers Hall of Fame, xiii, 35, 65, 67; Wolf Pack Hall of Fame, 125, 128
Harolds Club scholarship, xi
Harriman, Frank, 30
Harris, Judy, *100*
Harris, Walter C., Jr., *15*
Harry, Debra, 152
Hartigan, Frank, 83
Hartman, Leon W., xxi
Hartman Hall, 77
Harvey, Robert, 74
Hatch Hall, *20*, *48*
Hawaii, xx, 37
Hayes, Steven, 145
Hazard, Ben, xxiii, 74–75, 79–81
Hazard, Mark, 75, 79, 80
hazing, 55
health care, 30, 145–46
Heath, Stan, *37*, *62*
Heisman Trophy, 125
Helena, Joy, *11*
Hendrick, Archer W., xx, 34
Herz Gold Medals, R., xx
Hickey, Vive, *36*
Higginbotham, Alfred, 31

High Country News, 7
Hillman, Fred, 10
Himalayas, 18
Hispanic/Latinx people, xxiv, 84, 98, 99, 147, 157
Historical Society, Nevada, 2
Historic Preservation Program, 89
History Department, xi, xiii, 97–98
History of the University of Nevada (Doten), xxi
Hixson Softball Park, xxiv
Hobbins, Frank, *15*, 32
Hobbit Hole, 77–78
Holmes, Ida, 36
homecoming, xx, *131*
home economics, 26, 41, 45, 49, *49*
Homer, Dudley, *15*
Honor Court, *vi*, xxiv, 166, 167, *167*
Honors College, *134*
Honors Program, 57, 134
Hospital, University, 22, *23*, 71
Houwink, Willem "Wim," 57–58
Howard, Anne, viii, 82–84
Howard, Sherman, 60, *61*, *62*, 63–64, 129, 163–64, *164*, 165
Hug-English, Cheryl, 145
Hughes, Howard, xxiii, 73–74
Hulse, Berene C., *xii*
Hulse, Delora, *xii*
Hulse, James G., *xii*
Hulse, James W., xi–xiii, *xi*, *xii*, xxiii, 5, 16, 29, 41, 71, 74–75, 93, 98
Human and Community Sciences, College of, xxiii
Human Relations Action Council, xxii
Humphrey, Frances, *47*
Humphrey, Neil D., 93
Hunting, Alden D., *47*
"hy-flex" approach, 147
hyphen vs. comma, University name, 93–94

Illustrated History of the University of Nevada, An (Doten), 10
immigrants, 66, 68–70

inaugurations, University presidents, xx–xxv, 12, 71, 89, 123–24
Independent Association of the University of Nevada, xix
index cards, 123–24
Indian Association of California, 39
Indigenous people. *See* Native Americans; *individual peoples*
Indigenous relations, xxv, 101, 152
Indigenous studies, 84, 101
influenza, Spanish, xx, 29–30
Innevation Center, xxv, 121
Insight Magazine, xxiv
Intensive English Language Center, xxiii
International Collegiate Mining Competition, xxv
International Game Technology, 138
International Women's Day Parade, *95*
Irujo, Xabier, 70

Jackson, Robert D., xix, 10
Jackson, Stonewall, 15
Jacobsen, Virginia, 69
Jacobsen, William H., 69
James, Arthur, 129
Joe Crowley Student Union, xxiv, 54, *95*, *107*, 122, *137*, *142–43*, 147
Johnson, Marc, xxiv, 114, *121*, 122–23, 146–47
Jones, Stephen A., xix
Jot Travis Student Union, xxii, xxiv, *54*, 122
journalism, xxi, xxiii, 30–31, 94, 98, 150
Judicial College Building, 41

Kaepernick, Colin, 125–30, *128*
Kalmanir, Tom, *37*, *62*
Kappa Alpha Psi, 129
Kawar, Amal, 83
Kennedy Index, xxiv
Kent State University, 74, 75, 76, 77
Klaich, Dan, 92
Korean War, xi
Kosso, Lenore, xii
Ku Klux Klan, 15, 39
KUNR (radio station), xxii

laboratories, xix, 3, 9, 26, 56, 115, 132, 145, 153
Laird, Charlton, xii, 65
Lake Tahoe, xxv, 116, 152, 154; University of Nevada, Reno at, 116, 151, 152, 153
land grab, 7, 101
Landry, Tom, 163
languages, xxiii, xxv, 65, 69, 70, 152
Lansing (Michigan) Female Seminary, 1
Lara-Gutierrez, Lilly, 154
Lara-Gutierrez, Nayelli, 154–55
Larsen, Larry, 83
Las Vegas, xxi, xxii, 58; University of Nevada, xxiii, 93
Latinx studies, xxiv, 84. *See also* Hispanic/Latinx people
Lawlor, Erma, *94*
Lawlor, Glenn "Jake," 62, *94*
Lawlor Events Center, xxiii, *88*, *94*
Laxalt, Dominique, 66, 68
Laxalt, Joyce, 56, 68
Laxalt, Paul, 65–66, 68, 73–74
Laxalt, Robert "French," xxii, 35, 56, 65–66, *66*, 68, 69, *69*, 70
Laxalt Mineral Engineering Center, xxiii
Lee, Robert E., 15
Legacy Hall, xxiv
Legislature, Nevada, xxi, xxiii, 1, 5, 6, 9, 73–74, 79, 92, 101–2, 104
Lemon, Persia, *11*
Leon, Fred, *62*
Leslie, Sheila, xxiv
Letondal, Henri, *53*
Lewers, Charles, 32
LGBTQ, 84
Liberal Arts, College of, xxiv; as School of, xix
libraries, xxi, xxiv, 41, 68, 113, 116, 138. *See also* Getchell Library, Nobel H.
Lilley, John, xxiv, 122
Lincoln, Abraham, 7, 15, 101
Lincoln Hall, xix, 19, *20*, 23, 26, *52*, *54*, *76*, 122
Lippincott, Luke, 126
List, Robert, *94*

Lockhart, Gene, *53*
Lockman, Jerry, *3*
Loforth, Irma, 41
Lombardi, Vince, 163
Lombardi Recreation Center, *50*
Long, Leon, *15*
Love, Malcolm A., xxi

Mack, Margaret E., 32
Mackay, Clarence Hungerford, xxi, 13–14, 15, *15*, *33*, 34, 40, 44
Mackay, John W., xx, 13–14, 15, 34; statue, 13–15, *23*, *28*, *29*, *47*, *159*
Mackay, Mrs. Clarence, 36
Mackay Athletic Field and Training Quarters, xx, *15*, *57*
Mackay Bottle Sacrifice, 151
Mackay Day and Week, xx, 14–15, *48*, *91*
Mackay Field, *48*, *76*
Mackay Mineral Museum, xx
Mackay Muckers Women's Team, xxv
Mackay School of Earth Sciences and Engineering, xxiv
Mackay School of Mines Building, *xiv*, xx, xxi, xxiv, *23*, *47*
Mackay Science Hall, viii, xxi, *21*, *33*, 74
Mackay Stadium, viii–ix, xxii, xxv, 125, *130*, *148*, *149*, 151
Mack Social Science Building, xiii, *36*
Major League Baseball (MLB), 61
Manfredi, Sheridan, 147
Manzanita Bowl, vii, *22*, *75*
Manzanita Hall, xix, *24*, *52*, 59
Manzanita Lake, xiii, xx, 26, 44, *51*, *52*, *53*, 55, *110–11*
Maragakis, Manos, 95, 119
marching band, *130*, *131*, 138
Marine Corps, 55
Marjo, Ray, *100*
Marschall, John, 80
Martie, John E. "Doc," *48*
Martin, Anne Henrietta, 32, *32*
Martin, Charles, 62
masking, *144*, *146*, *148*, *149*
math, 118

Mathewson, Chuck, 122
Mathewson-IGT Knowledge Center, xxiv, 69, *107*, *113*, 122, 136, *138*
Mathewson University Gateway District, xxv, 151
Maxson, Bob, 92
May, Dixie, 122
Mayo, Lee, 87
McCammon, J. W., 8, 9
McCormick, Jim, 90
McFarland, Jennie, *11*
McIntyre, Mattie, 36, *36*
McKissick Opera House, xix, 11, 12, 14
McVicar, Neil, *15*
Mechanical Arts Building, 20, *23*, 74
Medicine, Center for Molecular Medicine, xxiv
Medicine, School of, xxiii, xxv, 71–74, *72*, *140*, 145, 154
Melendez, Brian, 7
Memorial Library, xxi
meteorology, 16–18
Milam, Max C., xxiii, 81–82, 84
military, xi, xxi, 10, 55–58, 62–64, 151; department, xxi, 74; GI Bill, 55, 63
Millennium Scholarship, xxiv, 103–4
Miller, Maya, *91*
Miller, N. Edd, xi, xxii, 76, 77, 78, 80, 89
Miller, Theodore H., xxi, 39–40, *39*
Miller, Walter McNab, *3*, 10
Mines, School of, xix, 9. *See also* Mackay School of Mines Building
mining, xxi, 14–15, 124
Mining Analytical Laboratory, xix
minorities, 80, 92, 97–99, 101, 103, 127–28, 165. *See also* racial discrimination; *individual groups*
mission, of University, xiii, 1–3, 9, 12, 89–90, 123–24, 130, 148, 154–55, 164–65
Mississippi State University, xxi, 61–63, 129
Mitchell, Paul, 98–99, *99*, 127–30
Modern English Handbook, The (Gorrell and Laird), 65
Molecular Medicine, Center for, xxiv
Monga, Natasha, 118

monuments, 70, *117*, 150–51, *166*, *167*, *167*. See also statues
Mordy, Wendall, 68
Morrill, Justin S., 9, 25
Morrill Hall, xix, *xxviii*, *3*, 6, 9, 19, *20*, *23*, *25*, *28*, 105, 151; restoration, xxiii, 87, 89
Morrill Land Grant Act: of 1862, xii, xix, 2, 3, 5, 7, 25, 39, 101; of 1890, 39
Morris, Bourne, 94
Morrison, Roger Barron, xxii
Morton, Adeline, 11, *11*
Moseley, John O., xxi, 56
Mother Is a Freshman (film), *52*
Motley, Marion, *37*, 60–60, *61*, 62, 63, 129, 163
Mount Rose, 16, 17–18
Mount Rushmore, 13
movies, xxi, 43, *52*, *53*, 66, 73, *142–43*
Museum of Art, Nevada, 17
music, 10, 38, 40, 96–97
Muti, Riccardo, 96

"N," the, 43, *43*, 47
name, University, xx, xxii, 93–94
Nash, Maude, 36
National Association for the Advancement of Colored People (NAACP), xxii
National Association of American Colleges and Universities, xx
National Collegiate Athletics Association (NCAA), 80, 92
National Football League (NFL), 61, 129, 163, 164
National Geothermal Institute, xxiv
National Guard, 74
National Landmarks of Democracy, 89
National Science Foundation (NSF), 120, 121, 153
Native American Alumni Chapter, 101
Native American Fee Waiver, 98, 101, 165
Native American Graves Protection and Repatriation, 101
Native Americans, xxi, 7, 37–39, 98, 100–101, 152, 165. See also *individual peoples*
Nazis, 57

NCAA (National Collegiate Athletics Association), 80, 92
Neff, Nelson, 72
Nelson, Evalyn, *47*
Nevada, state of, xix, 5, 68, 120–21, 145, 164–65; nature, viii, 100, *133*, 154
Nevada Art Gallery, 18
Nevada Business Review, 57
Nevada Center for Applied Research, 121
Nevada Division of Environmental Protection, 154
NevadaFit, xxv
Nevada Follies, 40
Nevada Foundation, 136, 145
Nevada Promise Scholarship, 104
Nevada Sagebrush, The, xxiv
Nevada Southern University, xxii, 93
Nevada State Journal, xi, 8, 9, 31, 34, 41
Nevada State Museum, 41
Nevada State Public Health Laboratory, 145, 153
Nevada State University, xx
Nevada State University Tri-decennial Celebration, May 28 to June 2, 1904, 16
Nevada System of Higher Education (NSHE), xxiv, 104
Nevada Taxpayers Association, 73
Nevada Today, 34
Nevada Urban Indians, 152
NFL (National Football League), 61, 129, 163, 164
Nicholson, Jordan, 149
Nixon, Richard, 74
Noble, C. R., 61
Norcross, Frank Herbert, xix, 11–12, *12*, 14, 15, 32
Normal School, 9, 11
North, Amelia, 36
North, Ruby, 36
Northwest Association of Secondary and Higher Schools, xxi
NSF (National Science Foundation), 120, 121, 153
NSHE (Nevada System of Higher Education), xxiv, 104

NV Energy, 35
Nye Hall, *95*

oaths, xx, 42
Obama, Barack, 81, *124*
Obama, Michelle, *125*
O'Brien, Katherine Mackay, *33*
O'Callaghan, Mike, *94*
Oddie, Tasker L., 29
Ohio, 34
Ohmert, Audrey W., xx
Oiarzabal, Pedro, 70
Oleevich, Annie, *11*
OLLI (Osher Lifelong Learning Institute), xxiv
Olympic Games, xxii
Olympic Valley, xxii
Omega Xi, *91*
online instruction, xxv
opera, 96–97
oral history, xxii, 58, 60, 70–72
orations, 11
Orlich, Dan, *62*
Orr Ditch, xx, *22*, *24*, 44, *46*
Orvis, Arthur E., xxii
Orvis, Mae Zenke, xxii
Orvis Ring Elementary School, 60
Orvis School of Nursing, xxii
Osher Lifelong Learning Institute (OLLI), xxiv
Ott, Sandra, 70
Overlook, the, xiii
Ox-Bow Incident, The (Clark), 66
Ozmen Center for Entrepreneurship, *141*

Pack Provisions program, 145
Page, Paul, 94
painting the "N," 43, 47
Paiute people, xxv, 100, 152
Palmer Engineering Building, xxi, *27*, 122
pandemics, viii–ix, xx, xxv, 29–30, 123, 144–50, 154
Pandori, Mark, 145, 153
Parker, Gilbert E., xxi
Parker, Mattie, *36*

Parker, Milton P., 41
Parson, Claude H., Jr., 60
Parson, Fred, 58
Parson, Jacqueline, 60
Parson, LaToyshia, 60
Parson, Matilda, 58
Parson, Naida, 60
Parson, Stella Mason, xxii, 58–60, *59*
Patterson, Maude, 36
Pavarotti, Luciano, 96
Peavine Hall, 122
Peavine Peak, xx, *47*, 55
Pennington, William N., 122
Pennington Engineering Building, William N., *115*, 122
Pennington Health Sciences Building, William N., 122
Pennington Student Achievement Center, William N., xxv, *113*, 122, *141*
people, as heart of University, vii–ix, 3, 10–11, 65, 89–90, 123–25, 155, 165
Phi Delta Theta, *91*
philanthropy, 13, 40–41, 73–74, 122, 166
Phillips, Virginia, 89
Physics Department, xx, *21*
Pine, Ed, 87
Pioche, NV, xi, *xii*
pioneers, 1–2, 14, 18, 100, 155
"Pistol" offense, 126
Placer, Eloy, *67*
planetary science, xxii, 73
police, 125
Pond, University, *44*
Pontius, C. I., 63
Powell, Jayde, 145
Pravosudova, Elena, 148–49
Preparatory Department/School, xix, 1, 3, 5–6
President's House, xix, *27*
President's Medal, 60, 90
Prim Library, *116*
"Professor Ex," viii
professors. *See* faculty; *individual instructors*
protests. *See* activism

Psychology Department, xiii, 66–67
public health, 30, 145–46; laboratory of, 145, 153; School of, 154
Puffer, Deena, 96
Puffer, Ted, 96
Pulitzer Prize, 99
Pyramid Lake Paiute Tribe, 152
Pyrenees, 66

Quad, *x*, xiii, xx, 13, 19, *25*, 28, *47*, 91, 108–9, *125*, *158*, *159*
quarantines, 29–30, 144, 148

racial discrimination, xxii, 13, 39, 59, 78–81, 164. *See also* ethnic studies; segregation; *individual groups*
radio stations, xx, xxii, xxiv
Raggio, William, 55, 92
"Ranch, The," 66–67
Rancho San Rafael Park, 70, 105
Rawson, Denise, *95*
Redfield campus, xxiv
Redfield Foundation, 122
regents. *See* Board of Regents, Nevada
Reid, Harry, xxiv
Reilly, Thom, 144
Reinhardt, Tom, *62*
Religion and Life, Center of, 80
remote work and instruction, 144–50
Reno, city of, 5, 8, 64, 66, 117, *131*, 150–51; University relocation to, xix, xxiii, 1, 6–7, 155
Reno Evening Gazette, 1, 2, 6, 13, 31, 34, 36, 56, 62, 80
Reno Gazette-Journal, 104
Reno Kindergarten Association, 2
Reno-Sparks Indian Colony of Northern Paiute, Southern Paiute, and Western Shoshone, 7
Renown Health, xxv
research, xxiv, xxv, 2, 106, 119–21, 123, 153. *See also* Desert Research Institute
Reserve Officers' Training Corps (ROTC), xxi, *57*, 58, 74, 75, 77–78
retirement, xxiii, 18, 34, 92

Reynolds, Donald W., xxiii
Reynolds School of Journalism, Donald W., xxiii, 94, 98
Rhoden, William, 164
Rhodes, Hattie, *11*
Richardson, James, 92–93
Riechers, Dorothy F., xx
Riverside Hotel, 14
Roberts, Kimberly, 34
Robinson, Carl, *62*
Robinson, Jackie, 61
Robinson, Vietta, 63, 163, 164
Ronald, Ann, 83
Roosevelt, Theodore, *30*
Rose, Delora, *xii*
Ross, George, *62*
Ross, John Tom, *94*
Ross, Silas E., xxii, 41–42, 65
Rostropovich, Mstislav, 96
ROTC (Reserve Officers' Training Corps), xxi, *57*, 58, 74, 75, 77–78
Rotunda, the, 69
Rowley, William, 35
Ruymann, Rosemary, 58

Sacks, Barry, 127
Sagebrush, xxii, xxiv, 53
Sagebrushers (team), 36–37
Sala, John, 87
Sanchez, Frank, *62*
Sandorf, Irving, 40
Sandoval, Brian, *vi*, *viii*, vii–ix, xxv, 104, *121*, *140*, *146*, 147–48, 150, 151, 152, 167
Sandoval, Lauralyn, 147
Sandoval, Marisa, 147
Santini, Clark, 35
Santini, James, 35
Savage, Lizzie, *11*
scholarships, xi, xxiv, 41, 58, 60, 97, 103–4
schools. *See* boarding schools; *individual schools*
science, 10, 16–18, *17*, 118, 120. *See also individual departments and fields*
Science, College of, xxiv
Scully, Thomas, *72*

segregation, 58–64, 129, 163. *See also* racial discrimination
selfies, *xviii*
Sessions, D. R., 5–6
settlers. *See* pioneers
sexual harassment, 104–5
Shaber, Lattie, *11*
Shaw, Henry G., 8–9
Shopping Angels, 145
Shoshone people, 100, 152
Shriver, Sargent, 125
Sierra Booster, 38
Sierra County Historical Society, 37–38
Sierra Nevada Mountains, 2, 17
Sierra Nevada University, xxv, 151–52
Sierra Seminary, 2
Sierraville Lumber Company, 38
Silver State Opportunity Grant Program, 104
Sinofsky, Ken, *62*
Sisolak, Steve, 144
Slavin, Isabelle, 30
smallpox epidemic, xx
Smith, George, 72, *72*
Smith, O. J., 14
Smith-Lever Act, xx
Smithsonian Magazine, 15
SNCC (Student Nonviolent Coordinating Committee), xxii
Snow, Mary, *11*
snow surveying, 16–18, *17*
social distancing, 144, 148
Sociology, Department of, 105
Sparkman, William, 135
Sparks, Ron, 92
sports. *See* athletics
Squaw Valley (now known as Olympic Valley), xxii
Stafford, Rebecca, 81–82, *81*
Stanfill, Dionne, 150–51
Stanford University, xi, 35
Stanley Palmer Engineering Building, *27*, 122
State Equal Rights Commission, 79
State Normal School, *11*

state universities. *See* funding; Morrill Land Grant Act; *individual schools*
State University of Nevada, 101
statues, 13, *69*, *144*; Mackay statue, 13–15, *23*, *28*, 29, *47*, *159*. *See also* monuments
Stella Mason Scholarship, 60
Stewart, Mary White, 104–5
Stewart, Omer, 68
Stewart Hall, *20*, *28*
Stewart Indian School, 37–38
Stiles, Maxwell, 37
Stone, Mike, 87
Stone Mountain, 15
Stout, Minard W., xxii, 65, 71
Strode, Woody, 61
Strosnider, Winnie, 36
Struve, Larry, 58
Stubbs, Elizabeth, 36, *36*
Stubbs, Joseph Edward, xix, xx, 12–14, *13*, *14*, 29, *30*, 34, 36, 123
Student Health Center, 145
Student Nonviolent Coordinating Committee (SNCC), xxii
Student Record, xix, xx, 35–36, 53
student unions. *See individual centers/unions*
Studies Abroad Consortium, 70
suffrage, 32
summer sessions, xx, xxi, *67*
Super Bowl, 125
Supreme Court, Nevada, 14
Sweet Promised Land (Laxalt), 66, *66*, 68

Tabor, Alva, 60, *61*, 63, 129, 163
Taeubel, Brayden, 150–51
Tahoe Science Consortium, xxiv
tanks, 77
taxes, 30
Team of the Century, 37
technology. *See* computers and technology
Teel, Claude, *15*
telemedicine, 145
tennis, 63, 147
Territorial Enterprise, 2, 9
textbooks, 65

Thomas, Christina, 152
Thompson Building, *53*
Tibbitts, F. Donald, 118
Tibbitts Distinguished Teaching Award, F. Donald, 118–19
Tillotson, Kenneth, *15*
Time magazine, 127
tobacco, 102, 104
Trachok, Richard "Dick," 62, *62*, *94*
track and field, 164
Tram, the, *22*, *24*, *52*
Trass, Tara, 58
travel, 18, 57
tricycles, *91*
Truckee Meadows and River, 8, 10
Truckee Meadows Community College, xxiv
tuition, vii, 6, 8, 102–3
Tulsa University, 63, 64, 129, 163
Tupper, Kate, 10
Turner, Gilberta, *47*
Twain, Mark, 2
Twentieth Century Fox, xxi

United Daughters of the Confederacy, 15
universities. *See individual institutions*
University and Community College System of Nevada (UCCSN), xxiii, xxiv
University High School, xix
University of California, Davis, xxiv, 50
University of Idaho, 61
University of Iowa, 63
University of Nevada, Las Vegas (UNLV), xxiii, 93
University of Nevada, Reno (UNR), xii, xix–xxv, 12, 93; founding of, viii, xii; funding for, xiii, 1, 5–15, 73–74, 92, 102, 124, 147–48; growth/evolution of, 3, 31–32, 34–35, 87, 103, 165; at Lake Tahoe, *116*, 151, 152, *153*; name of, xx, xxii, 93–94; stature of, 1, 3, 6–7, 64. *See also* anniversaries, University; mission, of University; people, as heart of University
University of Nevada: A Centennial History, The (Hulse), xi–xiii, xxiii, 5, 98
University of Nevada Press, xxii, 66, 69

University of Nevada System (UNS), xxii, xxiii, 93
U. of N. Sagebrush, The, xx, xxii
Upward Bound, xxii
Urza, Carmelo, 70
US *News & World Report*, 123

Vaczi, Mariann, 70
veterans, 55–58, 62–64
Veyrin, Phillipe, 68
Vietnam War, 74, 76, 77
virtual reality, *139*
Vista, 31
Vollstedt, Ann-Marie, 118–19
Voorhees, Vicki, *100*

Wainscoat, Damon, *100*
Wang, Eric, 119
Ward, Louise, 36, *36*
Warner, Glenn "Pop," 37
Washington, Kenny, 61
Washoe (chimpanzee), xiii, 66–67
Washoe City, NV, 5

Washoe County, NV, xix, xxv, 39, 59
Washoe Medical Center, 73
Washoe people, 37–39, 100, 152
Water Resources Building, 41
Wattis Petersen Foundation Athletics Academic Center, Marguerite, xxiv
Weather Bureau, US, 18
Webster, Elizabeth, 36
Wells, Karen, *100*
"What the University Stands For" (Wilson), ix
White, Linda, 70
whiteness, 7, 15, 42
Whittemore Peterson Institute, xxiv
Wiegand Fitness Center, E. L., xxv, *114*, 122
Wiegand Foundation, E. L., 122
Wilbur D. May Foundation, 122
Williams, Enid, *36*
Williams, Joseph, xx
Willis, A. H., 8, 9
Willis, Bill, 61
Wilson, N. E., ix
winter carnival, xxi

Winter Olympics, xxii
Wolf Pack, ix, xxi, *48*, 130, 163, 165; Hall of Fame, 125, 128; Wolfie Jr., xxv. *See also* athletics; people, as heart of University
Wolf Pack Radio, xxiv
women, xix, xxii, xxiii, 8, *11*, 31, 58–60, 104–5, 151; athletics, xxiv, xxv, 34–36, *36*, 92, 118; faculty, xxiii, 81–84, 96, 98, 104–5, 155; rights of, 2, 32, 81–84, *95*
Women in Science and Engineering Program, 118
women's studies, viii, 82, 83, 104
Woods, Tiger, 129
World Wars: First, 30; Second, 38, 55–58, 59, 62–64
writers, 66; Hall of Fame, Nevada, xiii, 35, 65, 67; in-residence, 66, 67

Zajick, Dolora, 96–97
Zoom, 144, 145
Zucker, Rueben, *72*
Zulaika, Joseba, 70